Vulnerable Places, Vulnerable People

D1532001

This book is dedicated to the memory of Konrad von Moltke, whose clear vision and commitment to a better world guided our work.

Vulnerable Places, Vulnerable People

Trade Liberalization, Rural Poverty and the Environment

Edited by

Jonathan A. Cook
WWF, USA

Owen Cylke
WWF, USA

Donald F. Larson
The World Bank, USA

John D. Nash
The World Bank, USA

Pamela Stedman-Edwards
WWF, USA

A co-publication of The World Bank, WWF and Edward Elgar

Edward Elgar
Cheltenham, UK • Northampton, MA, USA

Mixed Sources
Product group from well-managed
forests and other controlled sources
www.fsc.org Cert no. SA-COC-1565
© 1996 Forest Stewardship Council

ISBN 978 0 82138 099 4

Printed and bound by MPG Books Group, UK

Contents

Figures

Tables

Contributors

Anton Cartwright, Ecologic Consulting, Cape Town South Africa, and Stockholm Environment Institute, Sweden

Cao Chi Hung, Vietnam

Kanchan Chopra, Institute of Economic Growth, University of Delhi Enclave, India

Bobby Cochran, Clean Water Services, Oregon, USA

Jonathan A. Cook, WWF, USA

Owen Cylke, Macroeconomics Program Office, WWF, USA

He Daming, Asian International Rivers Center, Yunnan University, Kunming, China

Le Dang Trung, Centre for Analysis and Forecasting, Vietnam Academy of Social Sciences, Vietnam

Warren Evans, Environment Department, The World Bank, USA

Nicolo Gligo, Instituto de Políticas Públicas, Universidad de Chile

Liu Jiang, Asian International Rivers Center, Yunnan University, Kunming, China

Preeti Kapuria, Institute of Economic Growth, University of Delhi Enclave, India

Pushpam Kumar, Institute for Sustainable Water, Integrated Management & Ecosystem Research, Department of Geography, University of Liverpool, UK

Donald F. Larson, Development Research Group, The World Bank, USA

Jo Lorentzen, Science and Innovation Unit, Research Programme on Education, Science, and Skills Development, Human Sciences Research Council, Cape Town, South Africa

Bruno Losch, Sustainable Development Department, Africa Region, The World Bank, USA, and CIRAD (Centre de Coopération Internationale en Recherche Agronomique pour le Développement), France

Jacques Marcille, France

Philippe Méral, University of Versailles-St Quentin, France

Charles Meth, School of Development Studies, University of KwaZulu-Natal, Durban, South Africa, and Department of Sociological Studies, University of Sheffield, UK

Bart Minten, International Food Policy Research Institute, India

John D. Nash, Latin American and Caribbean Sustainable Development Department, The World Bank, USA

Tham Thi Ngoc Diep, WWF, Vietnam

Vu Ngoc Huyen, Faculty of Accounting and Business Management, Hanoi University of Agriculture, Vietnam

Edwin Niklitschek, Centro Trapananda, Universidad Austral de Chile

Mario Niklitschek, Instituto de Manejo Forestal, Universidad Austral de Chile

Raúl O'Ryan, Center for Applied Economics (CEA), Universidad de Chile

Le Phu Cuong, National Remote Sensing Center, Ministry of Natural Resources and Environment, Vietnam

Ha Thi Phuong Tien, Vietnam Academy of Social Sciences, Vietnam

Lalaina Randrianarison, Wye College, UK

David Reed, WWF, USA

Pamela Stedman-Edwards, Macroeconomics Program Office, WWF, USA

Johan Swinnen, Catholic University of Leuven, Belgium

Nguyen Thu Huong, Ageless Consulting, Vietnam

Mai Trong Thong, Institute of Geography, Vietnam Academy of Science and Technology, Vietnam

Tran Tuyet Hanh, Ageless Consulting, Vietnam

Andrés Ulloa, Universidad Católica de la Santísima Concepción, Chile

Ngo Van Hai, Institute of Strategy for Agriculture and Rural Development, Vietnam

Le Van Hung, UNDP, Vietnam

Hoang Xuan Thanh, Ageless Consulting, Vietnam

Preface

In today's increasingly integrated global economy, trade liberalization plays a key role in extending the dynamics of international markets to developing countries. Trade can catalyze economic growth but, like all forms of economic activity, trade-induced growth can also create new pressures on natural resources and on the rural poor who depend on those resources for their livelihoods. It is therefore not surprising that controversy has followed the widespread liberalization of economic policies and the dramatic expansion of trade in recent years.

This book is a joint effort on the part of The World Bank and the World Wildlife Fund (WWF) to move the discussion about trade, poverty and the environment beyond the theoretical and rhetorical and to shed light on the real impacts of trade liberalization. The conviction of both organizations that development must address the issues of environmental protection and poverty alleviation has brought us together in this effort to better understand the impacts of trade. The lessons drawn from the case studies in this book provide a critical first step in developing the appropriate policies and responses needed to ensure that trade, along with other aspects of globalization, plays a positive role in promoting truly sustainable development.

The innovative aspect of these six case studies lies in their effort to examine both the immediate and longer-term impacts of trade on some of the most vulnerable people and places in the world. This collaborative research project started with the recognition that trade, like any economic activity, has consequences for the environment through the use of natural resources and environmental services. These impacts, such as measured rates of deforestation, were generally understood in broad terms, at the level of national economies. Likewise, the economic impacts, such as changes in GDP, had been mostly studied at the national level.

However, missing in most analyses of trade was the critical link between people, especially the vulnerable poor, and the changing environment on which they depend. In particular places and for particular people, trade drives unique sets of responses that can only be understood by looking carefully at local conditions and results. That is where these studies dove into the heart of the complex relationship between trade, poverty, and the environment: by looking at specific outcomes in places of environmental concern.

Through these studies, we hear the stories of real people in real places – from the mountains of western China to the sugar-growing regions of South Africa to the salmon farms of Chile. Local research teams looked not only at the specific impacts of trade liberalization and associated socioeconomic changes on poverty and the environment, but also more importantly at their effects on the relationship *between* poor people and the environment. How did changes in the availability of environmental resources affect the poor? And how do changes in the natural resource constraints faced by the poor affect the use they make of environmental assets and services? Emerging clearly from these stories is the uniqueness of the factors shaping each place and the wide range of possible outcomes from essentially similar policies. While aggregate analyses of the impacts of trade liberalization generally tell a positive story of economic development, the stories of particular places and people make it clear that behind these aggregate figures lie a host of positive and negative impacts that will determine the long-term potential for sustainable development.

The fundamental importance of looking locally to understand the real impacts of global economic change, including trade liberalization, was recognized before these studies began. However, a rigorous methodology for examining the complex local impacts and clearly linking them to international and national policies did not exist. The research teams worked from a framework that emphasized the interconnected impacts of local, national, and international factors – laws and policies, demographics, culture – on local outcomes. Each team necessarily made use of a variety of traditional disciplinary methodologies to piece together the stories of local change and the various intervening factors shaping the impact of trade policies.

Over the period in which these studies were carried out, important advances have been made in our understanding of the relationship between trade, poverty, and the environment. Most importantly, human well-being has become widely accepted as a measure of development, replacing more limited measures such as income that emphasize only economic aspects. In equal measure, the Millennium Ecosystem Assessment has advanced an understanding of human well-being that gives a central role to the services and resources provided by the natural environment. It has also drawn attention to the precarious state of the natural resources on which human well-being depends. The Assessment is thus a major step forward in our understanding, but it too falls short in terms of providing a practical, applicable methodology.

Clearly we must now work towards a methodology that will better enable the donor community, development organizations, and national and local governments to better anticipate the environmental and poverty impacts of trade – or other global economic events – and to use that knowledge to design appropriate responses and interventions. Supporting a positive, sustainable relationship between the rural poor and the environment will allow these vulnerable people to benefit from the new economic opportunities created by trade without contributing to environmental degradation.

The case studies and the conclusions drawn from them by The World Bank and WWF in this book will contribute to this improved understanding. Here we highlight several important lessons that should shape an improved methodology for understanding the impacts of trade:

- The first lesson is that a robust analytical approach must be built on recognition that vulnerable people depend heavily on environmental resources in places of great value for conservation. Moreover, trade has the power to fundamentally alter traditional uses of environmental resources, as people take advantage of new economic opportunities or struggle to maintain their precarious existence in the face of increasing economic difficulties. Yet the impacts of trade cannot be isolated with certainty from the numerous socioeconomic changes occurring around the globe that likewise affect these places. Trade is often a central component of efforts to promote development through economic policy, but it is embedded within a larger set of changes to international, national and local markets, demographics, and culture.
- Second, from that starting point, we have learned that a methodology for understanding the impacts of trade must, like the studies in this book, look at the specific conditions in a particular place, and at the range of local, national and international factors that will shape the environmental and poverty outcomes. Perhaps the key lesson to take away from these studies is that trade policies aimed at increasing incomes may have beneficial effects in one place – for the environment, or for poverty, or both – and negative effects in another, depending on local conditions and local policies. The case studies highlight the fact that while some outcomes of trade can be clearly labeled positive or negative, in most cases trade-offs are being made. These trade-offs are, first, between different groups of people who may be "winners" or "losers" from trade liberalization, and, second, between people and the natural environment itself. Vulnerable people – the rural poor – have little or no say in the balancing of these trade-offs. And the environment is even more rarely given a voice. Only by understanding the complicated context and recognizing the forces shaping the trade-offs can we hope to predict and address the outcomes.

- Finally, we have come to learn that only by recognizing the complicated context of local responses can we begin to ensure that the outcomes of trade are beneficial. International negotiations cannot foresee the multiple local impacts of trade agreements. The recommendations provided in the final chapters of this book by The World Bank and WWF point toward some better ways to achieve core sustainability and human development goals. Most importantly, with an understanding of the multiple levels of economic activity and governance that affect local places, responses to changing opportunities can be implemented at the appropriate level of governance. Inevitably this will involve working to change conditions, incentives, and opportunities and to increase stakeholder participation at the local and national levels, rather than trying to address the local outcomes of trade at the international level. While trade will continue to play a central role in international development policies, the focus of development needs to be shifted back to the national and local levels in order to truly achieve its goals.

We have learned much from our collaborative work on this book. Long discussions about the case studies have made it clear that there are many places where a development bank and a conservation organization can agree. And while each organization drew its own overall conclusions, the differences between them reflect a difference of emphasis rather than fundamental disagreements. It is very clear that trade is affecting vulnerable people in vulnerable places, and that both development and conservation organizations must work through a variety of measures to ensure that these local changes are beneficial for the poor and for the environment. As the pressures of globalization and population growth increase, aggravated by the effects of global climate change, the need to solve the problems of the world's most vulnerable people and places will only increase. The lessons of this book will help guide us as we respond to those challenges.

Warren Evans   David Reed
Director, Environment Department   *Senior Vice President, Policy*
The World Bank   *WWF–US*

Acknowledgments

The editors would like to express their deep gratitude to Polly Means and Charles Huang for their creative help in designing the book's maps and figures; and to the following people for their insights and advice on early drafts: Moulika Arabhi, Ajay Chhibber, John Kornerup Bang, Hernán Blanco, Carter Brandon, Rachel Cleetus, Dipak Dasgupta, Eugenio Diaz-Bonilla, Ariel Dinar, Annie Dufey, Anantha Kumar Duraiappah, Hugo Garcia Rañó, Pablo Gutman, Norbert Henninger, Frank Jacobs, Walter Kennes, Piet Klop, Guo Li, William Lyakurwa, Richard McNally, Alejandro Nadal, Nanie Ratsifandrihamanana, Walt Reid, David Reed, Dirk Reinermann, David Tecklin, Hans Wessels, Wu Yusong and Moeed Yusuf.

Financial support for this book, and the project on which it was based, was generously provided by the European Commission and the Netherlands Directorate-General of Development Cooperation (DGIS).

Ministerie van
Buitenlandse Zaken

1. Trade liberalization, rural poverty and the environment

Jonathan A. Cook, Owen Cylke, Donald F. Larson, John D. Nash and Pamela Stedman-Edwards

As trade negotiators from around the world gathered for World Trade Organization (WTO) talks in Seattle in November 1999, a heated debate over the impacts of trade and trade liberalization reached its peak. A diverse group of protesters from countries north and south temporarily halted the controversial negotiations after years of slow but steady progress toward a global expansion of trade liberalization. While international development institutions and the governments of many developed and developing countries attempted to push forward with trade liberalization, protesters blamed trade for many of the problems facing the poor in developing countries and for the increasing degradation of the natural environment. At the same time, a deep schism emerged between developed and developing countries over agricultural trade and the protection of intellectual property rights (Bhagwati, 2005).

The rapid growth of international trade, supported by the liberalization of trade policies and by the efforts of many developing countries to expand exports, has dramatically transformed the international arena in recent decades. Trade liberalization and export promotion together have formed a policy keystone for many developing countries and for international development institutions. But the rapid changes brought in some places by opening markets, and the failed promise of change in others, have generated a highly polemical debate around the role of trade. Trade has been lionized – credited with fostering not only economic growth, but also poverty alleviation, environmental improvements and even democratization. And trade has equally been vilified – blamed for degradation of natural resources, disruptive social change and increasing inequality among social groups and nations.

While trade negotiations previously had been largely a technical matter for trade ministers and their staff, Seattle brought global attention to the significant impacts that trade deals have for people and places. Increasingly, international institutions and national governments have recognized that the environmental and social implications of trade liberalization can be significant and have begun to adjust their policies accordingly. Yet questions remain about the real impacts of trade liberalization, whether it delivers all that has been promised and about the role it plays in promoting sustainable development.

The Trade Liberalization, Rural Poverty and the Environment project, carried out over the past five years by the World Bank and WWF, attempts to answer some of those questions by looking at them in a new way. This chapter briefly reviews the state of the debate when this project was initiated, and the questions it aimed to answer, and describes the way the project was carried out. It also briefly summarizes the six case studies that are presented more fully in the subsequent chapters. Key findings and conclusions from the studies are not given here, but are presented from the perspective of each institution in later chapters. The volume concludes with a chapter that places the trade issue in a larger context of global economic, demographic and environmental changes, and offers some final thoughts about a way forward.

THE DEBATE ABOUT TRADE, POVERTY AND ENVIRONMENT

When the project began, the nature of the public debate made it clear that ideology, rather than careful study, informed many opinions about the relationship between trade, poverty and environment. In general, issues of trade and poverty and of trade and environment were addressed separately, without adequate consideration of connections among all three. And while these issues of trade and poverty and of trade and environment were considered from a variety of viewpoints (see Cleetus, 2005, commissioned as part of this project, for a detailed review), public debate was often dominated by advocates who fell into two camps: those in favor of trade liberalization, who were reluctant to admit any negative impacts, and those opposed to trade liberalization, who could see no good coming from it. Evidence was short on both sides of the debate.

As the developing countries suffered through the economic crises of the 1980s and early 1990s, international financial institutions and governments in developed countries worked from the premise that globalization, fostered by trade, investment and capital-flow liberalization, would provide the best solution to development woes. Many developing countries, faced

Billions of US dollars (constant 2002)

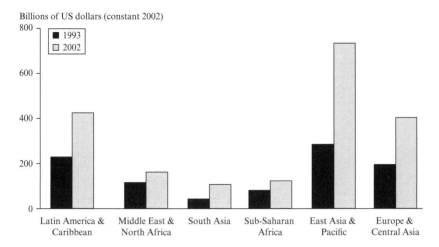

Source: World Bank (2008), *Development Data Platform* (electronic), Washington, DC: World Bank.

Figure 1.1   Exports of goods and services, 1993–2002

with overwhelming debts and financial instability, adopted liberalization with the hope that economic opening would lead them out of the development impasse they had reached.

World trade has expanded dramatically, with world exports of goods and services doubling between 1995 and 2000 and continuing to grow at a rate of 13 percent per year between 2000 and 2006 (UNCTAD, 2008). On average, developing countries have done well, with exports growing at almost 16 percent since 2000. But the results for developing countries have been mixed. In general, exports grew as did incomes in most countries (Figures 1.1 and 1.2). However, rates of growth were uneven among countries and among sectors. Importantly, even as average incomes grew and rates of poverty fell, the number of poor continued to grow in Africa and South Asia (Figure 1.3). At the same time, an increasing number of important and fragile ecosystems faced mounting demographic and economic pressures.

By the time of the Seattle meeting, many developing countries had become less willing to open their markets. While some trade barriers were being lowered, barriers for agricultural goods remained high, and the perception took root among developing countries that most benefits from international trade reforms accrued to the richer countries. Governments in developing countries began to look for more effective ways to benefit from the growing world economy.

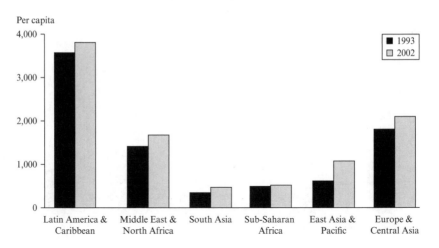

Source: World Bank (2008), *Development Data Platform* (electronic), Washington DC: World Bank.

Figure 1.2   Income growth, 1993–2002

TAKING A CLOSER LOOK AT THE TRADE–POVERTY–ENVIRONMENT RELATIONSHIP

At this juncture, the World Bank and WWF came together because of a shared view that the impacts of trade were more complex and nuanced than the public debate allowed. Trade outcomes were and continue to be important to WWF's conservation mission and the World Bank's goal of reducing poverty, and both institutions have a shared interest in sustainable development. Nevertheless, the two institutions approach trade policy from different perspectives and, in some cases, speak to different constituencies. Consequently, a collaborative effort between the World Bank, WWF and in-country research teams appeared to be a good way to help the governments of developing countries capture greater benefits from trade while averting negative social and environmental impacts.

The agreement between the World Bank and WWF on the need to better understand and address some critical aspects of the trade–poverty–environment relationship led to the collaborative project described in this book. The case studies presented here reflect the efforts of both organizations, along with local researchers in developing countries, to gain a more accurate understanding of the impacts of trade liberalization on the rural poor and on the land and water resources on which they depend. The lessons drawn from these case studies by the World Bank, WWF and local

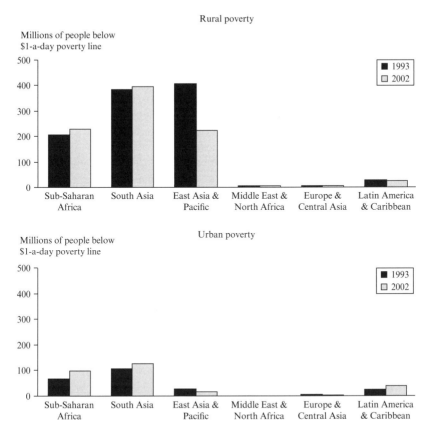

Figure 1.3 is described by the following:

Rural poverty

Millions of people below
$1-a-day poverty line

■ 1993
□ 2002

Urban poverty

Millions of people below
$1-a-day poverty line

■ 1993
□ 2002

Source: World Bank (2007), *World Development Report 2008: Agriculture for Development*, Washington, DC: World Bank.

Figure 1.3   Poverty rates

researchers vary because of our differing missions, but they reflect a deeper understanding of the complexity and interlinked nature of the relationships among trade liberalization, rural poverty and the environment for the same reason.

At the start of the project, several recently completed case studies pointed to the complex impacts of macroeconomic policy and trade reforms and to the importance of place-specific impacts (see Reed, 1996; and Wood et al., 2000). The studies showed that macroeconomic policies, intended to foster structural adjustment and long-term growth, had unexpected and sometimes detrimental consequences for both the poor and the environment. The case studies, carried out around the world, showed clearly that impacts of macroeconomic adjustment can vary substantially depending on the institutions, governance conditions and policies accompanying the economic adjustment. The studies suggested that both local- and national-level institutions play important roles in shaping environmental and social outcomes. The research concluded that the environment – particularly in natural-resource-based economies – was likely to suffer when economic incentives and policies accompanying adjustment favored short-term growth; and that poor populations were most likely to be hurt by policies that reduced access to natural resources.

It was also becoming clear that many of the world's most environmentally important and vulnerable places are also home to some of the world's most vulnerable people. Many of the characteristics of poverty – including restricted access to resources, education, health care and political influence – make it difficult for the poor to adapt to change. The problem is exacerbated because the poor have limited control over the natural resources on which they depend (see Reed, 2006; Millennium Ecosystem Assessment, 2003; Stedman-Edwards, 2005). In the literature on trade and poverty, much had been written about negative, downward spirals of poverty, overuse of resources and a resulting increase in poverty (e.g., Kates and Haarman, 1992). Likewise, much has been made of the balanced, sustainable use of resources by local peoples (e.g., Redford and Mansour, 1996). While most cases are more nuanced, it is clear that the rural poor are almost invariably highly dependent on the direct use of natural resources.

Because the public debate about the relationship between trade, poverty and environment had not addressed these complex interactions between policy and other factors, there was little understanding about how these macro-level trade events were likely to affect particular places. Knowledge was lacking about how trade affects the livelihoods of the rural poor, including some of the world's most vulnerable people; how trade affects the use of environmental services and resources, particularly the land and water that the poor rely on; and how trade affects global resources such as biodiversity. Moreover, given that trade is likely to have both positive and negative impacts for the livelihoods of the rural poor and environmental sustainability, there was little discussion of the institutions needed to make decisions about the inevitable trade-offs among income, equality and sustainability.

The studies in this book were carried out with the aim of better documenting the specific results of trade liberalization for vulnerable people in specific places. It was hoped that this improved understanding of the complex relationship between trade, rural poverty and environment would serve as the basis for identifying policy and institutional measures for local and national governments as well as international trade bodies – measures that would ensure that trade liberalization contributes to alleviating poverty and promoting environmental sustainability in rural areas. Each of the six case studies sought to answer three principal questions:

- How are trade policies and trade liberalization affecting land and water resources in environmentally significant rural areas, especially through their effect on livelihoods of the rural poor?
- How are trade policies and trade liberalization affecting vulnerable people, especially through their effect on use of land and water resources in rural areas?
- Can policy and institutional measures and other interventions be identified that will ensure trade liberalization contributes to alleviating poverty and at the same time promote environmental sustainability in rural areas?

A common thread in earlier WWF studies (Reed, 1996; Wood et al., 2000) was the use of a multidisciplinary framework that examined the local, regional or national, and international factors shaping the outcomes of policy changes. The studies relied on tools from economics, sociology, ecology, political science and other disciplines to draw a picture of the socioeconomic forces underlying environmental change and the institutional opportunities and obstacles to sustainable, equitable development. By examining the local, national and international contexts that were shaping local outcomes, these studies were more comprehensive than many examinations of poverty – environment relations. Rather than focusing exclusively on economic growth or environmental change, this approach sought to look at the impacts of policy changes on particular places and on the people who depend on the natural resources provided by local ecosystems. This cross-cutting approach was adopted for the project in order to move away from the narrow viewpoint of a single discipline and to better understand the myriad factors at play in determining the outcomes of trade liberalization.

The sample of case studies[1] – in Chile, China, India, Madagascar, South Africa and Vietnam – was chosen based on:

- high probability of experiencing significant impacts on land and water use
- high probability of experiencing significant impacts on rural populations
- finding a diverse, yet representative, set of examples of trade-related environmental and social impacts
- implementation or initiation of significant trade reforms
- local research capacity.

In each of the countries, a local research team carried out the study, focusing on a particular economic sector (or sectors) within a particular region of the country that was undergoing change related to new trade rules and opportunities. The cases range from shrimp production in the coastal regions of Vietnam and India, to corn production in the spiny forest of Madagascar, to forestry and salmon production in Chile, to rural development in mountainous western China, to horticulture in Madagascar, to sugar production in the Incomati River Basin of South Africa.

Each study carried out an overall assessment of the countrywide impact of a trade policy reform (or "trade event") in addition to looking carefully at the impacts on a particular rural site. Specific sites selected within the countries were rural areas where community livelihoods depend heavily on local environmental services, namely land and water resources. These sites were also places deemed of environmental importance according to WWF and other internationally recognized institutions. The studies aimed to describe the economic and environmental changes that occurred or could be expected to occur as a result of trade liberalization, and to understand how impacts on the poor's access to, control over and use of land and water resources intersected with these changes. Based on this analysis, the studies made specific recommendations for domestic policy and institutional interventions.

THE CASE STUDIES

The proposed framework called for looking at both the economic and environmental relationships at play and the sociopolitical and institutional context in which a trade event occurred. Generally, the trade event was a change in national and/or international trade rules. Each team adapted the framework, depending on the characteristics of the particular case and the availability of data. The analysis of trade liberalization's impact on land and water resources by the poor focused on the role of institutional, economic and social contexts. Each of these contexts has micro-, meso- and macro-level characteristics that were explored by the studies. Along with the environmental conditions of the country, these contexts shape the environmental and poverty impacts of agricultural and other natural-resource-based production (logging, fishing, etc.).

Land and water use provide the means to link the macro-level analysis with the micro- and meso- levels of analysis. The micro-level, or local-level, analysis looks at local environmental changes and local welfare and equity as they are affected by local resource-use decisions, incomes, markets and resource management institutions, among other factors.

The meso-level analysis looks at in-country institutions and patterns of change. The macro-level analysis looks at broader resource-use patterns, including cumulative, region-wide or global changes, as they are affected by national and international markets, national distribution of power and national institutions.

Put into operational terms, each case study examined how a trade event (past or present) influences the rural poor's access to, control of and use of land and water resources and, consequently, how a trade event affects income, equity and environmental sustainability. The case study is in essence a "bottom-up" approach, looking at the impact of "top-down" rules. The emphasis of the analysis was on the problems and opportunities that trade liberalization creates for poverty alleviation and natural-resource management.

The debate about the role of trade and trade liberalization has grown more sophisticated over the past decade, but it has hardly been put to rest. Without a better understanding of how trade really affects the poor and the environment, an understanding that is essential for making choices about trade and providing the institutional and policy support needed to make trade work for development, the debate will continue to be unfocused and polemical. The cases presented in more detail in the following chapters of this book identify some of the positive and negative impacts of trade liberalization for vulnerable people and places in developing countries and identify some of the key drivers that determine the outcomes of trade liberalization. Each case tells a different story – and this diversity and complexity is an important aspect in itself – but there are important commonalities among the cases, discussed in the concluding chapters, that can help us anticipate and interpret these complex impacts.

In choosing a case study approach for this research, WWF and the World Bank opted to look at the relationships among trade, poverty and environment in specific places under a microscope. The impacts of trade are varied and complex when examined in this way. Bringing together the six studies, however, reveals some commonalities or patterns at the micro level and supports some conclusions at the macro level. This micro-to-macro approach brings into sharp focus what is happening in particular places and to particular people in the short term, and begins to show us the likely long-term implications of changing poverty–environment relationships for both the environment and human well-being.

In a sense, the deck was stacked for this research. The cases were chosen because there was reason to believe, a priori, that trade liberalization was having significant local effects in these places in terms of both the environment and human well-being. Whether the patterns uncovered here prove to be widespread or peculiar to these particular places, they are important because they are affecting some of the world's most vulnerable people and places. And as trade liberalization continues to play a leading role in development policy, understanding how it actually affects critical ecosystems is important for us all.

Chile (see chapter 2) was one of the first developing countries to adopt extensive market and trade reforms, beginning in the mid-1970s. Today the country has a strong economy and relatively low poverty levels. However, the increase in exports is not equally benefiting all regions or the most vulnerable of the rural poor. This study examined two important sectors – salmon farming and forestry – in three poor regions of south-central Chile. Both sectors have benefited significantly from trade liberalization. However, salmon farming and forestry have had different impacts on poverty alleviation, inequality and migration because of their differing impacts on resource use and job creation. The salmon industry has been associated with broad job creation and increasing incomes; the forestry sector, on the other hand, has done little to reduce local poverty. While the environmental impacts of the two sectors are debated, the rapid growth of the salmon sector has set off some alarm bells concerning its potential environmental effects, and the expansion of industrial-scale forest plantations has generated substantial concern about the loss of native forest to large-scale, mono-crop, short-rotation stands of exotic trees. In general, the continued concentration of exports within natural-resource-based sectors raises questions about the overall sustainability of this aspect of Chile's economic development.

China's accession to the WTO followed as part of a successful long-term effort to modernize, liberalize and increase Chinese participation in the global marketplace (see Chapter 3). With its reserves of labor and natural resources and its massive industrial and manufacturing capacity, China was already poised to be a winner in global markets. Yet people living in the isolated mountain regions of western China, many of whom are ethnic minorities who live by farming some of the country's most environmentally fragile landscapes, were not expected to benefit from the liberalized trade regime. Nevertheless, through its indirect impacts, the rapid growth of trade has brought new opportunities to even these remote regions. This study looks at the case of Pingbian County, located in Yunnan Province. There, new opportunities to supply agricultural markets in eastern China and neighboring countries have brought not only reduced poverty and greater equity, but also a critical shift away from land-intensive agriculture, which was environmentally damaging, toward more sustainable labor-intensive crops. Forest conversion has slowed and environmental services remain largely intact because of the transition to horticulture and off-farm labor.

In the early 1990s, *India* (see Chapter 4) embarked on a program of economic liberalization that has given a much greater role to the market and has fostered an increase in exports. In the Sundarbans, the large delta region of West Bengal known for both its remarkable biodiversity and high levels of poverty, liberalization sparked expansion of an export-oriented shrimp industry. The last 20 years have witnessed the rapid proliferation of aquaculture farms and the development of a large processing and export industry in the region, which have generated employment and improved incomes for many. The use of land and water, however, has been greatly affected by all this development, with consequences for biodiversity, mangrove forests and the ecosystem services they provide. This study looks in detail at the effect of increased shrimp production on the people and the natural environment of the Sundarbans. The entire production and export process – from prawn-seed collection to farming, processing and transport – generates income and creates employment for many people who otherwise have very limited economic opportunities. At the national level, shrimp exports are earning substantial foreign exchange. But there are at least two important environmental impacts, namely land-use change and loss of biodiversity.

Madagascar (see Chapter 5) is one of the poorest countries in sub-Saharan Africa; it is also one of the world's richest areas for biodiversity. The predominantly rural population relies heavily on the natural resources that also support the island's remarkable assemblage of species. Liberalization of the Malagasy economy began in the 1980s and has led to a rapid increase in trade. But the growth of trade has had little impact on economic opportunities for Madagascar's rural population, and rural exports on the whole have declined. This study looks at two cases: first, rapid expansion of maize production in southwest Madagascar, a case that illustrates the contribution of trade to agricultural extensification and deforestation and its links to changing environmental governance; and second, contract farming of high-value vegetables for export to Europe, which illustrates the concrete opportunities trade can afford the poor and the contribution the private sector can make to sustainable agriculture through direct support for small producers.

The Incomati River Basin is a very poor and highly water-stressed area of *South Africa* (see Chapter 6). Liberalization of the country's economy, and particularly of its sugar policies, has contributed to the expansion of the region's sugar industry. The study analyzes how recent changes in the European Union sugar-subsidy regime are expected to contribute to an increase in sugar production in the Incomati River Basin. The opportunities presented by the sugar industry were crucial in helping black farmers to establish themselves on smallholdings. However, the sugar industry's heavy demands on water and land have significant impacts on environmental resources and on the large poor population, which has very limited access to land and depends on those resources for their livelihoods. Already the Incomati's watercourse ecology is severely compromised, and the area's natural vegetation has been irreparably damaged. The reduction of habitat has gone hand-in-hand with biodiversity loss. This increase is likely to generate negative externalities: less land available for the poor, increased water consumption and associated deterioration in the ecosystem services that will disproportionately affect the landless and the poor. A recent national water law offers some hope for more efficient and just allocation of water in the Incomati region and illustrates well the challenges of putting in place institutions to balance competing needs.

Vietnam (see Chapter 7) has dramatically reorganized its economy over the last 20 years, moving toward a market-based, open system. The economic and social results have been remarkable: production of export crops has soared and poverty levels have dropped substantially. The results for the environment have been more problematic, as changes in production have often moved ahead of environmental understanding and regulation. This study looks at the very rapid expansion of shrimp farming in Ca Mau Province in southern Vietnam in the wake of trade liberalization and increased farmer autonomy. The growth of shrimp exports has transformed the socioeconomic structure of Ca Mau. New economic opportunities have been created for both landowners and the landless in the region, and poverty levels have fallen. However, the sustainability of these improvements depends not only on international market prices but also on the adoption of appropriate shrimp-farming models and protection of the region's remaining natural mangroves and freshwater systems. The conversion of coastal mangrove forests and rice fields has had serious consequences for the natural environment, degrading ecosystems and reducing biodiversity, which in turn has reduced opportunities for many of the poorest people in the region.

NOTE

1. A seventh case study was carried out for the Santa Marta Biosphere Reserve in Mexico. That study focused heavily on providing small producers in that region with new information and capacity to improve the sustainability of their agriculture production model. The major conclusions were useful for the locality, but were not of sufficiently general interest to warrant inclusion in this volume.

BIBLIOGRAPHY

Bhagwati, J. (2005), "From Seattle to Hong Kong: are we getting anywhere?", *Global Economy Journal*, **5** (4), 1–12.

Cleetus, R. (2005), *Trade Liberalization, Rural Poverty and the Environment: A Wide-ranging Review of the Debates*, Washington, DC: WWF-MPO.

Kates, R. and V. Haarman (1992), "Where the poor live: are the assumptions correct?", *Environment*, **34** (4), 4–28.

Millennium Ecosystem Assessment (2003), *Ecosystems and Human Well-being: A Framework for Assessment*, Washington, DC: Island Press.

Redford, K.H. and J. Mansour (eds) (1996), *Traditional Peoples and Biodiversity Conservation in Large Tropical Landscapes*, Rosslyn, VA: The Nature Conservancy.

Reed, D. (1996), *Structural Adjustment, the Environment and Sustainable Development*, London: Earthscan.

Reed, D. (2006), *Escaping Poverty's Grasp: The Environmental Foundations of Poverty Reduction*, London: Earthscan.

Stedman-Edwards, P. (2005), *Strategic Vulnerabilities Assessment: Framework Paper*, Washington, DC: WWF-MPO.

United Nations Conference on Trade and Development (UNCTAD) (2008), *Globalization for Development: The International Trade Perspective*, New York: UNCTAD.

Wood, A., P. Stedman-Edwards and J. Mang (eds) (2000), *The Root Causes of Biodiversity Loss*, London: Earthscan.

World Trade Organization (WTO) (2007), *World Trade Report 2007*, Geneva: WTO

2. Trade liberalization, rural poverty and the environment: a case study of the forest and salmon sectors in Chile

Raúl O'Ryan, with Mario Niklitschek, Edwin Niklitschek, Andrés Ulloa and Nicolo Gligo

The rapid growth of the Chilean economy over the last few decades has earned the country its reputation as the most solid and dynamic economy in Latin America, with poverty rates now among the lowest in the region. Deep macroeconomic and microeconomic reforms, including a dramatic opening to international trade, that were initiated in the 1970s are credited for this export-led growth. However, these reforms came with significant social, economic and, possibly, environmental costs. The country's macroeconomic indicators are strong, but it is not so clear that the increase in exports is benefiting all local economies, or the most vulnerable of the rural poor, equally. And the concentration of exports in the natural-resource-based sectors – such as mining, forestry, agriculture, fishing and aquaculture – has raised questions about the environmental impacts, as well as the overall sustainability, of an economic model that relies heavily on natural-resource-based exports. Many environmental nongovernmental organizations (NGOs) and local organizations have argued against the current economic model on the grounds that it is unsustainable, contending that the environment has been degraded over the last 20 years. Other stakeholders, particularly producers, tend to dismiss the significance of these effects, pointing to the key role of exports in economic growth and poverty alleviation. Different studies have addressed some of these issues, without resolving the dispute.

This study aims to shed light on this complicated relationship among trade liberalization, the environment and rural poverty by examining two important sectors – salmon farming and forestry – in three regions of south-central Chile. Both sectors have benefited greatly from trade

14

Figure 2.1   Chile and regions VIII, IX and X

liberalization. Both sectors also have substantial impacts on natural-resource use and the environment, impacts that have been widely debated in Chile. And both sectors were established in areas of relative poverty within Chile. However, there are important differences between these sectors that could inform us about the impacts of trade: investment in the forestry and salmon sectors began at different times and faced different social and economic conditions and different environmental regulations and institutions, and the industries have different natural resource and labor requirements. This study looks at the role of trade liberalization in the growth of forestry and aquaculture and at the different impacts of the two sectors on natural resources and on rural poverty, particularly through the use of labor. It focuses on the three regions – regions VIII, IX and X – where these sectors have grown most rapidly and where poverty problems have been significant (see Figure 2.1).

This chapter begins with a discussion of the general economic liberalization process in Chile and its impacts on production, employment and poverty at the aggregate level. The development of the salmon and forestry sectors is then described. The next sections examine and compare the different socioeconomic and environmental impacts of the two sectors. The final sections look at the responses and interventions that have been made, particularly for the environment, and draw some conclusions about the relative impacts of the two sectors.

SITE DESCRIPTION

According to Global Forest Watch (2002), Chile has almost one-third of the world's few large tracts of temperate forest. Some of the most impressive forests in the world are located in the south, including araucaria forests, temperate rain forests, alerce forests and Chilean palm forests. The temperate rain forest was included by WWF among its 25 top priorities for conservation. These forests are of great ecological and conservation value. They contribute to global climate regulation, control flooding, cycle nutrients and soil, purify water and support a global reserve of biodiversity. One of the richest zones of native forest and biodiversity is in regions VIII to X. However, prior to 1973, these areas had suffered dramatic changes because of agriculture, fuelwood and timber extraction, forest degradation and clearing. After 1973, pressures increased as a result of the development of exotic plantations for the forestry industry.

Additionally, the coasts of southern Chile are rich in freshwater and estuarine ecosystems. Before 1973 there was very limited productive use of these aquatic ecosystems. However, estuaries, lakes and rivers near cities were used for discharging urban wastes and as recipients of other sources of nutrients and particulate matter originating in agriculture (fertilizer runoff) and erosion (resulting from poor agricultural practices and deforestation). Small-scale fisheries were mostly geared to the supply of the local and national market. These uses generated increasing environmental pressures on both lakes and marine waters. It was in this context that salmon aquaculture began its development in the late 1980s.

ECONOMIC LIBERALIZATION

Chile was one of the first developing countries to adopt extensive market and trade reforms (see Table 2.1). The reform process started in the mid-1970s and, after a long period of recession and adjustment, began to yield positive

Table 2.1   Evolution of the effective protection rate

Year	1961	1967	1975	1979
Average	133	168	90	13
Std. deviation	177	282	33	2
Range	488	1127	137	7

Sources: Behrman (1976) and Aedo and Lagos (1984), quoted in Hachette (2000).

results in the mid-1980s. The first period of reform (1974–84) included unilateral trade liberalization and other pro-market reforms, as well as contraction-based fiscal and monetary measures to correct severe macroeconomic imbalances. In this first decade, which also coincided with two major external shocks, considerable social and economic costs were incurred. Chile suffered two major economic crises, and average per capita yearly GNP (gross national product) fell by 0.3 percent. Unemployment soared to record levels during the 1982–83 recession, reaching 20 percent. Poverty levels rose to 45–50 percent. Despite these social costs, the military regime promoted and maintained its basic economic policy, particularly regarding macroeconomic stability and trade liberalization. Reforms were briefly halted and in some cases reversed in the mid-1980s as Chile dealt with inflation problems, but liberalization resumed in 1986. By the late 1980s, a real improvement in aggregate indicators – GDP (gross domestic product), unemployment, inflation – led to a consensus among Chile's political parties around export-led growth. The democratic government that took power in 1990 therefore maintained the basic policies and moved toward a second generation of macroeconomic and microeconomic policies that allowed the benefits of growth to be extended to more of the poor. Tariff cutting continued in the 1990s and, in addition to Chile's unilateral liberalization, the country signed a number of free trade agreements. Today, exports (mostly of natural resources and associated products) remain the cornerstone of Chile's growth strategy.

Once reform policies were fully implemented, from the mid-1980s to 2004, the Chilean economy grew at an average per capita yearly rate of 4 percent. This is well above the 2.7 percent growth rate achieved in the 40 years preceding liberalization (1933–73) and, in the 1990s, was triple the average growth rate for Latin America. Trade liberalization was certainly a key driver of this growth (De Gregorio et al., 2002; De Gregorio and Lee, 2003; Irarrazabal and Opromolla, 2005), together with other policies including macroeconomic stabilization, price liberalization, labor and capital market reforms and privatization of most productive activities (Corbo et al., 2005).

Although clearly Chile's economic growth has been remarkable, its quality has been mixed. While there are no comparable data to reliably track poverty rates before 1987,[1] available statistics indicate that following the initial economic reform and macroeconomic stabilization program, poverty increased significantly in Chile in the late 1970s and 1980s. This was followed by a dramatic decline in poverty that accompanied the economic growth starting in the mid-1980s. Studies in the mid-1980s found 45 percent of households in poverty, of which 30 percent were in extreme poverty.[2] National data place the poverty level at 39 percent in the period 1987–92 (CASEN[3]). With the restoration of democracy and the period of rapid economic growth in the 1990s, poverty fell rapidly to 21 percent of the population by 2000. In the same period, rural poverty fell from 41 percent to 24 percent. While both rural and national poverty indicators have fallen, rural poverty has decreased more slowly than the national average (3.2 percent decline per year versus 3.6 percent). Moreover, Chile's excellent economic performance had not yielded an improvement in income distribution, nationally or spatially, up to 2003. Income inequality in Chile remains among the highest in the world. The Gini coefficient improved slightly, from 0.58 to 0.56[4] between 1987 and 1998, but has remained fairly constant since then.[5] Table 2.2 shows macroeconomic indicators for 1974 to 2004.

However, after this extraordinary performance that led most analysts to predict future growth rates of 6 percent and even 7 percent, economic growth suffered another crisis because of external shocks between 1998 and 2002, resulting in an average growth rate of 2.3 percent over this period. As a result, more cautious expectations have developed and current per capita growth is believed to be around 5 percent per year.

Regional disparities have emerged and persisted. For example, the growth rate in region VIII has been half the national average since 1984. Poverty levels in regions VIII and IX reached almost 50 percent when the national average was 40 percent, and poverty reduction there has been slower than the national average. The three regions under study have had the worst income distribution in the country since 1987. Disparities between urban, rural and indigenous communities are also notable. In regions VIII and IX, rural poverty remains significantly higher than the national average and higher than urban poverty in the same region. However, in region X rural poverty has fallen significantly since 1987 and is now much lower than the national average. At the same time, the percentage of Chile's indigenous population falling below the poverty line is 50 percent higher than the national average. Of the three regions, region IX has the largest indigenous population, accounting for 30 percent of the region's population. This study focuses on analyzing how the liberalization

Table 2.2   Chile: macroeconomic indicators, 1974–2004 (period averages, percentages)

	74–75	76–79	80–81	82–83	84–85	86–89	90–93	94–96	97–2004
GDP growth	−6.2	7.4	6.7	−7.6	4.4	7.3	6.9	6.6	2.3
Unemployment rate	13.5	13.8	10.9	18.6	12.2	5.3	5.9	5.7	8.3
Inflation	358	69	20	22	25	18	18	8.7	4.2
Real wage variation	−4.1	14.3	8.8	−5.5	−2.1	2.6	3.9	5.1	1.6
Real exchange rate variation	83	1.4	−13.2	15.7	13.3	4.5	−2.8	−3.7	4.9
Term of trade variation	−33.1	2.6	−3.5	−3.6	−5.4	7.3	−3.6	1.6	7.3
Trade balance/GDP	−2	−2.8	−10.3	2.7	2.8	4.5	−2.3	8.6	2.1

Source: Chile's Central Bank.

process has influenced or mitigated poverty in rural populations located in these three regions of Chile.

How are poverty alleviation and income distribution related to trade liberalization? There are two main links. First, trade liberalization explains a significant part of growth and reduction of poverty at the aggregate level.[6] Exports have become a major engine for growth as production shifts toward meeting external rather than internal demand. Second, changes in Chile's productive structure have generated different impacts among regions, localities and populations. Given the country's large resource base, reallocation of productive resources to sectors with comparative advantages – which is the expected consequence of liberalization – has meant a general trend toward exports from natural-resource-based sectors. With liberalization, fruit production, fishing and mining increased their share of GDP. The manufacturing sector decreased in importance and its composition changed from a preponderance of basic industries to industries based on natural resources, notably food, wood products and pulp and paper.

The economies of the three regions included in this study have clearly adjusted toward goods that are more intensive in natural resources. Sectors such as forestry and aquaculture have been encouraged, while others, including traditional agriculture, livestock and other traditional industries, have lost relative weight. The composition of production has thus changed. Export demand has also resulted in scale effects notable in the rapid expansion of the forestry and aquaculture sectors. As a consequence of these significant trade-driven shifts in the productive structure of each region, some social groups have been negatively affected, losing their traditional means of subsistence, while others have experienced the positive impacts of growth. In addition to these socioeconomic impacts of the changing production structure, there are also different environmental impacts across the regions. Here we look in detail at the results of trade liberalization on the salmon and forestry sectors.

DEVELOPMENT OF THE SALMON EXPORT SECTOR

Commercial farming of salmonids[7] in Chile began in 1979. By 2003, Chile had become the world's second largest producer, close behind Norway. That year, 500,000 tons of farmed salmon were harvested, accounting for 22 percent of the country's fishery exports by weight and 51 percent (US$1,147 million) by value, and equaling about 6 percent of the country's total exports. Close to 80 percent of this harvest is produced in region X. From the mid-1980s to mid-1990s, production expansion – including the growth of coho salmon farming and the introduction of Atlantic salmon and rainbow

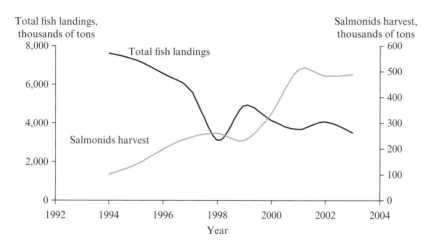

Total fish landings,   Salmonids harvest,
thousands of tons   thousands of tons

Source: Sernap (National Fisheries Service).

Figure 2.2 Salmon aquaculture harvest and total fish landings in southern Chile, 1992–2002

trout farming – was rapid. Beginning in the late 1990s, technological developments contributed to rising production levels. Salmon farming now represents more than 50 percent of total fisheries and aquaculture landings in regions X, XI and XII. The rapid growth of aquaculture contrasts with the decrease in other small-scale landings and industrial fisheries over the past two decades. Clearly, there has been a progressive replacement of wild fish by farmed salmon (see Figure 2.2). This substitution has allowed the regions to maintain and increase installed processing capacity and labor demand.

The development of the salmon sector began a decade after the process of trade liberalization was begun. Several successful pilot projects, initiated by private and public institutions in the early 1970s[8] that showed that salmon farming was both technically and economically feasible given southern Chile's climate and geography, triggered the sector's growth. Trade liberalization acted as a very important driver of this growth, not only by facilitating exports but also by opening the economy to external financial markets, foreign investments and new technologies. In particular, the Foreign Investment Statute (1974) gave security to foreign investors, allowing them to enter the salmon sector with their technology and practices. Most of the initial private investments were made by Chilean investors and by foreign companies already established in the country. The government helped with market identification and product promotion overseas.[9] The attractive exchange rate in the late 1980s played an important role in increasing returns and stimulating tenfold growth in production value between 1985 and 1994. This growth, together with Chilean policies that granted all national and foreign companies the same rights, attracted more foreign investors to the sector. Yet, although foreign capital has been very important in spurring the sector's development, its contribution has always been below 50 percent of total investment in the sector.

In its early years, the salmon sector was dominated by a large number of small and medium-sized salmon operations. Since 1990, the sector has seen important changes in the structure of the industry. As international markets began to react to the increase in Chilean production, prices began to fall. In recent years, this fall in export prices, aggravated by a change in the exchange rate, has promoted industry concentration and a significant level of integration between Chilean and European companies, which were formerly competitors. Foreign firms began to increase their share – estimates for 2005 indicate that foreign-owned companies produced about 40 percent of Chilean salmon. Both competition and integration have made it necessary to update local technology and to improve environmental standards to respond to external market preferences.

Production practices were initially rudimentary and dependent on imported inputs, including salmon eggs, smolts (young fish), cultivation tanks and processing machinery. Salmon feed was prepared locally by firms using fresh raw materials from the south of Chile and Peru. As the industry has grown, imports have been gradually replaced by national products (including eggs, hatchery equipment, feed and cages) – in part because of the support of local research institutions but mostly because of upgrading of the local industries by foreign suppliers – that have allowed the development of technology suppliers (Torres, 2006). This has created significant links with the local economy. A local service sector has also developed to support the industry and now supplies vaccines, nets and net maintenance, packaging material, transport services, software design and veterinary services. Although environmental and natural resources are the essential inputs of salmon production, the industry has gradually been moving toward the use of more knowledge-intensive inputs. Technological changes such as the use of larger cultivation tanks, automatic feeding systems and computerized monitoring systems have improved the rate of food conversion. Also, new firms dedicated to environmental activities have been emerging, including firms related to recycling and salmon-feeding services. In sum, there are now many linkages between salmon production and the local economy in region X, creating important multiplier effects for the rest of the economy (Schurman, 2001). For example, the 2003 input – output matrix showed that the multiplier effect of the sector was 21 percent higher than the average of all sectors.[10]

Regulations and rules have generally lagged behind the development of the sector. The legal and institutional framework for the fisheries sector prior to the growth of salmon aquaculture was focused on regulating and enforcing industrial and artisan fisheries. Only in 1991 did the General Fisheries and Aquaculture Law regulate the new salmon-farming sector. This law, the General Law for the Environment (established in 1994), subsequent rules and the four public agencies[11] involved in their application form the basic legal and institutional framework governing aquaculture in Chile today.

Two key areas of regulation, and of conflict among stakeholders, have been the distribution of aquaculture (spatial issues) and environmental impacts. Spatial restrictions have emerged from the unregulated situation that existed before 1991, with new regulations now under implementation. The first territorial planning instrument was the General Fisheries and Aquaculture Law, which mandated the fisheries authority to define Appropriate Areas for Aquaculture (AAA). Its application was unsatisfactory for the main local actors, in particular, artisanal fishermen. For this reason, 10 years later a new decree mandated regional governments to elaborate coastal management territorial plans with the participation of the local community, tourism sector, artisanal fishermen and environmental actors. As a result, the regional government of Aysen mandated the restriction of AAAs to about 75 percent of their original extent. It is uncertain how far this ongoing restrictive process will go and what its economic and environmental consequences will be.

Government concern about compatibility of economic growth and environment in coastal areas has been formalized in two main policy statements: the National Policy of Coastal Areas Use (Supreme Decree 474/1994) and the National Aquaculture Policy (Supreme Decree 125/2003). Few concrete actions or regulations can be attributed, however, to a systematic implementation of such policies so far. Two laws regulating environmental management of aquaculture have only been implemented fairly recently: the Environmental Impact Assessment System (SEIA) in 1997 and the executive decree on environmental norms for aquaculture[12] (RAMA). These regulatory tools together with their operational norms affect both the licensing and operation of fish farms.

DEVELOPMENT OF THE FORESTRY EXPORT SECTOR

The forestry sector has contributed significantly to the export expansion experienced by the Chilean economy. Plantation forestry is concentrated in the south-central regions of the country, particularly the coastal range

and the Andean foothills of regions VII, VIII and IX. Important plantation areas are also located in the sandy soils of the central valley in region
VIII and the northern coastal range of region X. The soil and climate of
south-central Chile are favorable for the cultivation of radiata pine and
eucalyptus, both exotic species, which achieve growth rates of more than
20 m³/2.5 acres/year, significantly higher than growth rates observed in
other temperate countries. These two species covered most of the 5.2
million acres of the planted area of the country as of 2001.

The plantations sustain an industry oriented to the export of pulp and,
increasingly, manufactured wood products such as plywood, medium-
density fiberboard, window and door frames and furniture. As of 2003, the
forestry industry accounted for 3.2 percent of total GDP and 12 percent
of exports. Region VIII accounts for a large share of the export-oriented
processing activities, concentrating the main pulp and sawmills and most
port facilities. The forestry industry provides over 42 percent of direct
employment, in the different levels of the industrial chain, in region VIII.

The Chilean state has long been actively involved in the development
of the forestry sector, beginning with the Forestry Law of 1931, which
encouraged afforestation of land classified as suitable for forest use
through generous tax exemptions on most property, income and inherit-
ance taxes. In 1939, Corfo, a public institution charged with promoting
productive activities, was created. Through this public institution, the
state provided financial mechanisms and direct shares to encourage plantations of radiata pine as well as the construction of paper mills and pulp
plants. In 1970, the government initiated a reforestation policy aiming
at planting 98,800 acres per year. The combination of direct government
intervention and private investment resulted in the development of an
important stock of radiata pine.

Trade liberalization, from its initiation in 1974, has directly affected
the forestry industry. High protection rates for pulp and paper were
significantly reduced, log and timber exports were liberalized and important forest and industrial assets were transferred to the private sector
(Wisecarver, 1992). A prohibition was established on the expropriation of
land under forestry plantations, a move considered important for increasing tenure security after the agrarian reforms of the previous regime. The
same law provided financial incentives – a 75 percent subsidy for planting
and management costs for afforestation of denuded forestlands – under a
program known as D.L. 701. This was designed as a temporary, 10-year
program intended to stimulate industry takeoff.

The forestry sector has shown a remarkable performance since 1970.
Forestry has been transformed from a highly protected activity, substitut-
ing imports, into Chile's second largest export sector. While the initial

comparative advantage of the sector was in timber production, following extensive technological innovation in the late 1980s and 1990s, the sector is now able to competitively export products with a higher value added. In its first stage, explosive growth of the industry allowed forest-sector value added to grow sixfold between 1970 and 1996, three times the value-added growth of the Chilean industrial sector as a whole. In addition, productivity, employment and the number of firms working in the sector have experienced higher growth rates than have those of the industrial sector as a whole (Katz et al., 2000). Commercial plantations expanded from 469,500 acres in 1970 to 5.2 million acres in 2002. Both general and sector-specific policies played a role in this transformation. Disentangling the impacts of these policy factors – trade liberalization, tenure security, subsidies – on the expansion of forest plantations is very difficult, since they were implemented simultaneously.

More recently, the forestry industry has become concentrated. Currently, two corporations – Arauco Group and Compañia Manufacturera de Papeles y Cartones (CMPC) – control over 52 percent of the planted area, 90 percent of pulp exports and over 80 percent of paper production. The high degree of concentration and use of outsourcing in harvest and transport activities is best explained by the large economies of scale in this industry. While this concentration may be necessary to compete in international markets, the lack of bargaining power on the part of the suppliers reduces the possibilities of generating stronger backward linkages (Izquierdo, 2002). In particular, small suppliers have very little incentive to invest and increase productivity, since most rents are captured by the large forest firms.

In terms of the ecological role of forests, the Chilean Forestry Law of 1931 established the first policies on sustainable management of forest resources, including the regulation of riparian vegetation, protection of springs and use of fire. The institutional development of the sector began in 1970 with the creation of the National Forest Service (CONAF). CONAF carries out such functions as forest fire control, management of the National System of Protected Wildlands (SNASPE) and the administration of the afforestation incentive programs. CONAF is also the enforcement agency for regulations on the exploitation of native forests. Specifically, it requires management plans when native forests are affected; CONAF practice has become increasingly less flexible in authorizing land-use changes toward plantations. However, these plans do not forbid partial or total substitution of native forest with plantation forest.

New legislation enacted in 1998, which partially replaced D.L. 701, redirected the state's focus from industrial growth to the protection of fragile soils, rehabilitation of degraded land and incentives for afforestation by smallholders. The impact of these reforms on afforestation by the industrial sector appears to be significant. The afforestation rate has declined from a yearly average of 191,500 acres (1993–94) to 105,500 acres (1999–2001). However, other factors, such as the declining availability of suitable land and higher investment risk in areas subject to land disputes and land-related violence in regions VIII and IX, are also important factors in this decline.

Sectoral policies are continuing to evolve as a result of local, particularly indigenous, and international pressures. International commodity markets and capital flows have played a critical role in these changes in sectoral policies. The long and somewhat frustrating policy-decision process regarding native forests revealed the difficulties that Chile's institutions face in reconciling conflicting views and interests among the sector's main stakeholders. Initially, the main concerns related to the negative impacts of plantations replacing native forest. NGOs were particularly vocal here. After 2003, the concern shifted toward the negative environmental impacts of the cellulose industry. Local communities began exercising pressure. Indigenous communities have been increasingly active in demanding that sector expansion in their territories be halted.

Many plantations are located on land with severe erosion problems.[13] At the national level, an estimated 85.5 percent of subsidized afforestation (up to 1994) occurred on moderately, severely and very severely eroded lands (Unda and Ravera, 1994). The continuation of traditional farming on these depleted, low-productivity soils could provide only a meager income for small landowners and was unlikely to be sustainable, making forestry plantations the profitable alternative for these landowners. In 2003, small owners accounted for 43.4 percent of the area afforested. The large companies were primarily engaged in replenishing harvested stock, rather than foresting new areas.

Small landowners mainly produce low-price pulp logs, and they have been notably slower than large companies to adopt new technologies, particularly intensive forest management techniques, which has led to large productivity gaps between company holdings and small landowners. The result is a very thin market for high-quality logs, which restricts opportunities for diversification toward higher-value products by small and medium-size processing firms. If these small producers could be integrated into the production chain for export of high-value products, the value of their landholdings would increase and, for many, it might be a chance to overcome poverty. Since most afforestation of new areas is now being carried out by small landowners, this need is particularly important.

The rapid development of the forestry sector has generated conflicts over land use with the agricultural sectors and with indigenous people.

The establishment of single-use plantation forestry dissolved many of the relationships that linked rural inhabitants to the land. As large properties were shifted from individual to corporate control, resident workers were expelled and relocated to urban areas or small towns in rural areas. In addition to the direct transfer of large landholdings, many small properties that had been used for agriculture began signing long-term contracts renting the land for 18 to 25 years for radiata pine or eucalyptus plantations. Many of these landowners, because of the depression of traditional agriculture, have moved off their farms to live and work in urban areas.

Traditional agriculture is, in general, more labor intensive than plantation forestry. The agricultural labor force was primarily composed of local residents. Forestry, in contrast, uses fewer workers per acre and relies heavily on seasonal migrants. However, many forestry sector activities – such as panel production – make more use of technology than traditional agriculture and thus require more skilled workers. As a consequence, although overall labor demand in these regions has been reduced as traditional agriculture has been replaced by forestry, productivity and wages may have increased, especially in manufacturing jobs in the forestry sector.[14]

CHANGES IN HUMAN WELL-BEING: COMPARING THE SALMON AND FORESTRY SECTORS

Salmon farming and forestry have had different impacts on poverty alleviation, inequality and migration, among other socioeconomic factors, because of their differing impacts on resource use and job creation.

Poverty

Poverty levels vary across Chile. During the period 1987 to 2003, regions VIII, IX and X were the poorest in the country. However, the situation was improving – all three regions experienced declines of over 50 percent in poverty over this period. The most rapid decline in poverty occurred in region X, where the salmon industry is most developed. In regions VIII and IX, where forestry has predominated, poverty reduction has now stagnated. These two regions remain among those with the highest levels of poverty; region X has moved out of this category and poverty levels continue to fall there (see Table 2.3).

In order to identify the causes of poverty in these regions, the researchers used panel data for 1992–2002 covering salmon and forestry municipalities. One of the hypotheses examined was that the evolution of

Table 2.3　Evolution of rural poverty in Chile (%)

	1970	1987–92	1994–98	2000
Country's poor	21.0	38.8	24.1	20.6
Rural poverty		41.4	29.7	23.8
Indigenous urban poverty				30.0
Indigenous rural poverty				36.1
Region VIII	22.6	49.9	35.3	27.1
Rural		*48.4*	*39.0*	*30.8*
Indigenous				*31.7*
Region IX	27.3	48.4	34.8	32.7
Rural		*47.4*	*35.2*	*34.9*
Indigenous				*42.1*
Region X	20.3	42.8	31.5	24.7
Rural		*38.0*	*27.2*	*19.3*
Indigenous				*35.0*

Sources:　MIDEPLAN (2005b) and INE.

employment, wages and migration has been different in the forestry plantation and salmon sectors after liberalization, with more positive impacts in the latter. The results showed that the most important factors in predicting a high poverty level were a large "inactive" population, inactive referring to children and older people; low education levels; and, finally, the nature of the productive sectors. Localities primarily engaged in the salmon sector have a lower poverty incidence, after controlling for other variables. Those with a larger proportion of people working in the forestry sector have a higher poverty incidence.

However, this result must be used with care, since correlation does not imply causality. It cannot be inferred that the development of the forestry sector generated more poverty. For example, the low productivity of traditional agricultural land together with the relatively low skill levels of the population of the areas where plantations developed could have resulted in higher poverty if this latter sector had not developed. More research is required to develop local studies and models to explore whether – and where – the development of this sector has resulted in immiserizing growth, or whether it has served to alleviate poverty in some localities where traditional agriculture was not sustainable.

Although poverty levels have fallen over the last 20 years, income disparity has not fallen so quickly. This disparity is evident at the regional level. Regions VIII, IX and X were among those with the highest level of income inequality as of 1987; 15 years later they still presented high

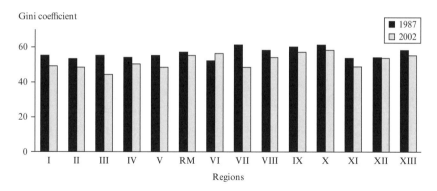

Source: MIDEPLAN (1987), (2002).

Figure 2.3 Income distribution by regions

levels of inequality relative to other regions, although all have improved. Notably, region X has the highest Gini coefficient, at close to 0.6. Even though wages have been increasing, returns to capital have grown at a much higher rate (see Figure 2.3).

Migration

In Chile, migration is closely related to poverty and to the performance of agriculture. A healthy agricultural sector is critical for the viability of rural communities. Localities with strong agricultural sectors report lower rates of migration and population distributions less skewed toward older ages. This is because of both the higher probability of finding a job in agriculture and the support the sector gives to nonfarming activities. Expansion of the agricultural export sector is associated with reductions in the incentives to emigrate.

In the salmon sector, there is some evidence that emigration rates may be lower than those of similar municipalities without salmon production. The forestry sector, however, appears to be associated with fewer economic opportunities. Our research shows that municipalities with high shares of forestry sector production have higher migration rates.

Migration can be a useful tool for translating economic growth into poverty reduction; the highest levels of out-migration are reported by the poorest regions. However, in Chile there are barriers to migration that stem from some poverty-alleviation policies. For example, housing subsidies are accompanied by a prohibition on the sale or rental of the house, effectively restricting migration from low-income locales (Soto and

Torche, 2004; Duran, 2005). Likewise, food subsidies for poor children may tie them to particular schools. Moreover, the costs of migration are important, particularly for indigenous people. Among those who do not migrate, poverty levels persist or worsen.

Indigenous Peoples

Although Chile's indigenous population is small, it is important in the regions studied, particularly regions IX and X. The main indigenous group in these regions, the Mapuche, is concentrated in rural areas. Socioeconomic indicators for the Mapuche are worse than the regional average. Moreover, at the national level, indigenous rural poverty was over 36 percent in 2000, above the national average for rural poverty of 23.8 percent in that period. Although elementary school attendance is good, Mapuche generally leave school before completing high school, and academic performance on national tests is poor. Unemployment rates and illiteracy rates are high. This situation persists despite the fact that many Mapuche are small landowners, perhaps reflecting the low productivity of their land. Moreover, land tenure policies – including collective property rights – may hamper migration. Thus, although the impact of trade liberalization on socioeconomic conditions among the Mapuche has not been examined, we conjecture that the presence of large indigenous populations in regions VIII and IX may explain the persistence of poverty in these regions as traditional agriculture declined.

Computable General Equilibrium (CGE) Models

The growth of these two sectors and their impacts on poverty and income distribution are the result of multiple policies, shocks and trends. To disentangle the importance of trade liberalization from other factors, a general equilibrium framework was used. This allowed the authors to construct a counterfactual scenario based on the specific policies applied for both sectors in order to look at the general equilibrium impacts of trade liberalization on wages and income distribution.

For forestry, the impacts of devaluation and plantation subsidies were simulated, together with trade liberalization, to replicate the conditions faced by the sector beginning in 1975 (see Table 2.4). The results show that devaluation has a significant effect on the sector's development. However, both the subsidies and trade liberalization have an effect too. The resulting growth of the forestry sector has had positive effects on wages for both rural and urban workers, and also for unskilled and skilled workers. The development of the forestry sector has had a small, positive effect

Table 2.4   Results of simulations for forestry sector

Variables		Plantation subsidy	World price of wood products	Trade closing
Output	Agriculture	0.01	0.06	−0.19
	Forestry	−0.52	−0.55	−0.05
	Wood products	−0.01	−14.45	−0.20
Sectoral labor demand	Agriculture	0.02	1.54	0.18
	Forestry	−1.99	−1.85	−0.13
	Wood products	−0.01	−26.88	0.03
	Manufacturing	0.02	2.38	−0.17
Wages	Urban skilled	−0.01	−1.94	0.28
	Urban unskilled	−0.01	−2.17	−0.03
	Rural skilled	−0.05	−0.58	0.01
	Rural unskilled	−0.02	−1.15	−0.15

Note: The Social Account Matrix for 1992 was used for these simulations.

on poverty alleviation. This benefit, however, must be weighed against the loss of jobs in traditional agriculture that occurs. Although unskilled workers may find jobs in the wood processing industry, the payment to capital rises more than the payments to labor. Moreover, the effects favor skilled labor over unskilled labor, particularly as the sector becomes more mechanized; the main wage benefits from forestry growth accrue to skilled labor. Thus, while the forestry sector has some positive impacts for lower-income groups, the highest-income groups benefit the most. Income inequality is aggravated and extreme poverty may worsen.

For the salmon sector, the impact of trade liberalization was simulated together with a devaluation and technological development (see Table 2.5). Sectoral production is very sensitive to price changes, so the devaluation of the peso in the early 1990s played a significant role in promoting growth. In the sector's initial phase of development, wages increased more for urban than rural workers and more for unskilled than skilled workers. This is important because the salmon sector employs a significant number of workers – especially women – with low levels of education. This has a positive impact on all income groups, but particularly on poor to middle-income groups and less so for the extreme poor and upper-middle and rich groups.

It can be concluded from this counterfactual exercise that the development of both sectors would alleviate poverty. However, in the absence of compensatory policies, salmon-sector growth would be more progressive than the forestry sector.

Table 2.5   Results of simulations for salmon sector

Variables		Productivity shock	World salmon prices	Unilateral trade closing
Salmon	Output	2.18	36.20	−0.39
	Employment	3.80	74.72	−0.53
	Exports	1.94	35.49	−0.37
Wages	Urban skilled	0.04	1.34	0.02
	Urban unskilled	0.05	1.83	0.03
	Rural skilled	0.03	0.79	−0.15
	Rural unskilled	0.03	1.34	−0.02

Note: The Social Account Matrix for 1996 was used for these simulations.

ENVIRONMENTAL IMPACTS

Salmon Sector

The rapid growth of the salmon sector over the last 15 years has set off alarm bells concerning its potential environmental effects. Although there are few scientific data as yet to determine or measure the impacts, concerns have been raised regarding local, regional and global impacts.[15]

Locally, the proliferation of unconsumed food, feces and antibiotics results in the physical, chemical and biological perturbation of sediments under the salmon cages. The level of impact is related to the production volume, local bathymetry and microcirculation patterns. Solid residues tend to accumulate on the bottom, forming a "shadow" under the cages with substantial effect on biota at a local scale. Chemical changes resulting from aquaculture have been observed in local levels of ammonia, nitrogen, phosphorous, carbon and particulate organic matter. A 50 percent lower level of species diversity has also been recorded (Soto et al., 2006).

Substantial quantities of antibiotics are released into the environment through unconsumed food and feces. Active antibiotic molecules and changes in the local bacterial communities in the cage shadow are evident several weeks and even months after treatment (Montesinos, 1999). The impact of these residual antibiotics is likely to include contamination of native fish and shellfish populations around the cages.[16]

At the regional level, no substantive evidence has been found linking salmon aquaculture to nutrient enrichment such as eutrophication or algal blooms. Nonetheless, as local impacts accumulate, regional impacts are expected to become evident. Long-term monitoring programs and modeling efforts to determine carrying capacity are needed. Another issue of concern at the regional level is the impact of escaped salmon. This impact includes predation on native fish, including species harvested commercially, and the long-term danger that escaped salmon will develop breeding populations. Playing a top predator role, escaped salmon could affect populations of schooling fish such as anchovies, sardines, silversides and juvenile hoki, as well as putting pressure on competing predators such as southern hake and adult hoki (Soto et al., 2001).

At the global scale, the high demand for fishmeal to support the salmon sector is a concern. Globally, salmon farming consumed an estimated 635,000 tons of fishmeal and 530,000 tons of fish oil in 2002, constituting 10 percent and 50 percent of total world production of fishmeal and fish oil, respectively (Tuominen and Esmark, 2003). Chile alone consumes approximately 30 percent of world production of fishmeal. This high consumption of fishmeal and oil has two potential global environmental impacts: an increase in pressure on already overexploited pelagic fisheries and the displacement of large quantities of nutrients from one ecosystem to another. Nutrients from highly productive ecosystems, such as the Peruvian upwelling zone, are being imported into the much less productive fjords of southern Chile. The long-term resilience of the upwelling systems to the current level of nutrient exploitation is unknown. Likewise, the long-term effect of importing these nutrients into low-productivity cold-water systems is unknown.

Another issue of global concern is the risk of developing bacterial resistance to antibiotics. The possibility, albeit low, that this resistance could be transferred to human pathogens (Smith et al., 1994) has generated intense debate.

Forestry Sector

The expansion of industrial-scale forest plantations has generated substantial controversy regarding the environmental implications of large-scale, mono-crop, short-rotation stands of exotic trees. In large part, the environmental impacts depend on the pattern of land-use change that plantation expansion entails.[17] Clearly, the impacts of converting degraded land are very different from those of converting old-growth forest. Understanding the land-use changes resulting from trade liberalization and from sectoral policies is critical to determining the environmental impacts on Chilean ecosystems. Conversion of land to forest plantations may have an important impact on biodiversity: to the extent that growth of forest plantations generates landscape changes – particularly the conversion of mature forest to other uses – flora and fauna may be significantly reduced. However, afforestation on degraded agricultural lands with plantation forests may increase biodiversity.

The impact of trade liberalization on land-use patterns is closely related to the impact on relative prices of land use. Forest plantations, producing exports, compete for land with rain-fed crops intended for domestic use, particularly wheat and beans, and with livestock. The comparative rise in export prices following liberalization drove the replacement of these crops with forest plantations on land suitable for forestry. In these cases, much of the land was degraded agricultural land. A positive impact of forest plantation growth is the reduction of soil loss on these degraded lands (Paredes, 1999; Unda and Ravera, 1994), given that soil loss has been identified as a critical environmental problem in Chile (Informe País, 2002). Approximately 80 percent of forest plantations have been established on lands suffering from erosion, with the result that forest plantations have significantly reduced soil erosion, especially in regions VIII and X.

The degree to which plantation forestry has replaced native forests in Chile is debated. While native forests have been converted, it is difficult to determine whether the primary cause of conversion has been collection of fuelwood and timber extraction – both of which are important sources of income for smallholders – or the demand for land for plantations. Conversion is not generally direct; native forest degradation on smallholder lands may be the result of many years' use. Based on available data, we estimate the conversion rate of native forests in the range of 10–20 percent, with evidence suggesting it is closer to 10 percent. Most of the converted forest is secondary growth, on lands that were cleared many years ago. The cases of greatest concern are the fragmentation of unprotected forests in regions VII and VIII. This leads to loss of biodiversity as corridors are lost, preventing animal migration. The potential impact of fragmentation is currently unknown.

Forest plantations may have a negative impact on water yields and flows. When forest plantations replace crops or sparse vegetation, the increased consumption of water could be significant. Further research is needed to determine the relevance of this issue in Chile.

Finally, at a global level, Chile's forest plantations, through carbon sequestration, have contributed very significantly to offsetting emissions from the country's energy sector. According to the Chilean National Environmental Commition (CONAMA), an estimated 44 percent of these emissions are offset by land-use change and forestry.

RESPONSES AND INTERVENTIONS: SOCIAL AND ENVIRONMENTAL CHANGES

During the 1980s, spending for social services was greatly reduced. The provision of services by the public sector was decentralized and private sector participation was promoted. Social programs with broad or universal coverage were reduced and expenditure focused on specific objectives such as the eradication of extreme poverty, provision of mother–child care and basic services. This targeting of spending allowed for significant improvements in human development indicators such as child mortality, illiteracy and schooling. However, the significant reduction in social spending and changes in economic structure discussed above resulted in extremely high poverty levels that reached 45 percent in 1987, almost double the level of 15 years earlier (Martin, 1998).

To reduce the problem of extreme poverty, beginning in 1990 public expenditure on social issues increased significantly. A new approach to social policies was implemented, focused on improving the quality of services and implementing specific instruments aimed at developing skills in the low-income population (Schkolnik and Bonnefoy, 1994; Baytelman et al., 1999). Social investment is preferred over assistance. This view was consistent with the new government's goals of economic growth and macroeconomic stability together with equality and poverty reduction, not merely as a consequence of growth. Social expenditure rose from 61 percent of total expenditure in 1990 to 68 percent in 2003, reaching almost 15 percent of GDP (see Table 2.6).

Together with the increase in public spending, nearly 400 social programs have been implemented by close to 80 different agencies (Raczynski and Serrano, 2005). These programs, aimed at the more vulnerable population, include Chile Solidario, to eliminate extreme poverty; Chile Barrios, to reduce informal urban settlements; Orígenes, aimed at the rural

Table 2.6   Chile: evolution of social public expenditure (as percentage of GDP)

	1990–91	1996–97	2002–03
Education	2.4	3.0	4.0
Health	1.9	2.4	3.0
Social security	8.2	7.2	7.6
Housing	0.2	0.2	0.2
Total	12.7	12.8	14.8

Source: CEPAL (2006); Raczynski and Serrano (2005).

indigenous population; Chile Joven, to build capacity among the poor young population; and the AUGE plan, which improves significantly the health care system for the poor. As a result of this effort and strong growth in the period, poverty fell from 45 percent in 1987 to 18.8 percent in 2003.[18] Despite this improvement, the social security safety net in Chile is still weak. The gap between rich and poor is substantial in education, health, housing and other social areas, requiring focused public social transfers to be maintained. Distribution of income is very unequal, with a Gini coefficient of 0.57 that has not changed significantly in the last 30 years.

Environmental management has changed significantly. Three stages of environmental management can be distinguished in Chile since trade liberalization began. Prior to re-establishment of democracy in 1990, authorities held the view that, in order to grow, it was necessary to pay some environmental costs. The government's approach was reactive. Environmental institutions, although numerous, were dispersed, lacked coordination and held overlapping responsibilities. Beginning in 1990, the approach to environmental management changed drastically. The government began to take preventive measures, negotiated regulations were introduced with the main actors, new standards were established to protect environmental quality, and environmental institutions were strengthened with the creation of a single coordinating agency, the National Environmental Commission. An Environmental Framework Law was approved, market instruments were introduced and preventive legislation was established. As a result, Chile has registered important advances in environmental management. In particular, the obligation of large projects to undertake environmental impact assessments has allowed increased control over the more significant impacts of new projects. Some important urban air pollution problems have also been tackled, though they are far from solved, as is the case with pollution by particulate matter in Santiago and close to copper smelters in the north.

Toward the end of the 1990s, Chile's growing insertion in international markets began to affect environmental management as well. Foreign export markets, through trade agreements and pressure from the private sector and consumers, began to require better environmental stewardship. Local communities and international organizations have also been pressing for better environmental stewardship. The state has begun to develop mechanisms that allow for the incorporation of these new actors. Despite these advances, Chile still has far to go in terms of efficiently implementing its environmental policies, particularly in monitoring and enforcement; further integrating environmental concerns into economic, social and sectoral policy making; and strengthening its international environmental cooperation (OECD-CEPAL, 2005).

CONCLUSIONS

The country as a whole, and even at the regional level, has benefited from falling unemployment and poverty that is driven in part by trade liberalization. Inequality has also been reduced, although rural and indigenous poverty remains problematic. The process has created both winners and losers.

Among the winners have been the communities of region X, where the development of the salmon sector alleviated poverty problems by increasing employment and encouraging immigration from other locations. Since the salmon sector is more labor intensive than other natural-resource-based sectors, unskilled workers have benefited. In addition, the multiple linkages that have developed with other economic activities – including transport and services – generate positive effects in employment and poverty alleviation. However, the sector is still evolving. Wages for unskilled labor are still low compared with other regions, and the quality of employment has been questioned.

Among the losers have been the small farmers, who have not been able to participate in the region's rapid forestry expansion. In regions VIII and IX trade liberalization was responsible, through consequent price increases for forestry products and competition faced by more traditional activities, for the land-use change from traditional agriculture to plantation forestry. Since the forestry sector is less labor intensive and more technologically oriented, unskilled rural labor has been negatively affected. Small farmers did not have access to the incentives provided for forestry under the Forestry Development Law (1974); nor did they have sufficient resources themselves to commit to long-term forestry investments. As a result, large forestry industries have displaced farmers from areas of high potential for forestry; many small producers from dryland areas have sold their land because traditional farming is unprofitable and viable agricultural alternatives are not available. Many unskilled workers and the young, elderly, women and indigenous population remained in rural areas, most of them unemployed or working in low-productivity agriculture or highly seasonal forestry activities. The most vulnerable populations, such as the elderly, indigenous and unskilled workers, have seen their relative condition deteriorate, evidenced by higher rates of poverty, higher unemployment rates and lower wages compared to other segments of the population. Migration patterns have been affected and, in the case of forestry, the youth have had to abandon rural communities in order to seek better opportunities. Skilled workers, however, have benefited, since those with higher education levels were able to find higher-paying jobs in the new manufacturing sector.

Trade liberalization generates environmental effects by changing the scale of production of a specific sector, changing the composition of production, promoting technological innovations and changing the demand for products. The final result is uncertain and may be very site specific, as the salmon and forestry cases illustrate. Significant scale effects have occurred in both sectors, raising concerns that this rapid growth could generate significant and even irreversible damage to the environment.

There was an important gap between the development of each sector and the creation of the institutional capacities and policies to mitigate the main environmental and social concerns. Only in the 1990s were specific policies applied to reduced poverty. Even then, most of the effort was concentrated on urban poverty, with a focus on rural poverty developing only since 2000. Similarly, environmental concerns became relevant for the government beginning in 1990. Improved environmental stewardship has resulted from the creation of CONAMA, the passing of the Environmental Framework Law and, in particular, the implementation of the Environmental Impact Assessment System. Even so, two key problems hamper more effective action: lack of information and models to examine the medium- and long-term environmental effects of both forestry and aquaculture, and weak monitoring and enforcement capacities.

NOTES

1. Unfortunately, systematic data on poverty are only available from the late 1980s, when the National Socioeconomic Characterization Survey (CASEN) began to be carried out biannually. Prior to this, poverty estimations were rare and inconsistent, with little local or regional focus. For this reason figures for 1973 should not be compared with those of the 1980s and 1990s.
2. See Torche (1987) (cited in Ihnen, 1987); Rodríguez (1984); and Pollack and Uthoff (1986).
3. CASEN is the National Socioeconomic Characterization Survey.
4. The figure for 1998 is 0.5 when adjusted for transfers of money and services.
5. The preliminary results of the 2006 CASEN survey suggested that this may be changing and some improvements in income distribution may be occurring.
6. This is shown by empirical studies available for Chile: De Gregorio et al. (2002); Levinsohn (1996)
7. These include coho salmon, Atlantic salmon and rainbow trout.
8. These were carried out by Nichiro, Mytilus and Fundación Chile.
9. This assistance was provided by ProChile, the Chilean Trade Commission charged with promoting Chilean exports.
10. This is the product multiplier that considers both direct and indirect effects.
11. Marine Undersecretariat, Fisheries Undersecretariat, National Fisheries Service and National Environmental Commission.
12. While this decree was promulgated in 2001, its operational standards were not issued until February 2003.

13. This land had been deforested as part of the settlement process, and soil degradation was aggravated by the wheat boom of the first half of the twentieth century.
14. Information on local wages for the first period of liberalization is not available, so this statement is made with some uncertainty. Moreover, in the last few years forestry wages, especially in logging, were lower than in agricultural activities.
15. This study did not examine the use of freshwater lakes for production, but focused exclusively on the marine environment. WWF Chile has recently produced a complementary report that fills this gap (Leon et al., 2007). This report mapped production and analyzed production trends by lake over the last eight years and reviewed all available literature on impacts. It found that production had doubled over this period, that 20 percent of lake concessions were already suffering from anoxia (oxygen deficiency) and that nearly all lakes studied were at or over carrying capacity for nutrient inputs before the doubling of production. Salmon production is the principal point source of nutrient inputs in these southern lakes, along with municipal sewage. Salmon farming is thus a major factor contributing to the ecological deterioration of many lakes, particularly on Chiloé Island.
16. This study did not look at the issues of disease and parasite transmission and management, which are both the industry's major production concern and a major area of environmental concern (WWF Chile, personal comment).
17. A major impact of the plantation forestry sector that is not considered by this study is that of the paper and pulp industry, which includes toxic spills that killed fish and bird life and degraded aquatic habitats in the Valdivia and Mataquito rivers between 2004 and 2007.
18. Even though these numbers were developed using different methodologies, reductions have been significant.

BIBLIOGRAPHY

Aedo, F. and F. Lagos (1984), "Protección efectiva en Chile: 1974–79", Working Paper No. 94, Pontificia Universidad Católica de Chile, Santiago.
Baytelman, Y., K. Cowan, J. De Gregorio and P. González (1999), *Política económica-social y bienestar: El caso de Chile*, Santiago: UNICEF Universidad de Chile.
Behrman, J. (1976), *Foreign Trade Regimes and Economic Development: Chile*, New York: Columbia University Press.
Comisión Económica para América Latina y el Caribe (CEPAL) (2006), *Panorama social de América Latina 2005*, Santiago: CEPAL.
Corbo, V., L. Hernandez and F. Parro (2005), "Institutions, economic policies and growth: Lessons from the Chilean experience", Working Paper 317, Central Bank of Chile, Santiago, available at: www.bcentral.cl/eng/studies/working-papers/317.htm.
De Gregorio, J., D. Contreras, D. Bravo, T. Rau and S. Urzua (2002), "Chile: trade liberalization, employment and inequality", in R. Vos, L. Taylor and R. Paes de Barros (eds), *Economic Liberalization, Distribution and Poverty: Latin America in the 1990s*, Cheltenham, UK and Northampton, MA, USA: Edward Elgar.
De Gregorio, J. and J. Lee (2003), "Growth and adjustment in East Asia and Latin America", Working Paper 245, Central Bank of Chile, Santiago, available at: www.bcentral.cl/estudios/documentos-trabajo/pdf/dtbc245.pdf.
Duran, G. (2005), "Subsidios en educación: impacto en la migración y convergencia regional", *Cuadernos de Economía*, **126**, 357–85.

Global Forest Watch (2002), *Chile's Frontier Forests: Conserving a Global Treasure*, Washington, DC: World Resources Institute.

Hachette, D. (2000), "La reforma comercial", in F. Larraín and R. Vergara (eds), *Transformación económica de Chile*, Santiago: Centro de Estudios Públicos.

Ihnen, P. (1987), "Reflexiones sobre la magnitud de la pobreza en Chile. Comments to paper by Arístides Torches, 'Distribuir el ingreso para satisfacer las necesidades básicas'", in F. Larrain (ed.), *Desarrollo Económico en Democracia*, Santiago: Ediciones Universidad Católica de Chile.

INE (National Institute of Statistics) (1970–2004), *Compendio Estadístico*, Santiago: INE.

Informe País (2002), *Estado del medio ambiente en Chile*, Santiago: Instituto de Asuntos Públicos, Departamento de Políticas Públicas, Universidad de Chile.

Irarrazabal, A. and L. Opromolla (2005), "*Trade reforms in a global competition model: the case of Chile*", Working Paper, New York University, available at: www.homepages.nyu.edu/~ldo202/homepage/traderef.pdf.

Izquierdo, F. (2002), "Los determinantes en los mecanismos de la organización industrial en el sector forestal Chileno", master's thesis, Agricultural Economics, Pontificia Universidad Católica de Chile.

Katz, M. and S. Molina (1975), *Mapa de la extrema pobreza*, Santiago: ODEPLAN, Instituto de Economía de la Pontificia Universidad Católica de Chile.

Katz, M., G. Stumpo and G. Varela (2000), *El complejo forestal Chileno*, Santiago: Proyecto CEPAL/CIID.

Leon, J., D. Tecklin, A. Farias and S. Diaz (2007), *Salmon Farming in the Lakes of Southern Chile – Valdivian Ecoregion*, Valdivia: WWF Chile, available at: www.wwf.cl.

Levinsohn, J. (1996), "Firm heterogeneity, jobs, and international trade: evidence from Chile", NBER Working Paper 5808, National Bureau of Economic Research.

Martin, M. (1998), "Integración al desarrollo: una visión de la política social", in C. Toloza and E. Lahera (eds), *Chile en los noventa*, Santiago: Dolmen Ediciones.

Ministerio de Desarrollo y Planificación (MIDEPLAN) (2005a), *Los objetivos de desarrollo del milenio: Primer informe del gobierno de Chile*, Santiago: MIDEPLAN.

MIDEPLAN (2005b), *Resultados de la encuesta de caracterización socio-económica 2003 (CASEN)*, Santiago: MIDEPLAN.

MIDEPLAN (1987), *Serie Casen 87*, Santiago: MIDEPLAN. available at: www.mideplan.cl/casen/.

MIDEPLAN (2002), *Serie Casen 2002*, Santiago: MIDEPLAN. available at: www.mideplan.cl/casen/.

Montesinos, A. (1999), "Resistencia de cepas bacterianas aisladas de sedimento marino de un ex-centro de cultivo de salmonideos frente a los antibacterianos Flumequina y Acido Oxolínico", Universidad Austral de Chile, Valdivia.

OECD-CEPAL (2005), *OECD Environmental Performance Reviews – Chile*, Santiago: CEPAL.

Paredes, G. (1999), "Chilean forestry", in A. Yoshimoto and K. Yukutake (eds), *Global Concerns for Forest Resource Utilization: Sustainable Use and Management* (47–62), selected papers from the international symposium of the FORESEA MIYAZAKI, Forestry Sciences, Netherlands: Kluwer Academic Publishers.

Pollack, M. and A. Uthoff (1986), *Distribución de ingresos y democracia: Materiales para una discusión*, Santiago: CED.

Raczynski, D. and C. Serrano (2005), "Las políticas y estrategias de desarrollo social. Aportes de los años 90 y desafíos futuros", in P. Meller (ed.), *La paradoja aparente. Equidad y eficiencia: Resolviendo el dilemma*, Santiago: Taurus Ediciones.

Rodríguez, J. (1984), *Distribución del ingreso y el papel del gasto social en Chile, 1983*, Santiago: Ilades, W.P.

Schkolnik, M. and J. Bonnefoy (1994), *Una propuesta de tipología de las políticas sociales en Chile*, Santiago: UNICEF/Universidad de chile.

Schurman, R. (2001), "Uncertain gains: labor in Chile's new export sectors", *Latin American Research Review*, **36** (2), 3–28.

Smith, P., M.P. Hiney and O.B. Samuelsen (1994), "Bacterial resistance to antimicrobial agents used in fish farming: a critical evaluation of method and meaning", *Annual. Review of Fish Diseases*, **4**, 273–313.

Soto, D., I. Arismendi, J. Gonzalez, J. Sanzana, F. Jara, C. Jara and E. Guzman (2006), "Southern Chile, trout and salmon country: conditions for invasion success and challenges for biodiversity conservation", *Revista Chilena de Historia Natural*, **79**, 97–117.

Soto, D., F. Jara and C. Moreno (2001), "Escaped salmon in the inner seas, southern Chile: facing ecological and social conflicts", *Ecological Applications*, **11**, 1750–62.

Soto, R. and A. Torche (2004), "Spatial inequality, migration and economic growth in Chile", *Cuadernos de Economía*, **41**, 124.

Torche A. (1987), "Distribuir el ingreso para satisfacer las necesidades básicas", in F. Larrain (ed.), *Desarrollo Económico en Democracia*, Santiago: Ediciones Universidad Católica de Chile.

Torres, C. (2006), "*Development of technology-intensive suppliers in natural resource-based economies: the case of aquaculture in Chile*", doctoral dissertation, Leipzig University.

Tuominen, T.R. and M. Esmark (2003) *Food for Thought: The Use of Marine Resources in Fish Feed*, Oslo, Norway: WWF Norway.

Unda, A. and F. Ravera (1994), "Análisis histórico de sitios de establecimiento de las plantaciones forestales en Chile", Instituto Forestal, Unidad de Medio Ambiente.

Wisecarver, D. (1992), "El sector forestal chileno: políticas, desarrollo del recurso y exportaciones", in D. Wisecarver (ed.), *El modelo económico chileno*, Santiago: Centro Internacional para el Desarrollo Económico (CINDE) e Instituto de Economía de la Pontificia Universidad Católica de Chile.

3. The impacts of trade liberalization in Pingbian, China

He Daming and Liu Jiang, with Bobby Cochran

When China joined the World Trade Organization (WTO) in 2001, it was already the leading producer and consumer of agricultural products in the world. Accession to the WTO followed as part of a successful long-term effort to modernize, liberalize and increase Chinese participation in the global marketplace. With its reserves of labor, natural resources and growing industrial and manufacturing capacity, China was poised to be a winner in global markets. Per capita incomes have already increased by 46 percent since the year 2000. The benefits of trade, however, accrue neither to everyone nor to all parts of China equally. People living in the isolated mountain regions of the western (inland) provinces, many of whom are ethnic minorities and who live by farming some of the country's most environmentally fragile landscapes, were not expected to benefit from the liberalized trade regime. However, through its indirect impacts, the rapid growth of trade has brought new opportunities to even the most remote regions of China.

This study looks at the case of Pingbian County, located in Yunnan Province along China's southern border with Vietnam. In communities like Pingbian throughout China and the developing world, economies are shifting from subsistence farming to export-led, cash crop agriculture. Labor is shifting from farm to nonfarm work. And local governments and people are struggling to anticipate and capitalize on the potential they see in expanding markets. This study used household and village surveys, stakeholder interviews, decision-maker workshops and land-use mapping,[1] along with government data and expert opinion, to better understand how a rural community anticipates and adjusts to ongoing economic, environmental and social changes that accompany trade liberalization.

SITE DESCRIPTION

Pingbian County is remote and mountainous. Elevations vary from 505 feet to 8,500 feet across the county's 471,000 acres. Pingbian is a Miao

Figure 3.1   Location of Pingbian, Yunnan, China

autonomous county, with 62 percent of the population belonging to ethnic minorities. The Miao people are ethnically tied to the Hmong of northern Laos and Vietnam. In Pingbian, they are given relatively greater control over policies compared to other counties, although this control is still quite limited. China's local government structures span a range of scales. Pingbian lies within the Honghe Prefecture, which is one of the administrative areas of Yunnan Province. Within Pingbian there are seven townships, 76 village committees and 694 villages (see Figure 3.1).

The total population, as of 2004, was 147,047. Ninety percent are farmers working small plots of land. Pingbian's agricultural economy remained isolated until recently because of its geographic remoteness and poor transportation. Corn is the primary subsistence crop, supplemented by rice, buckwheat and legumes. Cash crops include tropical fruits, oilseeds, hemp, tobacco, medicinal herbs, *caoguo* (a spice and medicinal herb) and bamboo. Prior to China's initial economic opening in 1978, the people of Pingbian did not have enough to eat. The poverty rate in 1993 was 71 percent. Today some 61 percent of the population are classified as poor (earning less than US$105 annually per capita). About half of these, 32 percent of the total population, are classified as absolutely poor (earning less than US$76 annually per capita).[2]

Yunnan Province is designated a Global 200 ecoregion by WWF and is home to two of the most biologically important regions of the world, namely the Mountains of Southwest China and Indo-Burma biodiversity hot spots.[3] Pingbian's subtropical mountains support both relatively intact ecosystems and corridors that connect forest patches from Laos and Vietnam up into the Red River Valley. The forests of Da Wei Shan Nature Reserve (115,200 acres), which protect much of Pingbian's ecological resources, are home to 3,619 plant species and 555 animal species. Pingbian's ecosystem services are largely intact – natural forests are protected and water is clean. However, new pressures are arising in the form of intensive land use and industrialization. Pingbian's steep slopes and rivers could generate up to 3 megawatts of hydropower, and the county has several important deposits of minerals. The forests, hot springs, a volcanic site and a rock cave are local tourist attractions.

In Pingbian there have been two major waves of ecosystem change. During the 1980s, major portions of Pingbian's natural forest were converted for shifting cultivation of corn, rice, wheat and other subsistence crops. In the 1990s, this pattern was reversed. Pingbian saw a decline in conversion of natural forestland and an intensification of agricultural land use. Production began to shift from traditionally grown, land-intensive crops, such as corn and wheat, to labor-intensive crops, such as fruit, vegetables and ornamental flowers. Slope-land farmers converted some of their land into forest plantations of fir or fruit trees. Former agricultural fields left fallow have reverted to shrub land. The resulting ecosystem is a mixture of agriculture, plantation forest and natural forest, which can be further divided by elevation. The middle elevations are most suitable for agricultural production, with temperate climates, low incidence of disease and good access to water. Here, too, there is better access to transportation, leading to a concentration of both population and farmland.

ECONOMIC CHANGE

China's market liberalization has unfolded gradually since 1978, marked by three distinct phases: import substitution (1978–84), export subsidies

(1984–92) and market economies (1992–present). These reforms have achieved remarkable results in terms of accelerating rural economic development. Market liberalization began internally, under the import substitution regime, with the introduction of the household responsibility system and other rural reforms that allowed farmers to sell their production above quotas in domestic markets. This spurred rapid development of rural markets for consumer goods and production materials. Beginning in 1984, when the government launched markets for production materials, capital, land, labor, technology and information to support export-led growth, rural liberalization deepened. The number of private enterprises and township-village enterprises (TVEs) grew substantially, land and labor markets emerged and intensive agriculture and animal husbandry developed rapidly. The latest stage of economic reform has moved China into the fast lane of liberalization. Capital and labor markets have developed further; direct government regulation has been replaced by more indirect regulation and less government involvement in microeconomic activities; and international trade and foreign investment have taken off dramatically. Now, throughout China, market mechanisms dominate urban and rural economic systems, capital and labor flow almost freely and private businesses are mushrooming.

The recent capstone to these reforms has been China's accession to the WTO. Occurring in parallel with several regional and bilateral trade agreements and regional development initiatives, WTO accession marked a major acceleration of the ongoing reforms. The production signals sent by Chinese macroeconomic policy in the years running up to WTO accession were clear. In the agricultural sector, more open markets were expected to drive production toward labor-intensive crops and away from land-intensive crops, in line with China's comparative advantage in world markets (Lu, 2001). Nationally, it was expected that farmers who had already been integrated into national and global markets would have the capacity to adjust to these new pressures, since they already had the necessary infrastructure and institutions to invest in new equipment or to shift cropping regimes. However, farmers just beginning to make the transition from subsistence to cash economies were not expected to adjust quickly to the new regime. On the one hand, they would lack the quality land, water supply, infrastructure and labor mobility needed to compete effectively. On the other hand, even if they were able to change production regimes, they would lack the supporting institutions needed to participate in international markets. Market forces were thus expected to direct the lion's share of benefits from WTO accession away from the poorest, least developed and most remote regions of China (Hertel et al., 2002; Huang et al., 2002; Sicular and Zhao, 2002).

Millions of US dollars

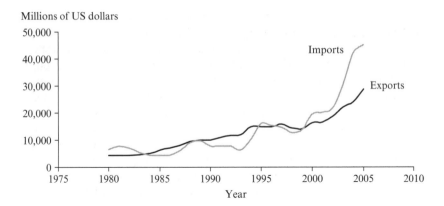

Source: WTO trade statistics.

Figure 3.2   China's agriculture imports and exports

Post-WTO accession there was a sharp national rise in agricultural product imports, primarily of soy oil, palm oil and raw soybean. Agricultural exports, primarily processed foods, fruits, vegetables, corn and pork, also rose sharply, up US$3 billion. This rapid expansion is expected to continue (Gale, 2005). These macro-level increases in imports and exports have sent ripples to micro-level markets around the country and have even affected the remote region of Pingbian. The increase in imports changed prices in the eastern coastal cities. These cities are major consumers of agricultural goods sent out from Pingbian; thus, the impacts of WTO accession are transmitted to Pingbian via shifts in major domestic markets. The impacts of these changes are explored in this chapter (see Figure 3.2).

In addition to the WTO, China has entered into several other international trade-oriented agreements that are relevant to the Pingbian region. China is a participant in the Greater Mekong Subregion (GMS) Cooperation Program, initiated in 1992 by the Asian Development Bank, along with Laos, Myanmar, Thailand, Cambodia and Vietnam. The GMS work program aims to promote regional economic development through improved transportation, increased power generation and transmission capacity, telecommunications, environmental conservation, tourism, human resources development and trade and investment. Pingbian lies in the middle of a GMS north–south economic corridor that connects Kunming and Hanoi. Plans include highway and railroad improvements and other infrastructure upgrades. China's cooperation with ASEAN (Association of Southeast Asian Nations) is also relevant. Trade between

China and the countries belonging to ASEAN has been growing rapidly[4] and will expand further when a China–ASEAN free trade zone is established in 2010.[5] In anticipation, regional tariff cuts on more than 7,000 commodities were granted in 2005. The opening of Chinese agricultural markets to the ASEAN countries was accelerated under the "Early Harvest Program," initiated at the time of WTO accession, that eliminated Chinese import tariffs on agricultural products from ASEAN countries. In exchange, ASEAN countries had to eliminate their tariffs by 2008. China's ongoing interest in supporting regional development and trade expansion is also evidenced by its participation in the 10+3 summits (ASEAN plus China, Japan and Korea) begun in 1997.

Given the major transformations that have occurred in China over the last 30 years, it is impossible to isolate the impacts of any single trade event. Trade liberalization has been constructed through a long series of macroeconomic policy decisions that have gradually created and promoted internal and external markets. While this chapter focuses on China's accession to the WTO as the latest, most significant, transition into a system-wide market economy, local actors throughout China have been affected by many economic policy decisions made in Beijing that have created market awareness and promoted changes in production patterns. The changes provoked by WTO accession are part and parcel of these other changes.

ECONOMIC CHANGES IN PINGBIAN

Pingbian County's economy grew rapidly from the beginning of liberalization in the 1990s. By 2003, Pingbian's GDP (gross domestic product) had reached US$4.8 million. With market development, agriculture was intensified, and new cash crops entered the mix. Pingbian's non-agricultural economy has also diversified. Government policy, farm-level decisions, expanding markets and the availability of investment capital have shaped these local production decisions.

Government Policy

In Pingbian, trade and production have followed the three phases of national economic liberalization with a delay of five to ten years. When liberalization began in the 1980s, high prices for grain increased production of corn and rice. In the late 1990s, Pingbian began to develop tropical fruit cultivation, local industries, including agricultural product processing, and ecotourism with support from government subsidies. Today,

Pingbian producers are moving from a mixture of land-intensive subsistence crops, forestry and animal husbandry into labor-intensive crops destined for sale outside of the county. The county government is promoting a shift from subsistence crops, particularly corn and wheat, to cash crops. Clear signals for production change are being sent in the form of propaganda, technical assistance and subsidies. The county is promoting use of more productive crop varieties, including hybrids,[6] and is supporting organic and more sustainable production to improve the quality of agricultural products. Producers are responding. Between 2001 and 2003, the total area of grains planted dropped by 882 acres and the area of cash crops expanded by 1,819 acres.

Government and market signals are also shifting the production mix in the forestry and livestock sectors. Timber trees are being replaced by multifunctional cash trees – that is, trees that provide not only timber but also food, medicine materials and other products. Non-timber products such as herbal medicines and ornamental flowers are also growing in importance. These products are consolidated and processed by businesses from outside the province and sold in domestic and Southeast Asian markets. Production of pigs, poultry and other livestock has grown to meet expanding domestic demand, with technical assistance provided by the county. Families are keeping greater numbers of animals, producing organic meats and exploring opportunities for meat processing.

County officials have zoned specific areas of the county for cash crop development and provide incentives in the form of technical assistance and free trees. While each township has cultivated area targets for a variety of cash crops, the county government has prioritized economic development in the central and southern parts of the county because of their relatively easy access to markets in Vietnam and other provinces of China.

Farmers

Most agricultural production choices are now made by farmers themselves, rather than imposed by a government quota system. Their decisions reflect traditional farming practices, geography, government signals, market infrastructure and the experiences of their neighbors. Government signals are very important, since many farmers lack other access to market information. Most farmers take a wait-and-see attitude: only when they see other farmers generating a profit with a new crop or technology will they follow suit. This leads to long delays in adapting to market signals, followed by periods of rapid change. Pingbian is now undergoing one of these periods of change.

Production decisions are also shaped by the physical factors that determine local comparative advantage. Water availability, climate and soil conditions differ by elevation, affecting livelihood possibilities. For example, desertification in Yanfeng Village makes corn the only suitable crop; Baiyun Village farmers raise pigs because water scarcity precludes other options; and Adakouxiaozhai and Huoshan villages, which have limited land, plant *caoguo* in the natural forest. These physical constraints limit the pace and extent to which economic liberalization shapes communities and ecosystems.

Producer responses to trade liberalization are not limited to the agricultural sector. Pingbian has seen significant growth in both industrial and service sector GDPs, which now rival agriculture in terms of economic value, although not in terms of employment or land use. Between 1990 and 2004, the number of local enterprises rose from 48 to 705, employing about 2,000 people in mining and processing, pharmaceuticals, tea making, electricity generation, textiles, wine, grain and oil refineries. This economic diversification coincided with the shift in investment sources from state to private capital just prior to WTO accession. Private funds have been directed toward industrial enterprises and urban services; county funds have also supported new industries, including mineral extraction and processing.

Markets

Markets in Pingbian are increasingly connected to other regions but are still immature. For most farmers, the weekly rural fair is still the primary place for selling agricultural products and for information gathering. Agricultural products, such as *caoguo* and anise, move primarily to urban centers in other Chinese provinces, such as Sichuan and Shandong. Growing wealth in these urban centers is also increasing demand for meat and specialty products, especially fruits and vegetables. Some vegetable products, such as potatoes and greens, go to Vietnam. Whether goods move to Vietnam or to other parts of China, they are, in effect, exports from Pingbian. They may be subject to different rules of exchange, but the market drivers are similar. As free trade expands regionally, markets in nearby countries are likely to become more accessible to Pingbian than distant national markets.

Because market participation is still immature, farmers have little ability to control prices and have to bear any losses related to price fluctuations. The long distance between the agricultural fair and farmers' homes forces them to sell whatever they have brought to market, with little information about prices available before they arrive. In this buyer-oriented market, most benefits flow to the middlemen, while the farmers bear most of the risk. The local government has taken some steps to build new institutions in order to improve the position of producers. Pingbian County has promoted and even funded "flagship" enterprises in agricultural processing industries, storage and transportation in order to facilitate agricultural industrialization. These have primarily benefited villages close to the county seat, which enjoy better access to information and multiple transportation nodes as well as a variety of employment opportunities.

Investment

Villages, other local government entities and farmers have increased borrowing in order to make the transition to cash crops. Villages raise small amounts of money directly from farmers to support highways, schools and water infrastructure; but most infrastructure development is funded by timber sales, primarily from commonly held plantations of monoculture pines, and borrowing. Households borrow from village credit cooperatives or the Agricultural Bank of China. These loans are small and not available to all farmers. Nevertheless, people borrowed heavily to finance the transition to intensive cash crop agriculture between 1990 and 1998. Likewise, in the following years, 1998–2000, average interest payments increased from 3 percent to 7 percent of total household expenditures. Access to capital is a two-edged sword. On the one hand, capital can be used to invest in new technologies and higher-value crops, lifting families out of poverty. Availability of credit increases opportunities for the poor. On the other hand, increasing debt burdens can limit available cash reserves for health care, education or natural disasters. With limited policies in place to protect borrowers, both local governments and households are now exposed to new financial risk.

HUMAN WELL-BEING IMPACTS

Across China, the absolute number of people in poverty has been dropping. The household responsibility system enabled families to clothe and feed themselves; poverty payments increased access to health and education; and growing nonfarm employment and agricultural exports increased cash incomes. Pingbian shows a similar pattern, with several years' delay. The incidence of poverty dropped from 71 percent of the total population in 1993 to 61 percent in 2000. Gross incomes have risen since 1980, with the fastest rise occurring between 2001 and 2003. However, while cash incomes have increased, so have payments on debt, so that net incomes improved very little among surveyed farmers in the late 1990s. Greater gains were made between 2001 and 2003, but other aspects of poverty, such as access to health services and education, remain problematic.

Household sources of cash income are shifting. Traditionally, live-stock served as a cash reserve for families. Since 1980, the total share of household income from livestock has declined, replaced by income from off-farm labor and cash crops. By 2003, 60 percent of average household income came from cash sales or nonfarm sources, such as part-time jobs in urban areas or small-scale trade. Clearly, as economic opening and trade developed, people have shifted labor from livestock production to off-farm employment. However, the share of labor devoted to crop cultivation (68–70 percent) and forestry (2–4 percent) has remained constant.

Since Pingbian's poor population increasingly resides in areas with relatively good transportation, communication, drinking water and sani-tation, poverty alleviation should be achievable with a combination of national policy and social supports. Eighty-two percent of households have access to improved dirt roads, 4 percent have access to national high-ways, and only 2 percent do not have road access. However, payments on debt have decreased cash reserves, leaving limited money to pay for edu-cation, health, taxes and capital investments, the elements need to make the next jump out of poverty. Part of the difficulty lies in rising education and health costs. Education costs jumped from 7 percent to 16 percent of household expenditures between 2001 and 2003 as the government transferred responsibility for costs to families. This policy was reversed the next year, when a national program was introduced to provide nearly free elementary education. Even so, higher-level educational opportunities remain limited. Although 95 percent of school-age children in Pingbian attend elementary school, few have access to middle, vocational, and high school education. For example, between primary school and middle school, student enrollment dropped from 16,816 students to 5,373 in 2001. Average household expenditures on medicine increased dramatically by 86 percent from 1980 to 1998. Expenditures leveled off from 1998 to 2001, but the annual rate of increase has been more than 15 percent since 2001. The health care system in Pingbian still relies heavily on traditional cures and rural medical clinics. Western medicine is in short supply in many villages, and some people who had shaken off poverty at one time have returned to poverty because of serious disease. This occurs even though nearly every village has a medical clinic staffed by 1 or 2 workers, funded by direct aid from Xuhui District, Shanghai.

Surprisingly, although income gaps between rich and poor, between east and west, and between rural and urban areas are growing across China, equity seems to be improving in Pingbian. The income gap, as measured by the Gini coefficient for surveyed households, decreased every year from 1980 to 2003. The reason is, in part, that while rural producers in mountainous areas have fewer opportunities for off-farm labor or intensive agriculture than do farmers on better land, their costs of living are also lower. The most important source of financial inequity in Pingbian is access to capital. While some farmers have access to capital through banks or through friends, some do not. Farmers with connections to the government generally have the best access to credit.

Pingbian's poverty-alleviation strategy has included several initiatives, including resettlement from the mountains to middle elevations. Resettlement is aimed at reducing pressure on steep slopes and encroachment on forestland while improving access to agricultural land. From 2001 to 2005, some 4,750 households, including 19,000 people, moved to three resettlement areas. By 2010, an additional 1,000 households (about 2,750 people) will move to four resettlement areas. The county provides land and infrastructure and offers houses at discounted rates. Within the scope of the plan, people are free to choose where they move. Many have moved from mountainous areas to the valley where the land resources and access to transportation are better. Resettlement is not always successful. In some cases, the resettlement areas do not have sufficient land to support the new farmers. In other cases, people are not happy in the new climate or community. As a result, older people tend to return to their villages, leaving the younger people in the resettlement areas. Out-migration from the region is insignificant, in large part because the language and culture of the Miao people provide an incentive for them to stay and create a barrier to finding work outside the region.

The county government has used the national Grain for Green/Sloping Land Conversion Program to ease the transition from higher to mid-elevations and to ease impacts of increasing population density on mid-elevation ecosystems. The Grain for Green Program delivers payments of cash and food to farmers to end cultivation on steep slopes. Pingbian participated in the program for two years between 2001 and 2003, with 10,400 acres enrolled. The program was used to help shift production from annual crops on marginal land to reforestation and perennial cash crops. Participating farmers were satisfied with the program because compensation in grain and cash was good. Pingbian County has also supported external employment by organizing migrant workers to find jobs outside the province and enacting policies allowing migrants to retain property ownership. The cumulative effect of these policies and economic growth has been positive for human well-being.[7]

China once had an "iron rice bowl," where people were assured food, a job, health care, and retirement. With market liberalization, the "iron rice bowl" has shrunk or even disappeared for many people, despite large and growing expenditures on safety net programs. In sum, Pingbian's rural poor are better off than before economic opening and incomes have become more equal. Still, poor farmers face a different set of risks associated with international price changes, natural disasters, or crop failure, which may affect their capacity to compete and succeed in future years.

ENVIRONMENTAL IMPACTS

In Pingbian, ecosystem change is being driven by people struggling to enter the market economy. In general, Pingbian's environment is good, providing forest products, drinking and irrigation water, productive soil and prevention of natural disasters. Conversion of forestland to agriculture was the driving force behind ecosystem change through the 1980s. As economic liberalization has progressed, however, forest conversion has been slowed by stricter regulations, increasing demand for non-timber forest products and intensification of agriculture on existing lands. However, new and alarming environmental changes are on the horizon. Rather than forest conversion, changes associated with increased market participation – primarily pollution, water diversion and infrastructure construction – are likely to degrade ecosystem services in the future. On the positive side, in order to support its new market participation, Pingbian is likely to make investments in maintaining its fundamental ecosystem services.

The switch from subsistence to cash crops and from land-intensive to labor-intensive crops has had important impacts on land use. Total farmland and forestland (including cash trees and natural forest) have both increased during the period of economic liberalization, largely through reclamation of fallow farmland. Barren and shrub land in the middle elevations is being converted to fruit plantations of pineapple and banana; and upper elevations are being planted with cash crop trees, including star anise and bamboo (see Figure 3.3).

Forests are more strictly protected and managed and public awareness of the services provided by forests has improved, but mature old-growth forests remain sparse and threatened. Roads have been built with government support at the request of village and local governments to meet market demands. The average distance from village committee offices to a road dropped by six-tenths of a mile between 1998 and 2003, and travel time to the county seat dropped by ten minutes. Road construction often increases soil erosion, limits habitat connectivity and increases local water and air pollution.

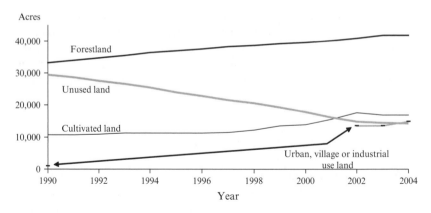

Figure 3.3   Pingbian land use

Forest Conversion

Much of the original forest was converted or degraded before 1980 (see
Figure 3.4), primarily to create agricultural land. As market liberalization
began in 1980, conversion of both original and secondary forest conversion slowed.

Demarcation of the Da Wei Shan protected area, which began in the
late 1950s, played an important role in slowing forest conversion. The protected area was expanded in the mid-1980s and again in the early 2000s,
and its status has been raised to that of a national nature reserve. The
actual protection of the natural forest remains tenuous. Because reserve
boundary demarcation is still underway, local people are not clear where
reserve boundaries and other management boundaries begin or end. The
reserve's staff and policy capacity have not been increased to handle the
expanded size of the reserve or to address emerging threats. Moreover,
while the reserve is an important habitat for the region's biodiversity, the
surrounding collective forest lands provide an important suite of ecosystem services. According to estimates of local residents and reserve staff,
some 60 percent of species found in the reserve also live in these forests.

A government initiative to promote a switch from wood to biogas has
also reduced forest degradation. The government provided cement, bricks
and other materials, and households provided labor and some funds for
this conversion. Forty-six percent of households in Pingbian now use
biogas. Biogas provides cheaper electricity, improves health and decreases
the cutting of forest wood.

Pingbian's population relies heavily on the ecosystem services provided

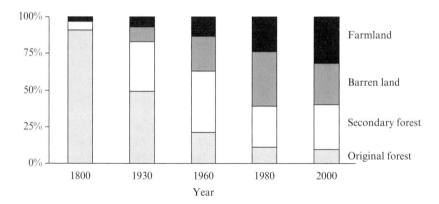

Figure 3.4   Pingbian: land cover by type, 1800–2000

by Da Wei Shan forest. Eighty-six percent of surveyed households get their firewood from the forest; 47 percent of households collect medicinal herbs from the forest; 38 percent collect mushrooms; and 54 percent of households rely on local springs and pools for drinking water. Overall, the Da Wei Shan Nature Reserve supplies almost 80 percent of the county's drinking water. Most people have access to safe drinking water, although many households experience seasonal water shortages. In the 16 villages surveyed for this study, water shortages averaged 78 days each year.

The county's agricultural production clearly relies on the productive soil and water and protection from natural disasters provided by the local forest ecosystem. Soil erosion and the regularity of drought increase with distance from the forest, according to the household survey. Most households in Pingbian are affected to some extent by soil erosion and/ or drought, though only 21 percent reported serious problems with soil erosion and 11 percent reported problems with drought. On average, households that never experience soil erosion live 0–0.8 miles from the forest. Households experiencing serious soil erosion or regular drought live, on average, over 1.2 miles away from the forest.

Collecting non-timber forest products (NTFPs) is traditional among local minority groups in Pingbian. Globally, markets for Chinese medicines and herbs are growing, and this demand is almost always met by collection rather than cultivation. Dozens of medicines are collected from the Da Wei Shan reserve, many for sale in Chinese urban markets. In recent years, business owners from outside the region, responding to growing markets, have purchased medicinal herbs, forest vegetables, flowers and trees in large quantities. Extracting these resources in large quantities changes the structure of ecosystems and may disturb the balance of ecosystem functions. Local income from NTFPs rose from less than US$150,000 in 2000 to almost US$800,000 in 2004. Forty-six percent of this income is derived from wild orchid sales, but the numbers collected seem to be dropping rapidly, indicating a level of harvest above carrying capacity. Sustainable levels of harvest for these products are not yet well known, but it is clear that expanding collection of NTFPs poses a growing threat to the forest ecosystem.

Cash-tree products such as star anise and *caoguo* and NTFPs such as orchids and medicinal herbs – all of which are enjoying increasing markets – can be grown under forest cover. In the early 1980s, Pingbian County issued small grants to farmers to encourage *caoguo* plantations, and 7,400 acres were planted in the primary forests of Da Wei Shan. Although the forest cover is retained, biodiversity decreases dramatically with the introduction of *caoguo* plantations. Research on sample plots conducted for this study found a drop from 130 to 50 species per plot (8,600 square feet). *Caoguo* plantations also decreased local drinking water supplies.

The county has made important investments in forest-based production. In the late 1970s, the county established more than 74,100 acres of pine tree plantations. Timber has been an important source of revenue for the county, accounting for 20–40 percent of revenue between 1985 and 1995. In 2000, Pingbian County issued a plan to increase forest production, calling for plantation of 24,700 acres of star anise, 16,500 acres of *caoguo*, 16,500 acres of bamboo, 1,600 acres of *Fibraurea recisa* Pierre,[8] and 8,200 acres of cinnamon, all of which are to be planted in large-scale monocultures.

In the agricultural sector, agricultural intensification – which has the great benefit of decreasing forest conversion – requires the use of larger amounts of fertilizers and pesticides. Average household fertilizer expenditures began to increase in the 1990s, followed before the end of the decade by pesticide expenditures. Part of the increase was a result of price increases, but the amount of chemicals used has also increased substantially. Nevertheless, most farmers (97 percent) still report that they face problems with crop disease.

The extent and dynamics of these new threats to Pingbian's ecosystems are still poorly understood but, clearly, rural communities are not well equipped to address pollution problems. More positively, forest conversion – the most severe threat to Pingbian's ecosystems – has slowed in the period of economic liberalization. According to the household surveys, water quality and air quality were generally considered good. Fifty-one percent of households feel the river quality near their homes is good; an additional 29 percent feel the water is drinkable; and 80 percent feel air quality is good near the forest.

Pollution

In past years, many of the challenges to the region's fragile ecosystem had to do with extensive agriculture, the collection of firewood from common forestland and the associated effects of deforestation and soil erosion. And, while policies and economic changes have worked to mitigate these problems, new challenges are emerging. Looking ahead, the most pressing concerns may have to do with air and water pollution stemming from new industry. Throughout China, rural industries have grown rapidly, beginning with a rapid growth in township and villages enterprises (TVEs).[9] The large number of new enterprises, their small scale and their distance from urban centers makes monitoring and regulation difficult.

In Pingbian, nascent enterprises include phosphorous and chrome processing firms, which rely on inexpensive electricity generated by a series of small hydropower stations along the Xinnian, Lushui and Nanxi Rivers. Pingbian now has 10,500 tons/year of yellow phosphorous processing capacity, 7,400 tons/year of refined antimony, and a 10,000-ton/year ferrosilicon factory under construction. These industries are located along streams and have the potential for sending polluted water into the region's river system, as well as generating air pollution. In addition, Pingbian has significant hydropower potential, but provincial restrictions on both developing large facilities and selling surplus power to the grid have limited construction to small hydropower plants directly tied to high-energy-use industries. In the future, this may lead county and private investors to invest further in energy-intensive industry. Taken together, these changes will bring about a different set of challenges than those faced in the past and will require an alternative set of approaches and institutions.

RESPONSES AND INTERVENTIONS

Interventions by various levels of government and by multilateral agencies and international NGOs in Pingbian have aimed to address changing production patterns, poverty alleviation and environmental concerns. The impacts of these interventions are varied, but few address the links among poverty, environment and economic change.

At the national level, the government's poverty-alleviation strategy in the context of the latest phase of trade liberalization has been to move capital from east to west and labor from west to east. The Great Western Development Program is investing in roads, energy and other infrastructure to facilitate connections between inland production and the coast. Key components of this program are environmental protection and sustainable development, which has been manifested in investments in protected areas such as Da Wei Shan. Other policies are designed to support rural incomes and reduce income differences between urban and rural areas. These include the phasing out of all agricultural taxes.[10] Price subsidies are likely to be transferred to infrastructure, technology extension or, potentially, payments for ecosystem services, which under the WTO fall into the category of green box payments. Government technical and financial assistance to farmers is expected to double agricultural exports by 2014 (Gale, 2005).

Honghe Prefecture has begun projects to support market infrastructure and the rural poor's capacity to compete. The prefecture's supply and marketing association established an Internet site to market local specialty products, providing information on the quantity, price and date of entry into the market of agricultural products and tropical fruits. The prefecture is also providing technical extension services; but not all farmers or government officials have access to these tools.

In Pingbian, the local government has responded with a mixture of central planning strategies and market facilitation activities. First, the government is promoting market-oriented production and protecting the mountainous regions by supporting development of the county's tropical areas. Poor mountain villages near natural forests are being relocated to tropical valley lands, as described above, where plantations of Chinese medicinal plants, tropical fruits and other mid-elevation cash crops are being promoted. Resettlement reduces population pressure in high-biodiversity and ecosystem-service source areas in the mountains and transfers it to the valley ecosystems in the form of agricultural intensification. For example, current government plans include development of large-scale monocultures in *caoguo*, bamboo, *Fibraurea recisa* Pierre and cinnamon. At the same time, the government continues to expand the protected area boundaries to reduce human disturbances caused by NTFP collection and tourism development.

Second, the local government is actively recruiting capital from outside the region to invest in TVEs, value-added agricultural production and industrial agriculture. While creating jobs and income through economic growth, the incentives offered, such as cheap electricity or the transfer of sections of the nature reserve to tourism companies, may threaten the natural resource base that is attracting investment in the first place.

Locally, some farmers have begun to organize producer associations, such as the *caoguo* growers association, in an effort to strengthen their capacity to guard against market risks. Through these unofficial organizations, farmers can access market information more quickly and reduce their losses.

Although remote, Pingbian has drawn substantial attention from multilateral agencies and NGOs because of the coincidence of poverty and conservation issues. The World Bank provided a US$1 million loan to the county to carry out "forest development in a poverty area" in 1998. In the same year, the Global Environment Facility (GEF) and the Ford Foundation together supported research on communities and reserve management in the Da Wei Shan Nature Reserve. The Center for Community Development Studies at the Yunnan Academy of Social Sciences has launched a case study that includes Pingbian.[11] All these projects have contributed to poverty alleviation and environmental sustainability in Pingbian.

Still, as the region's economy transforms itself from an isolated producer of traditional food crops into a more heterogeneous economy that is more closely tied to national and international markets, it will be important for policy makers to take into account changes in the economic structure that are driving changes in human well-being and ecosystems. The pace of change is likely to accelerate in Pingbian, and the effects of change will become increasingly complex, as will their implications for the environment and the livelihoods of the poor. Safeguarding the region's valuable ecology while addressing its pressing poverty will require strengthening the capacity of local institutions to provide needed services in education, health care, agriculture, and safety nets in case of economic crises or natural disasters.

CONCLUSIONS: LINKAGES AMONG POVERTY, TRADE AND ENVIRONMENT

Trade liberalization, to the extent that it is part and parcel of economic growth, is reducing poverty in China. Trade liberalization has clearly opened new markets for Pingbian. Recent income growth in the county is tied to the export of agriculture products to urban markets in China and Southeast Asia and to increasing off-farm labor opportunities. The resulting transition to intensive cash crops has slowed conversion of the natural forest. The new agricultural regime is heavily dependent on the ecosystem services provided by the Da Wei Shan Nature Reserve and the mountainous regions of the county, thus providing incentive for their conservation. At the same time, intensive agriculture raises a new set of environmental problems linked with fertilizer and pesticide use. Likewise, the growth of local industries that provide off-farm jobs also is raising new water-use and pollution issues. In addition, the increasing extraction of NTFPs is increasing pressure on the natural forests. These threats are not currently perceived by local people as a problem, but they will need to be addressed in order to maintain Pingbian's ecosystem services.

Environmental degradation and poverty are closely linked in China, where 70 percent of the poor population of poor counties lives in fragile environments. Poverty alleviation cannot proceed in these areas without functioning ecosystem services. For Pingbian, as for many rural communities throughout the world, the transition from subsistence living into an integrated global marketplace will draw from ecosystem services. The same natural constraints that have led to poverty in Pingbian have also protected much of the county's natural resource base. Isolated communities on steep slopes have not damaged water supplies, highland forests and other sources of ecosystem services. Agricultural production, NTFP collection, ecotourism, and water availability for drinking and irrigation have provided the backbone of Pingbian's achievement in food security and the transition into commercial agriculture. Human well-being and the global supply of ecosystem services will be shaped by the ability of these local communities to conserve ecosystems.

The story of trade, poverty and environment in Pingbian has been positive, but the final chapters have yet to be written. The human and environmental benefits of trade liberalization will not be sustainable without the development of new institutions to support growing market participation and to address emerging environmental problems. Pingbian's success has depended on the ability of local stakeholders to control how economic liberalization played out in their own communities. Its continued success hinges on building the supporting institutions to ensure that market participation contributes to poverty alleviation and to protecting the ecosystems that support livelihoods.

Mountainous, remote locations with limited market economies will always be at some disadvantage in a global marketplace. Time lags, missing information, incomplete transport networks and other constraints limit the benefits from trade that can be captured by these communities. In Pingbian, local government policy has focused on opening markets and moving toward market-based decision making. There has been much less attention paid to building the supporting institutions necessary to compete effectively or sustainably in national or international markets. Since economic liberalization, governments have less authority to determine production decisions, but they still have a considerable role to play in the development of institutions to support markets. Both local and national governments can contribute by providing the preconditions for successful markets: full information, physical infrastructure, access to technology and participation in decision making. They also have a substantial role to play in the creation of better safety nets for poor farmers, such as crop insurance, bankruptcy rules or government disaster relief, and social supports for education and health care. China is already beginning to redistribute the benefits of 20 years of liberalization to these impoverished regions; in the coming years the sustainability of the gains made through trade will depend on how that redirected wealth is put to use.

NOTES

1. The data on human well-being presented in this chapter are based on a household survey conducted with 94 households and a village survey of 18 villages in five townships. Sample households and villages were chosen to represent a diversity of land-use types, ecosystems and demographic profiles. The survey design was built from World Bank and China Agricultural Economy Survey experiences.
2. These classifications are made based on China's national living standard. In China, 60 percent of the nationally designated "poverty counties" are border provinces, such as Yunnan, and 40 percent of these poverty counties are minority autonomous counties like Pingbian (Fan et al., 2000).
3. Designated by Conservation International. See biodiversityhotspots.org/xp/ Hotspots.
4. Trade reached US$105.9 billion in 2005, up 35.3 percent over 2003. The ASEAN countries are Brunei, Cambodia, Indonesia, Malaysia, Myanmar, Laos, Thailand, Philippines, Singapore and Vietnam.
5. The China–ASEAN free trade zone will include a population of 2 billion, a combined GDP of US$2 trillion and a total trade volume of US$1.2 trillion.
6. The county hopes that 50 percent of its agricultural production will come from improved varieties by 2010.
7. The Grain for Green/Sloping Land Conversion Program has been extended, with the new program deadline set for 2016.
8. Known as Dutchman's pipe vine, this is a medicinal herb used to treat pain.
9. Their share of national GDP rose from 4 percent in the 1970s to more than 30 percent in 1999.
10. Most of the county's tax burden is shouldered by a small number of households. Although average taxes rose substantially with liberalization, most households in Pingbian pay little in taxes and the poor are largely exempt. Taxes began dropping from 2001 to 2003 as the central government started reversing policies. The rural tax burden will drop further as China moves to eliminate most agricultural taxes by 2010.
11. This study is entitled "Improve policy and strengthen community participation in environmental management, a case study of Yunnan." The project is funded by UNDP (the United Nations Development Program).

BIBLIOGRAPHY

Fan, S., L. Zhang and X. Zhang (2000), "Growth and poverty in rural China: the role of public investments", EPTD Discussion Paper No. 66, International Food Policy Research Institute.

Gale, F. (2005), "China's agricultural imports boomed during 2003–2004", WRS-05-04, U.S. Department of Agriculture.

Hertel, T., F. Zhai and Z. Wang (2002), "Implications of WTO accession for poverty in China", revised version of a paper prepared for presentation at the DRC/World Bank.

Huang, J., S. Rozelle and M. Chang (2002), "The nature of distortions to agricultural incentives in China and implications of WTO accession", University of California–Davis Working Paper.

International Institute of Sustainable Development (IISD) (1999), *Final Report on Trade and Sustainable Development in China*, Winnipeg, Canada: IISD.

Lu, F. (2001), *China's WTO Accession: Impact on its Agricultural Sector and Grain Policy*, Beijing: China Center for Economic Research at Peking University.

Sicular, T. and Y. Zhao (2002), "Employment earnings and the rural poor: impacts of China's WTO accession", paper prepared for presentation at the DRC/World Bank workshop "China's WTO Accession and Poverty", Beijing, China.

4. Shrimp exports, environment and human well-being in the Sundarbans, West Bengal

Kanchan Chopra, with Pushpam Kumar and Preeti Kapuria

In the early 1990s, India embarked on a program of economic liberalization that has given a much greater role to the market and has fostered an increase in exports. Given India's vast size and diversity, this policy change has had varied impacts across the country. In the Sundarbans, the delta region of West Bengal known for both its remarkable biodiversity and high levels of poverty, liberalization sparked expansion of the shrimp export industry. The last 15 years have witnessed the rapid growth of aquaculture farms and the development of a large processing and export industry in the region, which have generated employment and improved incomes for many. The use of land and water in the region, however, has been greatly affected by this development, with consequences for biodiversity, mangrove forests and long-term sustainability. This study looks at the effect of increased shrimp production on the people and the natural environment of the Sundarbans in order to better understand the links among trade, poverty and the environment. Two specific questions are addressed:

- What has been the impact of trade liberalization and consequent production of shrimp for export on the ecosystems of the Sundarbans in the last 15 years?
- What has been the impact of the shrimp industry on the well-being of different groups in the region?

To answer these questions, the authors made use of econometric analysis, remote sensing data, biodiversity indices and primary surveys about local livelihoods. These serve as the basis for identifying the trade-offs being made in terms of income, well-being and environmental stability and for developing policy recommendations that could increase environmental and social sustainability.

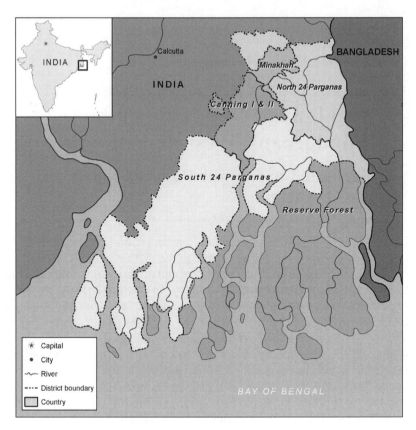

Figure 4.1   Map of the Sundarbans, India

SITE DESCRIPTION

The Sundarbans is the largest delta in the world, with a total area of 6.2 million acres in India and Bangladesh. The Indian portion is located in the state of West Bengal, at the northern end of the Bay of Bengal, and covers some 2.3 million acres. Administratively, the Indian Sundarbans includes a major portion of the districts of North 24 Parganas and South 24 Parganas (N24P and S24P). These districts are further subdivided into community development blocks (see Figure 4.1). The total population of the Sundarbans is about 4 million,[1] with a population density of about 3.8 per acre. The population is predominately rural, with most people employed in farming and fishing.

Environment

Protected mangrove forests cover 1.1 million acres of the Indian Sundarbans. Of this, 440,100 acres are inundated. This surface water is generally saline, making the region suitable for various types of brackish-water fish production, including shrimp production. Proximity to the Bay of Bengal and regular tidal flushing in the estuaries makes the climate of the Sundarbans quite moderate, with heavy rains during the monsoon season (July–October) averaging 65 inches. Salinity levels show seasonal variation that creates habitats for diverse fish species.

The Sundarbans is known for its rich biodiversity. The Tiger Reserve National Park and its buffer zone cover 638,800 acres of the Sundarbans. The park was declared a United Nations Educational, Scientific and Cultural Organization (UNESCO) World Heritage Site in 1987. Two wildlife sanctuaries are also located within the Sundarbans. In addition to the tiger, other notable fauna of the Sundarbans include the fishing cat, spotted deer, wild boar, Gangetic dolphin, water monitor, estuarine croco-dile, river terrapin, Olive Ridley turtle, ground turtle, hawksbill turtle and king (horseshoe) crab. There are some 64 plant species with the capacity to withstand estuarine conditions and high salinity.

Economy and Population

West Bengal has experienced rapid economic growth over the last two decades, and its economy is now the third largest in India. It is one of the fastest growing states in India, with the second highest rate of growth measured in terms of aggregate state domestic product (SDP). SDP growth was above 7 percent annually over the last decade. West Bengal has been successful in reducing poverty, as measured by income, in recent decades. The proportion of people below the poverty line fell from 55 percent in 1983 to about 32 percent in the year 2000.

Within the state, however, poverty is not evenly distributed. The Sundarbans districts are populated largely by poor scheduled castes (39 percent), scheduled tribes (5 percent) and minorities. These groups are generally economically disadvantaged. An estimated 50 percent of the population of 4.2 million live below the poverty line. Agricultural pro-ductivity is below the state average. Infant mortality and malnutrition are major problems, and other indicators of poverty, such as rates of anemia in women and young children, are above national averages. Most areas do not have access to electricity or safe drinking water, and other infra-structure and communication facilities are inadequate. The literacy rate is below 35 percent and education services are poor.

The majority of the Sundarbans people are agricultural farmers. Rice is the main crop, together with potatoes. Agriculture supports 89 percent of the local population. More than 90 percent of these farmers are small producers, with 56 percent of the rural population classified as landless laborers or marginal farmers (Katiha, 2001). About 13 percent of the population work as agricultural laborers, primarily during the monsoon and harvest seasons. The remainder of the year many seek employment on shrimp farms or collect shrimp seed (larvae) from the wild. An estimated 150,000 people depend on shrimp larvae collection in the Indian Sundarbans (Central Inland Fisheries Research Institute, 1999 and 2000). Yet, in spite of the prevalence of poverty in the region, people have been migrating there because of the rich natural resources.

CHANGING POLICIES

India embarked on a program of liberalization in the early 1990s in the face of a crisis in balance of payments. Key components of the liberalization program included reducing the role of the public sector, cutting the fiscal deficit and strengthening the financial sector. Domestic liberalization relaxed restrictions on production, investments and prices. External sector liberalization meant relaxed restrictions on international flows of goods, services, technology and capital.

Emphasis was given to the expansion of export-oriented businesses. The private sector was permitted to enter into areas previously reserved for the state sector; licensing for domestic manufacturers was abolished for most industries and the Indian rupee was devalued significantly. Following several partial adjustments between 1991 and 1994, full current account convertibility was established in mid-1994. This exchange rate adjustment was the single most important factor influencing exports.

India became a founding member of the World Trade Organization (WTO) when the Uruguay Round was ratified at the beginning of 1995. Under the agreement, India was obliged to eliminate all quantitative restrictions on imports and to reduce tariffs. Quantitative restrictions were eliminated in 2001–02. Many previously banned or restricted goods are now allowed access and import tariffs have been drastically reduced. India's trade-to-GDP (gross domestic product) ratio had been stable throughout the 1980s at around 14 percent. Three years into the reforms, it had risen to 18 percent, with the increase primarily attributable to a rise in exports promoted by the devaluation of the rupee in the initial years of liberalization. This pattern has continued. While both exports and imports have grown faster than GDP, pushing the trade-to-GDP ratio to 31 percent by the year 2003, the growth in exports has outpaced the growth in imports. And while the rupee has appreciated slightly against the dollar, it has continued to depreciate against the other major currencies.

In the years following this liberalization program, marine product exports from India increased substantially. The volume (in metric tons, or MT) of marine product exports more than tripled between 1990 and 2003 (from 139,419 MT to 412,017 MT). Growth was equally dramatic in value terms, from US$498 million in 1990 to US$1,331 million in 2003. Marine product exports now account for about 17 percent of India's total agriculture and food exports, up from 15 percent in the early 1990s. Frozen shrimp account for much of this expansion. The value of shrimp exports rose about 150 percent, from US$396 million to US$985 million over this period. India is now the world's second-largest shrimp exporter. Shrimp production and export from West Bengal played an important role in this expansion. Frozen shrimp exports from West Bengal now account for 11 percent of India's total frozen shrimp exports, up from 9.3 percent in 1991.

A number of factors contributed to this expansion, most notably the exchange rate devaluation. With changes in national economic policies, decision-makers in West Bengal have shifted from import-substitution approaches to export-led growth strategies. Shrimp, as a premium product in international markets, appeared an ideal choice for export-led growth. In the early 1990s, entering the international shrimp market was particularly attractive because production from the world's primary exporters – Thailand and Vietnam – was drastically reduced as over-intensive production led to disease outbreaks. The West Bengal tiger shrimp offered a good substitute.

This combination of more liberal domestic investment rules and international market opportunity led to increased private investment in shrimp-processing units, primarily by investors from Kolkata (formerly Calcutta). Government agencies provided substantial support. The State Department of Fisheries initiated policies favorable to production and export of shrimp, including extension and training, liberal credits and subsidies for nets and boats, insurance and savings schemes and infrastructure development such as establishing warehouses, processing units, roads and communications. The state government also established the Brackish Water Fish Farmer's Development Agency, which developed some 9,400 acres for aquaculture that now produce 45,000 tons of shrimp per year. The World Bank provided US$6 million to support the development of 1,100 acres for shrimp cultivation in the Canning and Dighirpur districts.

Exports of shrimp from West Bengal expanded, as a result of these policy changes and domestic supports, at a rate of about 4 percent annually from

1991 to 2003. Frozen shrimp now accounts for 96 percent of West Bengal's marine product exports. Relative prices in destination markets affected the pattern of exports. At the beginning of this period, the primary destinations for West Bengal shrimp exports were Japan, the European Union (EU) and the United States.[2] By 2003, the United States and Japan were the major importers (40 percent and 38 percent, respectively, by value), followed by the EU (11 percent).[3] Within the EU, the UK was the largest importer, followed by Belgium and the Netherlands.

One factor contributing to changing patterns has been the food safety and phytosanitary standards in the importing countries. These standards, which include labeling, processing and transport standards, have become increasingly stringent over the last decade and, at times, may have functioned as nontariff barriers to trade. Temporary declines in exports have occurred and some smaller companies have been driven out of business by these standards. Costs of compliance range from 1 percent to 5 percent of total production costs; an inverse relationship has been observed between the scale of operation and cost of compliance, making it harder for smaller firms to adapt. For the most part, however, exporting companies have been able to adapt to the changing standards because high international prices have given them leeway to make the necessary investments.

PRODUCTION CHANGES AND LANDSCAPE CHANGES

The increase in shrimp exports from West Bengal has changed the landscape of economic opportunities for the local population and caused changes in the physical landscape of the Sundarbans region. Aquaculture operations have expanded at a rapid rate in West Bengal, particularly in the Sundarbans, largely at the expense of agriculture. Of the eight community development blocks in the Sundarbans, all have registered an increase in land under shrimp. The Sundarbans now has around 103,800 acres under shrimp farming. The Sandeshkhali I and II, Minakhan, Hasnabad and Haroa community development blocks in the N24P district have about 81,500 acres under shrimp farming; Canning, Basanti and Gosaba blocks in S24P account for another 29,700 acres. Minakhan registered the largest conversion between 1986 and 2004 because of a number of favorable factors, including availability of vast agricultural fields, proximity to major markets, infrastructure facilities and good conditions for shrimp production. There are now 27 shrimp processing plants in West Bengal, mostly located in and around Kolkata. See Table 4.1.

To summarize spatial differences, Canning and Minakhan are the

Table 4.1   *Land converted to shrimp culture in the Sundarbans, 1986–2004*

Time period	Land converted in acres (million)
1986–1989	26.5
1989–1996	35.4
1996–2001	28.4
2001–2004	24.1

Source: National Remote Sensing Agency (NRSA) satellite data.

blocks with the greatest concentration of shrimp farms. In these blocks, different technologies for shrimp farming have been tried and polyculture with improved traditional techniques was found to be the best. These are also the blocks where land conversion has been from agriculture to aquaculture and then to brick kilns. Gosaba, which is relatively distant and inaccessible, is the area with the largest concentration of fishermen and prawn-seed collectors.

Stakeholders

Many people in the region are now involved in the shrimp export market. At the first step in the production process are the prawn-seed collectors. Because the region does not have shrimp hatcheries, aquaculture farms rely on a supply of shrimp larvae, known as prawn seeds, collected from the wild. In response to rapidly growing demand, many poor people in the Sundarbans have adopted prawn-seed collection as their primary activity. This can be carried out along with collection of crabs, ornamental fish and other fish sold in the local market. An estimated 150,000 people are involved, including a large number of children. These people are generally the poorest in the region, with no land and no livelihood alternatives.

Middlemen, known as *aratdars*, buy prawn seeds from the collectors and resell them to the farmers. In addition, an *aratdar* often serves as a financer, providing boats and nets to the collectors on condition that they will sell their catch to him. An *aratdar* will also lend money to the farmers, again on condition that the produce be sold to him.

Aquaculture farmers may either own their land or lease it. About 90 percent of the farmers in the region lease their land. Of these, about 80 percent have only a three-year lease. These leases, however, are often renewed; many leaseholders have been farming the same land for eight to 10 years, some for as many as 25 years. *Panchayats*, the local-level administrative and political units, play an important role in aquaculture activity, from the allocation of land to the farmer to the sale of the product. Farmers pay license fees to the *panchayat* of about 1,500 rupees per year. The *panchayat* influences the allocation of government assistance and subsidies, often favoring *panchayat* members and their relatives. Although shrimp production requires substantial investment and risk, it is often quite profitable for these farmers. Different technologies are employed, with varying investment and management requirements, as discussed below. An estimated 8,100 households are engaged in shrimp farming.

Farms employ two types of workers: temporary low-paid construction workers and permanent workers, including maintenance workers, supervisors and guards. There are an estimated 72,000 shrimp-farm workers in the Sundarbans.

Because shrimp production involves the use of a variety of inputs – shrimp feed, organic and inorganic fertilizers, lime, pesticides, medicines – and equipment for pond treatment and preparation, selling these inputs has become a profitable business for many suppliers in the region.

The processing plants are located in and around Kolkata. While some process a variety of marine products, most concentrate on shrimp processing and export. Those processing a variety of products operate 10 to 12 months of the year; those dedicated to shrimp operate about eight months a year because of the cycle of shrimp farming. In addition to jobs in the processing plants, there are also jobs created in packaging, transport, exporting, wholesaling and retailing. Processing plants in Kolkata employ more than 17,000 workers.

ENVIRONMENTAL IMPACTS

This study investigated two of the primary environmental impacts of the expansion of shrimp production – land-use change for aquaculture and loss of biodiversity attributable to prawn-seed collection. Notably, as the final step in the shrimp trade, the processing units do not contribute substantially to environmental problems through either solid waste or water pollution.

Land-Use Change

Two types of land-use change occurred in the Sundarbans as a result of the expansion of shrimp production:

- conversion of rice paddy (agricultural) land to shrimp ponds
- conversion of mangroves to shrimp ponds

The study used satellite images from the National Remote Sensing Agency (NRSA) to estimate the changes. Over the study period, 1986–2004, more than 24,700 acres were converted to aquaculture in the Sandeshkhali I and II and Minakhan blocks; about 13,300 acres were converted in the Canning block. Most of the land converted to aquaculture in these blocks was paddy land. Direct conversion of mangroves to aquaculture has been more modest. However, in the Namkhana and Kultali blocks, 6,200 and 2,700 acres, respectively, of dense forest were converted to aquaculture. Over the study period there was also some conversion of aquaculture lands to brick kilns in Minakhan.

The decision to convert land from paddy or mangrove to aquaculture is a result of increasing population density, labor productivity and relative net returns to the different land uses.[4] Increasing relative returns to shrimp production along with increasing population densities in the region have led to the rapid land conversion. Conversion from paddy land has occurred primarily in the northern blocks where population density had already led to the development of substantial paddy areas. Conversion of mangroves, which accounts for a much smaller share of the new aquaculture area, occurred primarily in the southern blocks where population was less dense.

Several aquaculture systems are in use in the region for shrimp, with different impacts in terms of land use and other environmental impacts. The prevalent systems for shrimp culture in the Sundarbans are as follows:

- The *traditional system* uses large areas that are naturally inundated during high tide. Very little management is required. No supplementary feed is added and water is exchanged infrequently. Production per acre is low.
- The *extensive* or *improved traditional* system is the most commonly used in the Sundarbans. Ponds of 2.5 to 12 acres with low stocking density (approximately 20,000/acre) are maintained with moderate management. Water is exchanged twice a month during high tide and occasional feed and fertilizer additions are made. Production per acre is moderate.
- The *modified extensive system* uses a high stocking density (40,000/acre) in smaller ponds of 1.2 to 7.4 acres. Management requirements are greater to maintain water quality, food and soil. Ponds require preparation before stocking, water is exchanged six to eight times per month and supplementary feed, such as oil cake, is added. Production is about 0.5 tons/acre.
- The *semi-intensive system*, which used even higher stocking densities (80,000/acre) has been banned since 1997 by a supreme court ruling

because of its harmful environmental impacts, including impacts on the forest, fish biodiversity, agriculture and the environment in general. This system required intense management and substantial inputs; yields averaged 1.48 tons/acre.

Some 81,500 acres in North 24 Parganas and 29,700 acres in South 24 Parganas are devoted to shrimp farming. The potential area that could be brought under shrimp farming is substantially greater, about 444,800 acres in these two districts alone. The implications of land-use change for this ecologically rich region are many and need to be studied in depth.

Biodiversity Loss

The expansion of aquaculture production has affected biodiversity through the conversion of land and through the rapid growth of prawn-seed collection. The collection of tiger prawn seed from the wild, using various kinds of dragnets, is affecting biodiversity primarily through loss of the bycatch. Several studies have shown that many non-target species, including juveniles of many finfish and shellfish species, are trapped in the nets. These are thrown away, causing major damage to the juvenile fish community of the area. These juvenile fish, known as ichthyoplankton, are a critical component of the marine and estuarine ecosystems, which constitute not only the next generation of adults but also a major food source for larger bony fish, sharks, turtles, dolphin and other species.

Several studies have made estimates of the bycatch loss resulting from prawn-seed collection. One study found, for example, that almost 11 tons of finfish (juveniles) were wasted per day, including an average of 48 species per net per haul (Mitra, 2005; MOEF, 1996). This bycatch loss clearly contributes to a decline in the variety of the biological resource base.

While such one-time estimates of biodiversity loss are useful, given the rapid expansion of prawn-seed collection, it is important to look at how this loss has evolved along with the shrimp industry. This study reviewed available time-series data to establish the trend in biodiversity loss.[5] Because prawn-seed collection appears to be spread over the whole region, three representative sites were selected in the coastal zone for their different salinity levels and diversity.[6] Monthly data for 10 years on the number of species lost in the bycatch were used to construct indices of biodiversity loss for the period.[7] An average annual decline of 0.03 in the index was found. Analysis of the decline in biodiversity at the three sites over the ten years showed that biodiversity loss was more pronounced in the regions where prawn-seed collection coincided with other anthropogenic pressures, particularly conversion of mangroves to other uses. Because prawn seeds are transported all over the region, it was assumed that an aquaculture farm's contribution to this biodiversity loss depends on its size and stocking density, not its location. Further expansion of shrimp production would aggravate this loss of biodiversity. On a more positive note, the banning of semi-intensive culture practices has resulted in lower average stocking densities and consequently has reduced the loss in bycatch.

Since biodiversity loss resulting from prawn-seed collection is one of the major negative impacts of the shrimp export industry, this study undertook to investigate the feasibility of internalizing this cost. The data used for costs of production were based on field surveys conducted at aquaculture farms in the three representative blocks in 2005. The authors found that, given the present structure of costs and prices, aquaculture farmers would be able to absorb the social cost of biodiversity loss caused by prawn-seed collection if seed prices were raised to cover these costs.

CONSEQUENCES FOR HUMAN WELL-BEING

The benefits of the shrimp export industry for the region are many. Shrimp exports are earning substantial foreign exchange. The entire production and export process – from prawn-seed collection to farming, processing and transport – generates income and creates employment for many people who otherwise have very limited opportunities. Shrimp exports in 2003–04 were worth about 5,080 million rupees at international prices. This generated domestic income of 6,555 million rupees. Every rupee of export results in income accrual of 1.29 rupees. This income was distributed approximately as follows: shrimp farmers, 61 percent; shrimp-farm workers, 14 percent; prawn-seed collectors, 8 percent; transporters and retailers, 14 percent; and processing units, 4 percent. See Table 4.2.

These very positive economic changes, however, must be weighed against the environmental and social changes that have accompanied the expansion of shrimp production. Poverty is a question not just of income but of many other factors that affect human well-being. These factors have been defined in a variety of ways, but are well summarized by the Millennium Ecosystem Assessment as follows: basic material for a good life (adequate livelihoods, sufficient food, shelter, access to goods); health (including access to fresh air and water); social relations (such as social cohesion); security (including personal safety, secure resource access, security from disasters); and freedom and choice.

This study made a comparison – across regions and stakeholders – of the impacts of the shrimp industry on human well-being.[8] The comparison looked at income, food security, health and life security, and conflict and

Table 4.2   Income and employment from shrimp production and processing
           for export in the Indian Sundarbans (annual)

	Number (in thousands)	Income (in billion rupees)	Attributable to export activity (in million rupees)
Shrimp farmers	8.1	5.68 (7.79)*	3.98
Prawn-larvae collectors	150	0.75	0.52
Shrimp-farm workers	72.14	1.29	0.90
Processing unit value added		0.24	0.24
Transporters and agents		0.90	0.90
Total		8.88	6.55

Notes:

All figures are annual for the year 2004–05. No shrimp-farm worker reported from Gosaba in the survey.
*Figures in parentheses in the category of shrimp farmers are estimated on the basis of land-use data from NRSA.

social cohesion. For the purposes of the comparison, the following groups were selected: shrimp farmers, agriculture farmers and mixed-income households in Canning and Minakhan, selected because of the rate of land conversion from paddy to aquaculture in those blocks; prawn-seed collectors and fishermen in Gosaba, selected because many fishermen in this block have moved into prawn-seed collection; and prawn-seed collectors and salary and wage earners in Gosaba, selected in order to examine the options if prawn-seed collection were banned. Results are based on a household questionnaire administered in Minakhan, Canning and Gosaba.

The study found that the shrimp farmers in Minakhan and Canning were better off than the agriculturalists in terms of per capita income. However, the security of their income was much lower because of the frequency of lost harvests. Also, while agricultural farmers are not exposed to conflict, shrimp farmers have a relatively low level of social cohesion that is associated with frequent conflicts. Many of these conflicts are over property rights; land for ponds remains the most critical resource and most conflicts arise around land-rights issues. Mixed-income households have lower levels of income than shrimp farms but enjoy greater income security. They also face lower levels of conflict.

In Gosaba, prawn-seed collectors had increased incomes compared to fishermen. They also enjoy greater life security, since they do not have to go out to sea. However, they do suffer more chronic health problems as a result of their work and often face conflicts over the price of their catch. About 87 percent rely on the *aratdar* for credit, and then must sell the catch to him. Not surprisingly, salary and wage households had even higher levels of income security and health security and lower levels of conflict. However, prawn-seed collectors lack the skills, particularly literacy, needed to move into this category of worker.

RESPONSES AND INTERVENTIONS

The expansion of shrimp production and processing that has followed trade liberalization is expected to continue. Growing markets and the existence of substantial areas suitable for shrimp farming will support the continuing land-use change and increased prawn-seed collection. Well-designed responses will be critical for ensuring economic and environmental sustainability in the region and for ensuring that the poor benefit from the continued development of the shrimp export industry. Investment by the West Bengal State Department of Fisheries in the following measures is essential:

- *Accurate and timely information about markets.* Processing units can internalize compliance costs arising out of food safety regulations in importing countries, provided they receive accurate and timely information. This adaptive capacity has been demonstrated but needs to be strengthened to prevent disruptions in the industry that would affect all stakeholders. Scaling down of production or going out of business means loss of income to the whole supply chain from the prawn-seed collector to the processing units. The national government and industry associations have an important role to play in assuring fast and accurate transmission of information regarding prevailing food safety, phytosanitary or other standards of importing countries. A public–private partnership to provide this information could ensure that incomes from shrimp processing are sustained in the region.
- *Appropriate technology choices.* Disease related to use of intensive stocking technologies illustrated how inappropriate choices can lead to economic and environmental problems. The combination of economic and legal action resulted in a shift into more sustainable technologies. The continued adoption of such sustainable aquaculture practices should be supported.
- *Innovative policies to address the biodiversity loss associated with livelihoods that sustain the poor.* Prawn-seed collection has become a very important livelihood for large numbers of poor people in the region. While making an important contribution to poverty alleviation, prawn-seed collection is having damaging effects on biodiversity. Several policy options could be considered to address this conflict:

○ *Internalizing the cost of biodiversity loss into the cost of shrimp production.* The money generated could be put into a designated fund for mangrove generation or, more generally, biodiversity conservation. This is economically feasible, but administratively difficult to implement.

○ *Providing alternative livelihoods for the prawn-seed collectors and establishing hatcheries to provision shrimp farms.* This option would require extensive investment. In some cases, civil society organizations and NGOs have been able to foster such livelihood changes.[9] Such efforts need to be developed on a much larger scale.

• *Cooperation to find new policy solutions.* Many diverse stakeholders in the Sundarbans have an interest in the long-term sustainability of the shrimp export industry. Yet the incentives facing each stakeholder group, especially in the short run, may jeopardize the benefits over the long run. Exporters and processing plants are reliant on continuing favorable international prices and their ability to meet importers' standards. Processing units also require a continuous supply of shrimp. But this supply is vulnerable because of the risks of intensive farming, particularly the risk that disease will wipe out a harvest. Continued expansion of the land under shrimp farming to meet the demand of processing plants reduces agricultural production and lessens biodiversity. Vulnerable people rely on prawn-seed collection for their basic livelihood, maximizing their daily catch of tiger prawn seeds using techniques that cause biodiversity loss. Faced with limited choices, all these stakeholders may be forced to make choices that are not in the long-term best interests of the economic or ecological stability of the region. This study from the Sundarbans has lessons for the other regions – such as Orissa, Andhra Pradesh and Gujarat – where mangrove forests are being cleared and coastal biodiversity is under threat. Working cooperatively, with support from civil society and government, and making use of diverse experiences and knowledge systems, more effective ways of managing these valuable ecosystems and more effective ways of meeting the needs of India's vulnerable people could be achieved.

NOTES

1. As per the 2001 census the population stood at 3.7 million, but it was estimated to have reached 4.2 million by 2006.
2. Shares by value were Japan, 68 percent; EU, 18 percent; and United States, 7 percent.

Shares by volume were Japan, 52 percent; EU, 29 percent; and United States, 12 percent.
3. Shares by volume are slightly different: United States, 35 percent; Japan, 37 percent; and EU, 17 percent.
4. A model was devised for the study that showed that, for a 1 percent decrease in the relative yield ratio between paddy and aquaculture, 0.47 percent of the land will be converted to aquaculture. For every 1 percent increase in the population per 247 acres, 0.4 percent of paddy land will be converted to aquaculture. In the case of mangrove to aquaculture conversion, a 1 percent decrease in the relative yield ratio will correspond with a 0.11 percent conversion rate, and a 1 percent increase in population density will correspond with a 0.55 percent conversion rate.
5. This rich data set was made available and analyzed as part of this project thanks to the collaboration of the Department of Marine Sciences, University of Kolkata. See Mitra (2005).
6. These were Diamond Harbor, Sagar South and Junput.
7. The sample size for the computation was a 10 g composite sample of the wasted material obtained by a random mixing of the take of 15 nets.
8. This comparison used shrimp farmers and agricultural farmers in Canning and Minakhan.
9. For example, development of livelihood options and nonconventional energy sources in areas like Chhotamullakhali has improved incomes and reduced environmental stresses. Development of small-scale tourism involving local people, such as projects by the Wildlife Protection Society of India and WWF, has also offered alternative livelihoods with reduced environmental impact.

BIBLIOGRAPHY

Central Inlands Fisheries Research Institute (1999, 2000), *Annual Reports*, Kolkata: Central Inlands Fisheries Research Institute.
Directorate of Census Operations (2001), *Census of India (2001), Provisional Population Totals*, Series 20, Paper 3, New Delhi: Registrar General, Census.
Economic Survey (2004, 2005), New Delhi: Ministry of Finance, Government of India.
Katiha, P.K. (2001), "Profile of key aquacultural practices and fishing technologies in India", paper presented during the First Regional Workshop on Strategies and Options for Increasing and Sustaining Fisheries and Aquaculture Production to Benefit Poor Households in Asia. ADB, RETA 5945. Penang, Malaysia, 20–25 August.
Millennium Ecosystem Assessment (2003), *Ecosystems and Human Well-being: A Framework for Assessment*, Washington, DC: Island Press.
Ministry of Environment and Forests (MOEF) (1996), *Annual Report*, New Delhi: Government of India.
Mitra, A. (2005), "Study of the evaluation of fin fish juvenile loss due to wild harvest of tiger prawn seeds from coastal West Bengal", report commissioned by the Department of Marine Science, University of Calcutta, for the project "Trade, Environment and Rural Poverty", Delhi: Institute of Economic Growth.

5. Trade liberalization, rural poverty and the environment: two studies of agricultural exports in Madagascar

Bart Minten, with Philippe Méral,
Lalaina Randrianarison and Johan Swinnen

While Madagascar is one of the poorest countries in sub-Saharan Africa, it is also one of the world's richest in biodiversity. The predominantly rural population relies heavily on the natural resources that also support the island's remarkable diversity of species. Madagascar has drawn international attention in recent years because of its environmental assets, and substantial investments have slowed environmental degradation. Liberalization of the Malagasy economy began in the 1980s and has led to a rapid increase in both imports and exports over the last 20 years. But the growth of trade has had little impact on economic opportunities for Madagascar's rural population, and rural exports on the whole have declined (Cadot et al., 2005; Moser et al., 2005). Rural poverty still runs above 77 percent, despite the economic reforms. This aggregate picture, however, conceals the fact that new international trade opportunities have had dramatic impacts for some rural people and places.

This study looks at two cases where changing trade rules have had important effects on poverty and the environment. First, we look at the rapid expansion of maize production in southwest Madagascar, a case that illustrates the contribution of trade to agricultural land extensification and deforestation and its links to changing environmental mores. Second, we look at contract farming of high-value vegetables, which illustrates the opportunities trade can afford the poor and the contribution the private sector can make to sustainable agriculture through intensification. To carry out these studies, surveys were conducted with agricultural households and communities in different parts of the country about trade, poverty and environment, and secondary data were used complement and corroborate the findings. From these cases we draw some lessons about the challenges that arise with trade liberalization and about how Madagascar could better take advantage of trade opportunities to improve the livelihoods of the poor and contribute to sustainable use of the country's environmental resources.

MADAGASCAR

Economy, Population and Environment

From independence until the 1990s, Madagascar faced both a rapidly growing population and falling GDP (gross domestic product). Per capita GDP fell to a low of $229 in 1989 and, as the 1990s began, an estimated 70 percent of the total population was living in poverty. Of the poor population, 80 percent lived in rural areas. Today, the economy remains predominantly rural, with agriculture accounting for about 30 percent of GDP.[1] Most agricultural production is carried out by smallholders, with farm sizes averaging just over 2.5 acres. Rice is the primary crop and the food staple, accounting for the majority of land in agricultural production and for 45 percent of calories consumed (Dorosh et al., 2003). However, Malagasy rice yields are among the world's lowest.[2] Yields for other food and export crops are also consistently low, reflecting poor water management, lack of nutrient replenishment and limited adoption of improved agricultural technologies.[3]

Madagascar's geographic isolation, together with its highly varied geomorphology and microclimates, has resulted in some of the most distinct biodiversity in the world. It is considered one of the world's 17 mega-diverse countries. An estimated 80 percent of Madagascar's plant species are endemic, along with an even greater percentage of the fauna. The coastline supports coral reefs and mangroves with the highest level of diversity of flora and fauna in the region (World Bank, 2003). This unique biodiversity is threatened by rapid degradation of habitats. Between 1960 and 2000, Madagascar lost 50 percent of its forest cover, some 29.7 million acres (World Bank, 2003). Most of this loss occurred in the 1970s and early 1980s, when the government actively promoted food self-sufficiency through expansion of slash-and-burn agriculture. Since the mid-1980s, Madagascar has been the focus of international conservation efforts, with substantial international assistance provided for environmental objectives.

By the end of the 1990s, only 29 percent of Madagascar remained under forest cover,[4] including evergreen forest (32 percent), dry and spiny forest (24 percent), secondary forest (42 percent)[5] and mangroves. Almost 13 percent of the country's forests have protected area status (World Bank, 2003). The Mikea forest of southwest Madagascar, the area of the first case study, is classified as spiny forest. Because of high levels of endemism, spiny forests are considered among the most valuable in the world in terms of biodiversity and have been widely identified as a conservation priority. However, as of the early 2000s, only 3.2 percent of Madagascar's spiny forest was protected (WWF, 2000; Gorenflo et al., 2005).

Trade Event

At the beginning of the 1980s, the Malagasy economy was plagued by severe macroeconomic imbalances. The development strategy of the socialist period led to a huge surge in imports, an unsustainable balance-of-payments deficit, large budget deficits and, consequently, inflation (Dorosh, 1996). High tariffs and quantitative restrictions along with the licensing of foreign exchange and various bureaucratic hurdles, which reflected the government's inward-looking development strategy of the 1970s and early 1980s, combined to severely constrain trade. State intervention was particularly notable in the agricultural sector: most trade in agricultural products and inputs was in the hands of the state. Efforts to stabilize agricultural prices through government controls had the effect of discouraging both production for export and production of domestic food products.

Under the aegis of International Monetary Fund (IMF) agreements and a succession of World Bank and bilateral adjustment loans, internal trade liberalization began in 1983 with the state officially abandoning its monopoly on commerce in agricultural products. External trade liberalization was initiated six years later and continued into the 1990s. The import licensing and quota system was abolished; export taxes for cash crops were eliminated; the exchange rate was gradually adjusted and finally floated in 1994; and banking arrangements for imports and exports were simplified.

With liberalization, the combined value of exports and imports as a share of GDP rose from less than 30 percent in 1986 to more than 70 percent in 2004. Yet, while overall exports increased, agricultural exports showed little growth. This stagnation reflects, in large measure, the fall in coffee exports. In the early 1980s, when agricultural exports accounted for over half of exports, coffee was by far the largest export (64 percent), followed by cloves and vanilla. Coffee now represents just 1 percent of agricultural exports. This collapse is attributable to the entry of newcomers into the international market, notably Vietnam, and to the degradation of Madagascar's plantations. Vanilla exports, on the other hand, have benefited from rising prices. Fresh and prepared tropical fruits and fiber crops have also expanded.

In short, the importance of agricultural exports has declined significantly, in absolute as well as relative terms, since trade liberalization

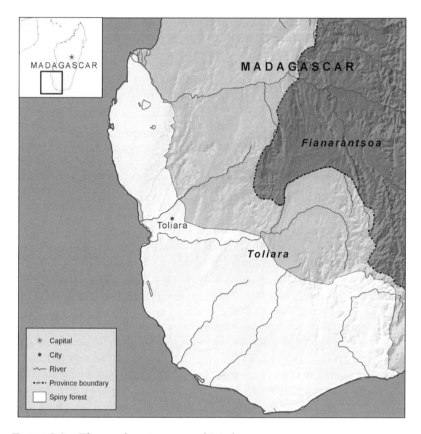

Figure 5.1   The southwest region of Madagascar

began. The rural majority appears to have been bypassed by the benefits of trade liberalization. However, there are rural places where trade has made a big difference in the last 10 years. The following two case studies look at places where there have been significant changes in the livelihoods of rural people and in the environment.

MAIZE EXPORTS AND THE LOSS OF THE SPINY FOREST IN THE SOUTHWEST

The southwest of Madagascar is one of the poorest regions in this very poor country, and the region's unique spiny forest has suffered one of the highest rates of deforestation in recent years. This deforestation has been linked with export of maize to Ile de la Réunion, an export market that was opened by a particular set of European development policies. The study explored this link to determine how the maize trade with Réunion affected the people and environment of the area around Madagascar's Toliara port.

Trade Event

As Madagascar was liberalizing its own trade rules in the late 1980s and early 1990s, the European Union (EU) put in place some specific policies intended to promote the development of its outermost regions, including Madagascar's neighbor, Ile de la Réunion, which is an overseas department of France. The new policies, known as Posei,[6] were intended to speed up integration of these regions and promote regional collaboration with other developing countries.[7] Beginning in 1992, two types of policies were implemented that benefited Ile de la Réunion: policies promoting imports of agricultural supplies to support agribusiness and livestock production; and policies promoting development of local agriculture. Under these policies, Réunion was allowed to give tax breaks on imported cereals as a way to facilitate livestock production.

As a result of Posei,[8] meat production expanded rapidly in Ile de la Réunion. Production of pork and chicken increased by 51 percent and 92 percent, respectively, between 1990 and 2003. This expansion was dependent on the import of maize for feed. Maize imports to Réunion came from only three countries: France, Argentina and Madagascar. Madagascar had the great advantage of proximity to Réunion, which should have kept Malagasy maize prices competitive. Toliara, Madagascar's southern port, is only 1,100 miles from Réunion (as compared to the 8,100 miles between Argentina and Réunion).

Initially, Malagasy maize production expanded to meet this new demand. By a conservative estimate (Georges, 2002), Madagascar exported 160,000 tons of maize to Réunion between 1988 and 1998. Approximately 38 percent of maize production was exported (Escande, 1995), and as much as 72 percent of this went to Réunion (Fauroux, 1999). By 2001, however, Malagasy maize exports to Réunion had fallen substantially, and Réunion was importing maize almost exclusively from France and Argentina. Madagascar lost this export market for several reasons. First, in order to assure cheap and regular supplies of feed, Réunion created a cereal port and constructed a large-capacity silo. This allowed it to focus on supplies in large quantities rather than managing multiple small shipments, such as those from Madagascar. Second, because of local monopolies at the port of Toliara and the small size of ships and maize shipments leaving Madagascar, handling and transport costs from Madagascar were relatively high. Third, Madagascar was not able to provide the regular supply needed by Réunion's livestock producers. Thus, what appeared to be a large trade opportunity fizzled out almost completely for Madagascar.

Southwest Madagascar

In the 1980s, maize was used only as a food crop in southwest Madagascar. While a maize marketing chain existed, it was primarily geared toward local consumption. Cotton, the primary cash crop in the region, had experienced a boom in the 1970s and early 1980s that attracted new farmers to the region and led to a shift among local farmers from subsistence crops toward cash crops. The cotton boom ended in the middle of the 1980s but left the structures for commercial agriculture in place. In the late 1980s, these structures supported the expansion of maize production for export. The principal cooperative of Réunion (Unacoopa) started trading with Madagascar at the end of the 1980s and, in 1990, established a local subsidiary, known as Sopagri, in the region, attracted by improved export conditions and more liberal investment rules. In the early 1990s, Sopagri built a 12,000-ton capacity silo in Toliara and set up a local collection system in the southwest. Thus, when the opportunity for increased maize trade with Réunion came along under the Posei policies, maize production in the southwest expanded rapidly. In the 1990s, about a dozen companies in Toliara were exporting maize to Réunion, each with a capacity of 2,000 to 4,000 tons annually.

The collapse of exports to Réunion has not substantially reduced maize production in the southwest. Sopagri's presence has made it possible to maintain production in the region. Some 5,000 to 10,000 tons per year are still sold for export to countries in the Indian Ocean (Comoros, Mayotte, Seychelles), to two small companies from Réunion and to a domestic company in Antananarivo.

Human Impacts

Poverty is very high in southwest Madagascar. The head-count poverty ratio was estimated at 85 percent in 1993, significantly above national levels (Razafindravonana et al., 2001) as well as above the average for rural areas in the province of Toliara. Since 1993, poverty in the area of maize production has decreased, suggesting that, despite the collapse of exports to Réunion, maize has been beneficial for the local population.

Two data sets were used to look at the impact of increased maize production and trade on human well-being in the region. The first are five national household surveys conducted between 1993 and 2004 (by INSTAT, the National Institute of Statistics) that look at poverty dynamics for the study region around the port of Toliara. (Some caution is warranted in interpreting these data, given a large change in sample composition and size.) Second, focus-group interviews were carried out in 80 communities in the area in 2004 to better understand the dynamics in the region. Focus groups were chosen to be as representative as possible of the population of the communities. These data were mapped in order to link them with other spatial data (Minten and Méral, 2005).

Poverty levels remained high in the study area, but they did improve. The head-count poverty ratio decreased to 73 percent in 2004. Because it is difficult to attribute this evolution to specific causes, we compare it to the rest of the province of Toliara in order to look at differences within the region. The poverty head count for the study area was 2 percent higher than the rest of rural Toliara in 1993; by 2004, it was 4 percent lower. This strongly suggests that the area that produced maize exports, and consequently experienced high rates of deforestation, fared a bit better than the rest of the province in terms of per capita income. Access to social services and social capital has also improved over the last 15 years, according to the evidence from the focus groups. The majority of focus groups also believe that the health of the population has improved and that newborn mortality rates are lower.

Most of the communities no longer produce maize for export.[9] Despite improved transport conditions, fewer traders come to the region. While traders now visit some communities that previously were not involved in trade, other communities now report that they see fewer traders. One quarter of the communities still are not involved in any marketing of agricultural produce.

Environment

Deforestation rates in southwest Madagascar were the highest in the country over the 1990–2000 period (Agarwal et al., 2004). Based on long-term land-use data, deforestation rates in the area are estimated to have increased from 124 acres per year for the period 1949–67 to 4,100 acres per year for the period 1986–96 (Razanaka et al., 2001). The increase in the deforestation rate in the area east of Toliara, known as the *plateau calcaire*, is even more dramatic.

The total area deforested in the study area between 1990 and 2000 was 630,600 acres (Steininger et al., 2003). How much of this deforestation can be attributed to export maize production? Based on the total amount of maize exported and local productivity measures, about 123,600 acres

(20 percent) of the area deforested can be directly related to international trade.[10] The farmers are estimated to have obtained about \$51,800 per square mile of forest converted to maize.[11]

While trade clearly played an important role in regional deforestation, there are many other contributing factors: deforestation is linked with maize production for subsistence and local sale. Maize for local consumption and national markets is estimated to account for 33 percent of the deforested area.[12] Deforestation is also linked with fuelwood and charcoal consumption. An estimated 197,700 acres (31 percent) were lost for energy use between 1990 and 2000 (ASE-PSO-PNEBE, 1998).

Links between Poverty and Environmental Degradation

To better understand the causes and impacts of deforestation, qualitative analysis was carried out with the community focus groups. The focus groups were in agreement that deforestation was a growing problem. Land for agriculture and livestock was reported to be becoming scarcer, and declining yields were noted for major crops. The most dramatic change reported was a decrease in the availability of water over the last 15 years, including reduced water flows from springs, shorter rainy seasons and increasing droughts. While the water scarcity is problematic for local agriculture, it cannot be clearly linked to deforestation.[13]

Various causes of deforestation were discussed with the focus groups. Most agreed (70 percent) that deforestation has increased because of improved opportunities for selling agricultural goods. Blame for deforestation was largely placed on the shoulders of poor farmers practicing slash-and-burn agriculture. However, in the communities with the highest rates of deforestation, the focus groups were *less* likely to attribute deforestation to the poor. This suggests that deforestation is not only a survival strategy for the poor but also a way of profiting from trade opportunities.

The growth of profitable opportunities has led to migration flows to this region, mostly from the south and the highlands (Fenn et al., 1999). According to several researchers,[14] the arrival of these migrants has affected the resource-use practices of local communities. Migrants may have been more destructive of the forests because they are not bound by local social or customary obligations (Fauroux, 1999).[15] In some cases, in-migration has led to the degradation of social cohesion and the collapse of traditional forest management structures. This collapse provoked a race to claim land through deforestation and exacerbated the typical problems of an open access resource.[16] Migrants, therefore, may contribute to a change in attitude on the part of the population as a whole, and to an increasingly common view of the forest as a consumption good.

However, the role of migration may have been overstated. In the eyes of the focus groups, in-migration was not considered a major cause of deforestation. Only about 5 percent of the local population was estimated to have arrived within the last 15 years, and only one-third of the focus groups linked migration with deforestation. Nevertheless, population growth, which has some links with migration, was considered a driving force of deforestation by 80 percent of the focus groups.

Traditional land-use controls were recognized by the focus groups as contributing to deforestation. Under customary systems of land tenure in the southwest, forests are considered a common resource, and agricultural land becomes the property of those who have cultivated it (World Bank, 2003). Any signs of previous use will deter newcomers. This can lead to inefficient land use and is an important factor forcing migrants to cut forested areas rather than cultivate unoccupied agricultural land. This was confirmed by the focus groups, especially those in the high-deforestation areas. While in most of the communities migrants have to ask for authorization from community authorities to cultivate the land, they can become landowners. This process apparently is easier in the high-deforestation areas.

On the other hand, the role of traditional authorities in managing the forest undoubtedly reduces deforestation. There is a striking difference between management levels in the high- and low-deforestation communities. In the low-deforestation communities, only 8 percent of the focus groups reported that anybody can do as they wish with the forest. In the high-deforestation communities, the figure was over 50 percent. The link between lack of local customary management practices and deforestation in the region is clear.

In short, the evidence of this case study seems to indicate that slash-and-burn agriculture and the increasing opportunities to sell agricultural produce contributed to deforestation in southwest Madagascar. However, trade was not the only reason. Even without the peculiar new trade opportunities afforded by the EU Posei policy and their unintended environmental consequences, deforestation would have occurred, though to a lesser extent. Perhaps one of the most important causes has been not the trading opportunity itself but changing attitudes toward use of the forest and agricultural land.

EXPORT OF VEGETABLES AND RESOURCE MANAGEMENT IN MADAGASCAR'S HIGHLANDS

The mountainous highlands region, located in the middle of the country, is one of Madagascar's most densely populated regions. While some authors argue that this region was completely forested before human arrival, other authors dispute this claim (Klein, 2002). Today, forested areas are limited and scattered. Smallholders cultivate rice in the lowlands and other crops such as maize and cassava on uplands. Access to infrastructure is relatively good; however, modern input use (fertilizer, pesticides, improved seeds) is low, and agricultural yields have shown little improvement in recent decades. Erosion rates are high. The region is also characterized by out-migration to the cities and to less densely populated rural areas.

Trade Event

Madagascar has enjoyed preferential access to EU and US markets under several agreements, including the EU–ACP Lomé Convention and the US African Growth Opportunity Act (AGOA). Under Europe's Everything But Arms (EBA) agreement of 2001, Madagascar, along with 47 other least-developed countries, gained duty-free and quota-free access to the EU for goods including fruits and vegetables. The Malagasy government also took its own steps to increase exports, notably through the establishment of an Export Processing Zone, or EPZ (Zone Franche) in 1989, modeled after the successful experience of Mauritius. Export enterprises in the EPZ enjoy tax holidays, exemptions from import duties and taxes and free movement of foreign exchange.[17] Much of the economic growth in Madagascar in the late 1990s was a result of the growth of exports, reflecting in part the rapid expansion of activity in the new EPZ (Glick et al., 2004). Output from EPZ enterprises increased by about 20 percent annually (1997–2001) as foreign investors took advantage of the country's low labor costs as well as the trade initiatives giving preferential access to developed country markets. Most of these enterprises were textile and apparel manufacturing firms located in Antananarivo and Antsirabe; however, some firms in the EPZ invested in the agricultural sector. This study looks at the impact of Lecofruit, the largest firm involved in the vegetables-for-export business, on the poor and the environment.

Lecofruit, a locally owned company founded to take advantage of the EPZ, produced gherkins in small quantities in the early 1990s. To develop its export markets, it linked up with a French company, Segma Maille, which assured regular outlets for its products in Europe. As a result, Lecofruit began to diversify its production and today produces French beans, snow peas, gherkins, asparagus and mini-vegetables for the European market. Because the products are hand picked, quality is perceived to be superior and fetches a high price in European markets. The firm now directly employs hundreds of permanent and seasonal workers as well as day laborers in processing. Lecofruit buys vegetables from almost 10,000 contract farmers around Antananarivo. Contracted farmers are guaranteed a fixed price for their output and are given seeds and small quantities of fertilizers and pesticides, as well as some technical assistance. In return, they must follow the rigid instructions of the firm. The firm, for its part, signs yearly contracts with its clients in Europe, primarily supermarkets, which cover not only product quality but also employment practices and hygiene standards.

Human Impacts

Contracts with Lecofruit provide participating farmers with important cash income, reduce the seasonality of their income and reduce risk inherent in agricultural production. Although the areas cultivated under contract are relatively small, contract income represents 50 percent of the cash income for the average household. The average contract income (2003–04) was about US$45, of which more than half came from French beans. To put this figure in context, the average agricultural household income at this time, including subsistence production (i.e., non-cash income), was only US$315 (Randrianarison, 2003).

Agricultural production in Madagascar is characterized by high seasonality. During the year's lean period – which in the region of Antananarivo lasts about 4.5 months – consumption levels fall for the poor and the incidence of disease and mortality rises. Contract farmers, however, report a substantially shorter lean period of less than two months. Most contract farmers reported that access to a source of income during the lean period was a major reason for signing a contract. Other reasons mentioned for participating were access to inputs on credit and learning new technologies. Higher overall income was mentioned by very few farmers. In fact, when asked if they would still sign a contract were Lecofruit to lower its prices by half, almost half the contract farmers said they would still participate. This loyalty is best explained by high transaction costs in local marketing, reduction of risk, and spillover effects on land use and habit.

Environmental Impacts

In terms of environmental impacts, the most important contribution of Lecofruit is in improving the sustainability and productivity of agriculture. The company teaches the farmers to prepare and use compost. This compost is a mixture of manure and vegetable matter, which is then combined with chemical fertilizer in the field. Its main benefit is in maintaining the soil structure, especially in promoting retention of moisture, and providing nitrogen and other minerals needed for healthy crop growth.

The benefits of compost are long lasting, often improving soil fertility for several years.

The introduction of composting is important also because of the spill-over effects – it will not only improve the fertility of the soil in plots used for contract agriculture with Lecofruit, but farmers may extend its use to other plots. Most farmers confirmed that, since the introduction of composting by Lecofruit, they are now using compost on all their plots, including those not under contract. Moreover, most stated that they would continue to use compost even if they did not continue working with Lecofruit. While teaching the use of composting may seem a small contribution, it illustrates the possibility of simple but important techno-logical improvements in rural areas where the state has failed to provide good extension services and where most agricultural practices are fairly primitive.

Contracts with Lecofruit seem to have changed the way farmers care for their plots in other ways too, which may have long-lasting impacts on productivity and sustainability. Most state that they have changed the way they cultivate off-season crops, with 90 percent noting that they now use compost and inputs on these plots and 70 percent stating that they also do more weeding. However, very few have changed the way in which they cultivate rice, probably because of the large differences between cultiva-tion methods for rice and off-season crops. Nevertheless, composting for off-season production has improved rice productivity.

Links between Poverty and Environment

Given the central role of rice in the Malagasy economy and diets, the impact of farming improvements on rice is clearly important for poverty impacts. Evidence from the Lecofruit farmers shows that composting and other techniques used for off-season crops have greatly improved rice pro-ductivity. Higher rice productivity has been shown, through modeling as well as empirical analysis of primary data, to have large effects on welfare in Madagascar.[18] Higher rice productivity would especially benefit the poor, since improved productivity would lead to relatively lower food prices and higher real wages for unskilled laborers (Minten and Barrett, 2005).

Households were asked about the constraints to rice productivity. Nutrients were considered the main constraint on lowland plots.[19] Access to labor was considered the second-most-important constraint. Access to cattle manure – again an issue of nutrient replenishment – ranked third. These results are consistent with previous studies in the highlands.[20] This suggested that composting and other inputs related to vegetable

production in the off-season might improve the productivity of rice production in the same plots. In order to compare the performance of contract and noncontract plots, farmers were asked detailed questions about
the productivity of both types of plots.

Clear differences in productivity were found. Rice productivity is 64
percent higher on the contract plots compared to those plots without
a contract; and yields increase from 1.4 to 2.4 tons/acre. Moreover,
while labor productivity stays the same, agricultural output increases
significantly, evidence that there is greater labor absorption on contract
land. This suggests that diffusion of this technology at a larger scale in
Madagascar has potential to decrease incentives to deforest by increasing
employment and boosting productivity on existing agricultural lands. The
higher productivity of rice would also lower food prices, particularly benefiting poor consumers (Minten and Barrett, 2005).

RESPONSES AND INTERVENTIONS

The Malagasy government and stakeholders have tried to address the
problems of increasing rural poverty and environmental degradation
in recent years. The government developed a comprehensive Poverty
Reduction Strategy Paper (PRSP) in 2003 that put forward three priorities:
better governance, social sector development and growth through increasing investments and economic opening. Under this strategy, the government remains committed to trade liberalization, and continuation of the
EPZ has strong support. Madagascar has joined the Common Market
for Eastern and Southern Africa (COMESA) and the Southern African
Development Community (SADC). Trade barriers between members of
these organizations will increasingly be lowered or removed. Moreover,
the long neglect of agriculture may be ending: while the budget allocated
to agriculture had declined for several years, recent agricultural budgets
have been stable.[21] The government is also increasingly relying on infrastructure development, especially roads, to better connect poor farmers to
the economy.

Environmental awareness has greatly improved among policy makers,
in part because of significant investment from donors (notably, the World
Bank and US Agency for International Development). All new investments now require rigorous social and environmental impact studies.
Moreover, the president himself committed the country to more than tri-
pling the forests in protected areas, from 4.2 million acres to 14.8 million
acres. The Mikea spiny forest that was threatened by maize expansion
now has special protected status.

Environmental lobbies have been active. Increasing environmental outreach to rural communities has been paying off throughout the country. In 1990, 69 percent of focus groups at a community level stated that access to forest resources in their community was regulated. This figure increased to 79 percent by 2005. Some of the most dramatic impacts of outreach have been in the southwest. There the percentage of community-level focus groups reporting that access to forest resources was regulated increased from 41 percent to 70 percent over the same period. Other indicators show similar results. For example, in an effort to improve property rights for forest resources, the government started Gelose programs (Gestion local securisée des resources renouvelables) in the late 1990s. Under these programs, user rights and property rights over natural resources are transferred to the villages. Countrywide, 22 percent of communities participate in a Gelose program; in the southwest, 49 percent report participating. The number of community focus groups that report needing formal authorization from the Ministry of Environment to use forest resources has also increased significantly. However, governance problems continue to plague the Ministry.

CONCLUSIONS AND RECOMMENDATIONS

International trade liberalization bypassed the majority of the rural population of Madagascar, and rural poverty has increased steadily even as trade barriers have been lowered. Structural constraints appear to prevent rural areas from profiting from new trade opportunities. However, some communities and areas have been dramatically affected by trade liberalization, as documented by these two case studies.

Neither of these cases is typical of the impact of trade liberalization and agricultural exports from Madagascar. There are only a few firms that produce vegetables for export. Destruction of primary forest for production of agricultural exports using slash-and-burn methods is likewise an exception. The most important agricultural exports from Madagascar remain perennial crops such as vanilla, lychees, coffee and cloves. While it is likely that some of these perennial crops have been planted at the expense of forests, there is no evidence that, in the absence of these opportunities, deforestation would have been less. Without these perennial crops, people might have planted annual crops that would have been more environmentally destructive (Freudenberger and Freudenberger, 2002).

Nevertheless, these two cases allow us to draw some lessons about the potential benefit and harm of international trade for countries such as Madagascar. In the absence of a strong regulatory and institutional environment, of well-defined property rights and of an environmental monitoring and evaluation system, norms are set by the private sector. The private sector may have an incentive to care about its impact on the environment – for example, because of its reputation or sales potential. This is the case for the production of vegetables, given the clear traceability from producer to end product and the quality requirements of the customer. Demand for high-value, high-quality exports promotes investments and long-term commitments to specific rural areas to ensure profits. In the case of maize, however, private firms had little reason to be concerned about the environment, given the difficulty of tracing the end product to environmental damage. Low-quality, low-value products such as animal feed do not seem to foster long-term investments; spot transactions and fast-changing trade behavior is the rule.

In a situation such as occurred in the spiny forest, where incentives for environmentally sound use of resources on the part of the private sector are insufficient, there is a role for public policy to limit environmental damage. Several policy options are discussed here.

Eco-certificates

Implementation of a certification program for agriculture, providing proof of sustainable production methods, could be implemented for international trade. However, to effectively reduce deforestation it would also be needed for national trade, and other interventions would be necessary to deal with forest loss to subsistence agriculture.

Protected Areas

Protected areas have been shown to effectively reduce deforestation in environmentally sensitive areas in Madagascar (World Bank, 2003; Gorenflo et al., 2005). However, this approach to conservation may simply displace deforestation to other sensitive areas. Agricultural and forest products must be taken into consideration for appropriate planning that addresses the needs of conservation and rural stakeholders. Initiatives undertaken by environmental organizations, such as WWF and Sage (Service d'Appuie à la Gestion de l'Environnement), need the participation of all stakeholders, including the private sector.

Malagasy environmental agencies have been struggling financially, and their impact on poverty is unclear. Madagascar is currently experimenting with two alternative financing schemes: an environmental trust fund and a carbon fund. Both funds promise to attract international monies to pay for international environmental public goods in Madagascar. Conservation contracts are another option that might be more beneficial for the local populations in or near protected forest areas. Conservation contracts would allow them to receive more revenues directly, rather than through park management fees or indirect development assistance (Ferraro and Simpson, 2002). A growing body of literature is appearing on implementation of conservation contracts internationally (Pagiola et al., 2002; Gutman, 2003) that makes it clear that the design of such a program presents major challenges, including the development of long-lived institutions and financial support and the identification and allocation of individual or group property. Experiments in Madagascar[22] could add to our knowledge of this approach.

Environmental Monitoring

Environmental monitoring has an important role to play in preventing or halting degradation. In the case of deforestation in the southwest, it seems that irreversible damage occurred before stakeholders were alerted. Despite concern with environmental issues in Madagascar, the first national-level deforestation maps only became available in the early 2000s. This lack of monitoring and data has hampered forest protection.

Environmental Impact Analysis

Some countries, including the EU, now require environmental impact analysis of proposed policy actions. Such an assessment for the EU's Posei policies would probably have predicted increased exports from Madagascar. This analysis might well have failed to foresee the production of maize in fragile ecosystems, but only a thorough analysis of this sort offers the possibility of identifying such unintended consequences.

Property Rights

Property rights to forest resources are not well defined and, in large parts of Madagascar, forests are still treated as open-access resources. Deforestation in the southwest was especially high in those communities where traditional management systems were weak. Efforts toward establishing better property rights could reduce deforestation; toward this end, an evaluation of the impact of transfer-of-management programs such as Gelose that have been developed in Madagascar over the last decade would be useful.

NOTES

1. As of 1989 (Dorosh, 1994).
2. About 2 tons per 2.7 acres, consistent over the last 40 years (Dorosh et al., 2003).
3. Minten and Barrett (2005); de Laulanié (2004); World Bank (2003).
4. Dufils (2003), based on 1998 and 1999 satellite images.
5. Secondary forest is often the fallow stage of slash-and-burn agriculture.
6. Abbreviation for Programs with Specific Options for Remoteness and Insularity.
7. See Meyer and Clément (2000); Fauroux (1999).
8. Posei program funds were used primarily to promote local hog and poultry production: 63 percent of the grants in Ile de la Réunion were used by the poultry and hog sectors, and 86 percent of the subsidies received by these sectors were put toward maize imports. These data are for 1992–97 (Meyer and Clément, 2000).
9. It must be noted that farmers may not always know what happens to products they have sold to local collectors – thus, exports may be underestimated.
10. This estimate is based on total maize exports of 200,000 tons and productivity of 4 tons/2.5 acres. Given a productivity level of 6 tons/2.5 acres, the deforestation linked with international trade would be 82,300 acres, or 13 percent of the total.
11. This estimate is based on an average producer price reported by Fauroux (1999), and productivity of 4 tons/2.5 acres. Assuming a higher productivity level of 6 tons/2.5 acres, earnings would be $30,000 per 247 acres converted.
12. Based on data from Escande (1995), extrapolated to the regional level.
13. See Brand et al. (2002); Calder (1999); and Kaimowitz (2001).
14. See Fauroux (1999, 2001); Razanaka et al. (2001); Georges (2002); Blanc-Pamard and Rebara (2001).
15. Under local customs all over southern Madagascar, forests are generally treated with respect and fear as a place where sacred spirits live; notably, migrants often leave forests untouched in the places they come from (see WWF, 2000; Fenn et al., 1999; Moizo, 1997).
16. See Fenn et al. (1999); Abel-Ratova et al. (2000); and Fauroux (2001).
17. See Cadot and Nasir (2001); Razafindrakoto and Roubaud (2002); Glick et al. (2004).
18. See Goletti and Rich (1998); Dorosh et al. (2003); Minten and Barrett (2005).
19. Seventy-one percent of farmers ranked this "very important" or "important."
20. For example, Freudenberger (1999) found that rice farmers in the province of Fianarantsoa considered access to manure to be a bigger constraint than access to land. Randrianarisoa and Minten (2005) came to similar conclusions in the Vakinankaratra and Fianarantsoa regions.
21. Agricultural project money fell by 60 percent in real terms between 1997 and 2004; own funds of the administration fell by 10 percent over the same period (Loi de Finances).
22. The Durrell Wildlife Conservation Trust is currently experimenting in the Menabe region of Madagascar with direct payments for conservation.

BIBLIOGRAPHY

Abel-Ratova, H., F. Andrianarison, T. Rambeloma and R. Razafindraibe (2000), "Analyse des causes racines socio-économiques de la perte de la bio-diversité dans l'écorégion de forêt tropicale de Madagascar", mimeo, WWF-Madagascar.

Agarwal, D.K., J.A. Silander Jr, A.E. Gelfand, R.E. Dewar and J.G. Mickelson Jr (2004), "Tropical deforestation in Madagascar: analyses using hierarchical, spatially explicit, Bayesian regression models", *Ecological Modeling*, **185**, 105–31.

ASE-PSO-PNEBE (1998), "Evaluation de la consummation de charbon de bois

dans la region de Tuléar", Association de Sauvegarde de l'Environnement–
Project Sud-Ouest–Programme National d'économie de Bois Energie.

Blanc-Pamard, C. and F. Rebara. (2001), "Lécole de la forêt: dynamique pionièreet
construction du territoire", in S. Razanaka, M. Grouzis, P. Milleville, B. Moizo
and C. Aubrey (eds), *Sociétés paysannes, transitions agraires et dynamiques
écologiques dans le Sud-Ouest de Madagascar*, Actes de l'atelier CNRE-IRD,
8–10 November 1999, Antananarivo: CNRE/IRD, pp. 117–38.

Brand, J., B. Minten and C. Randrianarisoa (2002), "Etude de la déforestation sur
la riziculture irriguée", *Cahier d'Etudes et de Recherches en Economie et Sciences
Sociales*, FOFIFA, No. 6, December.

Cadot, O., L. Dutoit and M. Olarreaga (2005), "Subsistence farming, adjustment
costs and agricultural prices: evidence from Madagascar", mimeo, World Bank,
Washington, DC.

Cadot, O. and J. Nasir (2001), "Incentives and obstacles to growth: lessons
from manufacturing case studies in Madagascar", Discussion Paper No. 117,
Regional Program on Enterprise Development, World Bank, Washington, DC.

Calder, I.R. (1999), *The Blue Revolution: Land Use and Integrated Water Resources
Management*, London: Earthscan.

de Laulanié, H. (2004), *Le riz à Madagascar: Un développement en dialogue avec les
paysans*, Antananarivo: Editions Kathala.

Dorosh, P. (1994), *Structural Adjustment, Growth and Poverty in Madagascar: A
CGE Analysis*, Monograph 17, Cornell, NY: Cornell Food and Nutrition Policy
Program.

Dorosh, P. (1996), "Rents and exchange rates: redistribution through trade liberalization in Madagascar", in D. Sahn (ed.), *Economic reform and the poor in
Africa*, Oxford: Clarendon Press, pp. 29–61.

Dorosh, P., S. Haggblade, C. Lungren, T. Razafimanantena and Z. Randriamiarana
(2003), *Moteurs économiques pour la réduction de la pauvreté a Madagascar*,
Antananarivo: INSTAT.

Dufils, J.M. (2003), "Remaining forest cover", in S.M. Goodman and J.P.
Benstead, *The natural history of Madagascar*, Chicago: University of Chicago
Press, pp. 88–96.

Escande, C. (1995), "Etude des réseaux commerciaux et de la formation des prix
des produits agricoles", Thesis, CNEARC Montpellier.

Fauroux, E. (2001), "Dynamiques migratoires, tensions foncières, et deforestation
dans l'ouest malagache", in S. Razanaka, M. Grouzis, P. Milleville, B. Moizo
and C. Aubrey (eds), *Sociétés paysannes, transitions agraires et dynamiques
écologiques dans le Sud-Ouest de Madagascar*, Actes de l'atelier CNRE-IRD,
8–10 November 1999, Antananarivo: CNRE/IRD, pp. 91–106.

Fauroux, S. (1999), "Instabilité des cours du mais et incertitude enmilieu rural: le
cas de la deforestation dans la région de Tuléar (Madagascar)", Mémoire DESS,
Paris X Nanterre, GEREM (IRD/CNRS).

Fenn, M., M. Robinson, D. Whyner and K. Bernard (1999), "Les tendencies
actuelles de la migration des peoples et son impact dans la région écologiques
des forêts épineuses á Madagascar", mimeo, WWF, Washington, DC.

Ferraro, P.J. and R.D. Simpson (2002), "The cost-effectiveness of conservation
payments", *Land Economics*, **78** (3), 339–53.

Freudenberger, K. (1999), "Flight to the forests: a study of community and household resource management in the commune of Ikongo, Madagascar", mimeo,
Landscape Development Interventions (LDI).

Freudenberger, M.S. and K. Freudenberger (2002), "Contradictions in agricultural intensification and improved natural resource management: issues in the Fianarantsoa forest corridor of Madagascar", in C.B. Barrett, F. Place and A.A. Aboud (eds), *Natural Resource Management in African Agriculture: Understanding and Improving Current Practices*, New York: CABI Publishing, pp. 181–92.

Georges, E. (2002), "Analyse des dynamiques économiques impliquées dans la deforestation de la forêt des Mikea á Madagascar", Cahier du C#EDM, No. 1, Antananarivo.

Glick, P., F. Roubaud and J.B. Randrianasolo (2004), "The urban labor market in Madagascar through growth and crisis, 1993–2002", Ilo program, INSTAT/ Cornell University, Antananarivo.

Goletti, F. and F. Rich (1998), "Analysis of policy options for income growth and poverty alleviation", Part 5 in *Structure and Conduct of Major Agricultural Input and Output Markets and Response to Reforms by Rural Households in Madagascar*, Washington, DC/Antananarivo: IFPRI/FOFIFA.

Gorenflo, L.J., C. Corson, K.M. Chomitz, G. Harper, M. Honzák and B. Özler (2005), "Exploring the association between people and deforestation in Madagascar", mimeo.

Gutman, P. (2003), *From Goodwill to Payment for Environmental Services: A Survey of Financing Options for Sustainable Natural Resource Management in Developing Countries*, Washington, DC: WWF-MPO.

Kaimowitz, D. (2001), *Useful Myths and Intractable Truths: The Politics of the Link Between Forests and Water in Central America*, Bogor: CIFOR.

Klein, J. (2002), "Deforestation in the Madagascar highlands – established 'truth' and scientific uncertainty", *Geojournal*, **56**(3), 191–9.

Meyer, P. and T. Clément. (2000), *Evaluation de l'impact des actions réalisées en execution du volet agricole du Poseidom*, Final Report, Auzeville, France: Oréade-Brèche.

Minten, B. and C. Barrett. (2005), "Agricultural technology, productivity, poverty, and food security in Madagascar", mimeo, Cornell University/World Bank.

Minten, B. and P. Méral. (2005), "International trade and environmental degradation: a case study of the spiny forest in Madagascar", WWF-Madagascar.

Minten, B. and M. Zeller (2000), *Beyond Market Liberalization: Welfare, Income Generation and Environmental Sustainability in Rural Madagascar*, Vermont: Ashgate.

Moizo, B. (1997), "Des esprits des tombeaux, du mile et des bouefs: perception et utilization de la forêt en pays Bara Imamono", in *Mileux et sociétés dans le Sud-Ouest de Madagascar*, Collection Iles et Archipels, No. 23, pp. 44–66.

Moser, C., C.B. Barrett and B. Minten (2005), "Missing markets or missed opportunities: spatio-temporal arbitrage of rice in Madagascar", mimeo.

Pagiola, S., J. Bishop and N. Landell-Mills (2002), *Setting Forest Environmental Services: Market-based Mechanisms for Conservation and Development*, London: Earthscan.

Randrianarisoa, C. and B. Minten (2005), "Getting the inputs right for improved agricultural productivity in Madagascar: which inputs matter and are the poor different?", mimeo, World Bank, Washington, DC.

Randrianarison, L. (2003), "Les revenues extra-agricoles", in B. Minten, J.C. Randrianarisoa and L. Randrianarison, *Agriculture, pauvreté rurale et politiques économiques à Madagascar*, Antananarivo: Cornell University/FOFIFA/ INSTAT.

Razafindrakoto, M. and F. Roubaud (2002), "Les entreprises franches à Madagascar: atouts et contraintes d'une insertion réussie", Afrique contemporaine, **202–203**, 147–163.

Razafindravonana, J., D. Stifel and S. Paternostro (2001), *Dynamique de la pauvreté: 1993–1999*, Antananarivo: INSTAT.

Razanaka, S., M. Grouzis, P. Milleville, B. Moizo and C. Aubrey (eds) (2001), *Sociétés paysannes, transitions agraires et dynamiques écologiques dans le Sud-Ouest de Madagascar*, Actes de l'atelier CNRE-IRD, 8–10 November 1999, Antananarivo: CNRE/IRD.

Steininger, M., G. Harper, D. Juhn and F. Hawkins (2003), "Analyse de changement de couverture forestière nationale: 1990 et 2000", Conservation International, Center for Applied Biodiversity Science (CABS), U.S. National Air and Space Administration (NASA).

World Bank (2003), *Madagascar: Review of Agricultural and Environmental Sector*, Washington, DC: World Bank.

WWF (2000), *Une vision de la biodiversité de la region écologique des forêts d'épineuses*, WWF-Madagascar.

6. Trade liberalization, rural poverty and the environment: a case study of sugarcane production in the Incomati River Basin in Mpumalanga, South Africa

Jo Lorentzen, Anton Cartwright and Charles Meth

The Incomati River Basin is a very poor and highly water-stressed area of South Africa. Sugarcane production, primarily for export, is the most important commercial activity, despite the heavy demand that cane production places on water. Liberalization of the South African economy, and particularly of the country's sugar policies, has contributed to the expansion of the sugar industry. This expansion has provided development opportunities for some farmers in the region. However, the sugar industry's demands on water and land have important impacts on the region's environmental resources and on the large poor population that depends on those resources for their livelihood. Recent changes in the European Union (EU) sugar-subsidy regime are expected to affect world sugar production, including production in the Incomati Basin. This study examines the role that sugar is currently playing in the Incomati and how the changes in the EU sugar regime and the global sugar economy may affect the prospects of poor rural people and their environment.

The conflicts and trade-offs examined in this chapter epitomize the conflicts that affect many other parts of southern Africa, and indeed the rest of the world. Global water usage has increased sixfold over the last 100 years and is forecast to double again by 2050 (FAO Aquastat; Falkenmark, 1997). Clearly, in South Africa there is excess demand for water. Resources in three of the country's four catchments – Gariep, Limpopo and Incomati – have been over-allocated. When, in 2003–04, South Africa experienced a drought, harvests and livestock were lost, and water restrictions were imposed in residential areas. In 2005, three provinces resorted to trucking emergency supplies of water to rural areas that usually rely on springs and

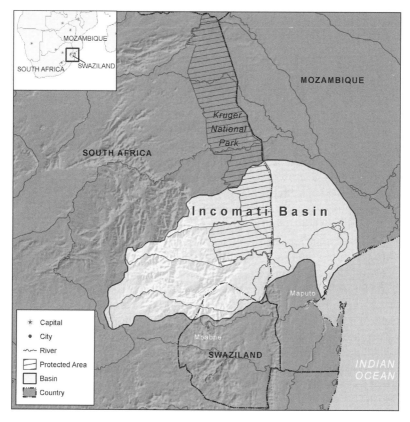

*Figure 6.1   The Incomati Basin, South Africa, Swaziland and
Mozambique*

boreholes. The poor were especially hard-hit. Although the rains returned
in 2006 and reservoirs were refilled, at least 7 million people in the country
still do not have adequate access to water. Today, a new national water
policy offers some hope for more efficient and just allocation of water in
South Africa, with the Incomati Basin as a starting point.

SITE DESCRIPTION

The Incomati Basin straddles three countries – South Africa, Swaziland
and Mozambique – with the largest part flowing through South Africa
(see Figure 6.1). Apart from the Incomati River itself, four other major
rivers contribute to the catchment area: the Nwandedzi, the Crocodile,

the Sabie and its tributary the Sand. They converge into the Incomati in Mozambique. The basin covers over 7.7 million acres in South Africa and Swaziland alone.

Topographically, the Incomati Basin is divided into the western plateau (Highveld) and the eastern coastal plain (Lowveld) by a north–south escarpment. The basin spans three vegetation biomes: Afromontane Forest on the escarpment and North-Eastern Mountain Grassland and Savanna Bushveld in the eastern regions (Low and Rebelo, 1996). The Savanna Bushveld consists of three distinct veld types – Lowveld, Lowveld Sour Bush and Zululand Thornveld (Peel and Stalmans, 1999). This diversity of habitats accounts for the high levels of species diversity and endemicity (Vas and Van der Zaag, 2003). The eastern section of the Lowveld area of Mpumalanga Province, which forms a wedge of land between the 4.9-million-acre Kruger National Park in the north, Mozambique to the east and Swaziland to the south, is the focus of this study. See Figure 6.1.

Mpumalanga is one of South Africa's least developed provinces. According to most studies, household income in the province is below R18,000 (US$257) per year; unemployment is over 33 percent; life expectancy is under 50 years; and inequality is high, with an estimated Gini coefficient of 0.63 (StatsSA, 2001; SoER, 2001; Pauw, et al., 2005). Many poor households are rural subsistence farmers and would have been classified as "black" under South Africa's apartheid policies (Pauw, et al., 2005).

Mpumalanga's economy is based on primary activities. Just under a fifth of formal sector employment is in agriculture and forestry; agriculture contributes about 5 percent of the provincial gross geographical product. More than half of agriculture's share comes from the 160,600 acres under sugar, which employs some 65,000–70,000 people. Citrus, vegetables and forestry are the other main crops. There is also a small limestone quarry.

Forward linkages from the local primary sector are poorly developed. Agro-processing is limited to sugar refining at two mills, fruit packing and small-volume fruit juicing. Although agriculture and agro-processing are likely to remain important, policy makers are increasingly turning to manufacturing and the rapidly expanding tourism sector for future economic growth and employment. Reflecting a trend throughout southern Africa, economic expansion in the Incomati can be expected to bring the region's natural resource limitations into stark focus (Sachs, 2005). Most critical among these is the scarcity of water.

Nowhere are the acute and complex pressures on South Africa's scarce water resources more manifest than in the Incomati.[1] South Africa's Department of Water Affairs and Forestry (DWAF) estimates that the mean annual runoff for the Incomati is 3,022 million m^3. But current water use exceeds available water by 26–29 percent. Consequently, natural stream flows are being depleted; the Incomati is considered the third most water-stressed catchment in South Africa. In 2006, Mozambique lodged an official complaint alleging that South African farmers were extracting so much water illegally from the Incomati River that the flow across the border was reduced to a trickle.

In the context of the water deficit, the absolute volumes of water consumed by sugarcane – a particularly "thirsty" crop – mean that the water resources available for other water users are restricted. In the Incomati Basin itself, sugarcane accounts for more than 80 percent of the irrigated land and an even greater proportion of the water used for irrigation. Existing activities that compete directly with sugarcane for water include mining, manufacturing, steel production (in the Mpumalanga Highveld), fruit and vegetable production, shrimp (in the Incomati Estuary in Mozambique) and ecotourism in the Kruger National Park.

THE POLITICAL TRANSITION AND TRADE LIBERALIZATION

The South African economy was highly protected until the early 1990s. The inefficiency of import substitution in its late stages, combined with the lifting of sanctions against the country and a global trend toward liberalization, motivated a shift toward a more open, competitive economy when the first democratically elected government took office in 1994. South Africa negotiated membership in the World Trade Organization (WTO) and improved its economic relationships with its regional neighbors in the Southern African Customs Union (SACU) and the Southern African Development Community (SADC) as well as with overseas trading partners, notably the EU. However the new government, led by the African National Congress (ANC), inherited a very difficult economic and social situation. The large majority of the population, who for too long had been deprived of the most basic means of achieving productive livelihoods, rightly expected that the new government would provide them with access to jobs, shelter, food, medical services and so on. But rampant fiscal deficits and a burgeoning public debt required macroeconomic austerity, without which, it was clear, the hoped-for international capital flows would never materialize.

The government opted to focus on monetary austerity, international competitiveness and economic efficiency before attempting to redress the infrastructure and services deficit that affects much of the population. One of the immediate steps of the ANC government was to curtail support for agriculture. Gradual reductions in support along with agricultural market liberalization had begun in the late 1980s. But in support of its urban

electorate and in compliance with its WTO obligations, the ANC government withdrew support for commercial agriculture almost completely
after 1994. By 2002, state support for agriculture in South Africa was at an
all-time low.[2] Once fiscal consolidation was achieved in the early 2000s, the
government turned to a more expansive fiscal policy to improve the country's low growth rate. Decision makers began to examine the potential of
public infrastructure investments and industrial policies. In early 2006 the
Accelerated and Shared Growth in South Africa strategy (ASGISA) was
accepted, a strategy that aims to halve poverty by 2015, in part by raising
long-term growth rates to 6 percent.

Important social policy objectives – including land reform, poverty
alleviation through distribution of child support, old-age and disability
benefits and the provision of basic housing and sanitation services – have
had to be pursued within a conservative fiscal framework. The budget constraints, combined with capacity constraints especially evident below the
national level of government, have slowed progress on social investments.

Sugar Industry and Trade

The specific trade changes considered in this study concern sugar. The
international event with the largest expected impact on people and ecosystems in the Incomati River Basin is the ongoing liberalization of the
EU sugar regime. But in the past decade sugar trade between South Africa
and its neighbors in southern Africa has already been subject to a slow
liberalization process, and the South African government has gradually
deregulated the domestic sugar industry. These reforms have had important consequences for South African sugar producers. They also illustrate
supply responses, thus helping us to predict the impact of the recent EU
regime change, whose full effects have yet to materialize.

The global production and trade of sugar are highly regulated and
distorted by trade barriers and national subsidies, with the result that the
world price is always lower than domestic (protected) prices.[3] Almost a
third of world production is traded, but under present conditions most
producers prefer to sell domestically. Although the protection afforded
sugar has been under fire both in the global arena and in national contexts,
farmers and industry worldwide continue to produce sugar because sugarcane is a profitable and relatively secure crop.

Sugarcane in Incomati

Sugarcane is grown in three provinces in South Africa – KwaZulu-Natal,
Eastern Cape and Mpumalanga – on a total of about 1.1 million acres,

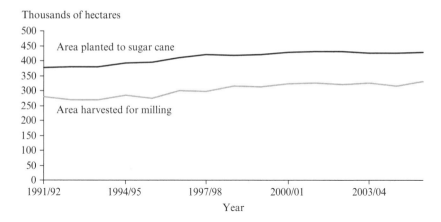

Source: South African Sugar Association (SASA).

Figure 6.2   Area under sugar

and generates about 2.5 million tons of sugar per year (see Figure 6.2). The per-acre sucrose yield of the Incomati area is reportedly the highest in South Africa and higher than in many competitor locations elsewhere. Historically, about half of production has been exported. The industry employs about 350,000 people. In addition, there are about 50,000 cane growers, mostly small-scale farmers, who produce about 22 million tons of cane per year. About 80 percent of sugarcane is grown by the 1,700 large-scale producers, another 10 percent by the mills themselves and 11 percent by small-scale farmers. The industry operates a total of 14 mills, including two in Mpumalanga. These two, Malelane and Komati, both operated by Tsb Sugar RSA Ltd,[4] together produce 3.7 million tons of sugar. Tsb Sugar employs about 2,400 people in Incomati and provides support services to about 100 commercial and 1,400 small-scale farmers operating on 66,700 acres (27,000 ha) and 24,700 acres (10,000 ha), respectively.

In South Africa, the sugar industry has traditionally been highly organized. Growers and millers cooperated so as to achieve a measure of stability in a market that was subject to high price volatility and distortions introduced by export subsidies, especially those paid to European producers. Until 2000, the sugar sector was largely insulated from the sweeping deregulation and curtailment of state support that characterized the post-1994 period. Under the supervision of the Department of Trade and Industry (DTI), rather than the Department of Agriculture, the South African Sugar Association (SASA) was entitled to determine the maximum domestic industrial price and the quantities of sugar released onto the domestic and export markets. SASA divided the proceeds among growers and millers according to a set formula. However, the 2000 Sugar Industry Agreement (SIA) changed this cozy state of affairs. The SIA has substantially increased the role of the market in sugar production and sales, albeit gradually. It replaced fixed domestic and export quotas with flexible market shares, factored transport costs into the price of sugar, allowed millers to deviate from the previously fixed floor price, gave more efficient and better quality growers higher prices for their cane and virtually abolished SASA's monopoly.

In addition to the growing role of market-based prices, South African producers have increasingly had to contend with regional competitors, most notably Swaziland and Zimbabwe, within SACU and SADC, which is gradually implementing a free trade agreement. South Africa is relatively cost competitive globally, but lower labor costs in other SADC countries, such as Zambia and Mozambique, have increased regional competition. Although South Africa remains the largest producer in the region, the country's share of the sugar market in SACU[5] fell from 95 percent in the early 1990s to 78 percent at the end of the 1990s. The 2000 SADC Trade Protocol includes an annex that regulates regional sugar trade. The agreement permits surplus-producing countries to sell tariff free within SACU but under a quota system, thereby forcing millers to sell increasingly (and unprofitably) to the world market. In view of the objective of essentially free trade in sugar in SADC after 2012, increasing access of non-SACU SADC members to the SACU market is likely to further erode South Africa's market share.

Two other factors must be considered, however. First, South African millers control a very substantial share of the production in other regional countries. For example, Illovo, which accounts for almost half the South African market, controls between roughly 25 percent and 100 percent of the milling in the five other countries in which it has operations. Therefore, it clearly makes sense for the millers to restrict domestic output and export surpluses, thus keeping domestic prices throughout SADC as high as possible. Second, most SADC members belong to the African, Caribbean and Pacific (ACP) group or are classified as Least Developed Countries (LDCs) and thus benefit from certain concessionary terms in international trade. Over the next few years they will be granted phased-in tariff-free access to the EU market (see below). As a result, SADC sugar producers from Zambia, Mozambique, Swaziland and perhaps Zimbabwe are likely to replace the less competitive Caribbean producers in their exports to the EU. This will tend to limit the effect of SADC liberalization on South African producers by reducing the amount of sugar in the SADC market.

EU Sugar Regime Liberalization

For decades the EU managed to reconcile top export status in refined sugar with a production cost structure that was two or three times above the world price. This was possible thanks to a complex system of quotas, import controls, price supports and export subsidies introduced in 1968 as part of the Common Agricultural Policy (CAP). Although the CAP has been the subject of reform since 1992, the sugar regime was left largely untouched. Nor was reform of the sugar regime on the table at the WTO Uruguay Round.

In addition to its substantial export role, the EU is also the world's second largest importer of raw sugar. Imports are governed by two preferential agreements with former European colonies in the ACP group, of which South Africa is not a member.[6] Under the 1975 Lomé Convention, ACP countries are guaranteed a collective duty-free import quota of 1.3 million tons of white sugar equivalents known as "preference sugar." An additional import quota of 200,000–350,000 tons was allocated in 1995, at a slightly lower price. In 2001, the EU made unilateral trade concessions to the LDCs under its Everything But Arms (EBA) initiative that include a gradually increasing sugar quota with a high tariff on imports above the quota.[7] The effects of this change essentially favor more efficient African producers to the detriment of the Caribbean producers since less efficient producers will not be able to produce at the new EU price or the lower world price.

The EU sugar regime has depressed world prices and discriminated against more efficient producers. These producers brought the EU before the WTO in 2002. The WTO decision, reached in 2005, finally forced the EU to reform its sugar regime. The reform entails a 36 percent reduction in the EU guaranteed price, phased in from 2006–07 over four years, followed by the dismantling of the intervention price system.[8] The reduction of the EU intervention price is expected to lead to production cuts of 6 million to 7 million tons, which will increase the world price of sugar.

To summarize, the reform of the EU sugar regime and the gradually increasing access under the EBA program will affect the world price of sugar in at least four ways:

- Subsidized sugar will be removed from the world market. European sugar exports are expected to decrease from 3.1 million tons to 0.4 million tons by 2012–13 (CEC, 2005).
- Many ACP countries will not be able to produce at the new EU price, let alone the lower world price. More efficient ACP producers will replace them with exports to the EU, thus withdrawing some supplies from the world market. By the same token, Swaziland may divert some exports from South Africa to the EU.

- Sugar from the EBA-eligible countries will replace up to a third of the sugar previously produced in the EU by 2012–13, again withdrawing supplies from the world market (CEC, 2005). Those producers that stay in the market will increase production.
- The world price of sugar will increase by as much as 11 percent.[9]

South African Response

In South Africa, the reform will affect production in two ways. One is the increase in the world price; the other, the likely withdrawal of Swazi sugar from the South African market. Domestic regulation to date has not fundamentally altered the incentive structure of the South African sugar industry. Nor is the impending trade liberalization likely to change that structure, either. We therefore estimate South Africa's supply response to changes in the world price based on historical data.

The model used in this study (Lorentzen et al., 2007) explains the production of raw cane as a function of the world price, the producer price in South Africa and previous sugar production in South Africa. The model estimates that every 1 percent increase in the world price of sugar will lead to a 0.49 percent increase in South African sugar production. It also estimates that a 1 percent increase in the producer price will lead to a 1.04 percent decrease in production. This counterintuitive result reflects the dynamics of the local sugar market in which it makes sense for millers to limit supplies in order to increase the domestic sugar price. Finally, production is trended in the decade under observation (1994–2000): a 1 percent increase in production is associated with a 0.28 percent increase the following year. This may be because of a variety of reasons, including weather patterns, availability of land and inefficiencies or information failures within the sugar supply chain. With a point estimate of 0.49 for the coefficient on world price, there is a 95 percent confidence level that a 1 percent increase in the world price will increase production between 0.22 percent and 0.77 percent. Thus, if the world price increases by 11 percent as a result of liberalization of the EU trade regime, production of raw sugarcane in South Africa will expand by 5.4 percent. Using the confidence interval, the EU reform will lead to an increase in production of between 2.42 percent and 8.5 percent.[10]

HUMAN WELL-BEING CHANGES

The Incomati Basin is home to some of the poorest people in the country, women and children especially. Official unemployment in the Nkomazi

Municipality – one of the poorest in the catchment – is over 40 percent, and up to 70 percent of households earn less than the national poverty rate (R800/month, equivalent to about US$114/month). Forty-four percent of people over 20 have no formal schooling. Almost two-thirds of households do not have piped water, and more than half do not have adequate sanitation facilities. A considerable share of households get their water from unsafe sources. Life expectancy at birth dropped from 62 years in 1980 to approximately 50 years in 2001, chiefly because of HIV/AIDS, the impact of which is compounded by the prevalence of tuberculosis, malaria, cholera and typhoid.

Poverty in the Incomati Basin is in part a legacy of the colonial and apartheid administrations that took valuable land from the African population. Black South Africans were moved into the so-called "homelands" where neither the quality nor the quantity of land was sufficient for sustainable livelihoods and where basic infrastructure in health and education was severely deficient. Incomati belonged to the KaNgwane Homeland, which shared these features of deprivation, many of which persist today.

Post-apartheid attempts to redress this situation are a mixed bag. On the one hand, agricultural development based on land reform has seen a considerable number of black small-scale farmers emerging, most of whom are cane growers. On the other hand, it has been primarily privileged people who have managed to gain access to land earmarked for cultivation, so that inequalities have been reinforced. The very poor have not benefited from land redistribution. To the contrary, households that were disenfranchised in the past are often not much (or not at all) better off now.

The opportunities presented by the sugar industry were crucial in helping black farmers to establish themselves on smallholdings and in guaranteeing an outlet for their crop. The establishment of smallholder contract sugarcane farmers began in the early 1980s (and predates the land reform initiative). Expansion accelerated under democracy, so there are now more than 1,400 smallholder farmers on some 21,500 acres. This represents more than a quarter of land under sugar in the Incomati, and these growers contribute 20 percent of the cane supplied to Tsb (this compares with 10 percent supplied by small farmers nationally). In the context of disappointingly slow land reform, the small cane out-grower schemes have been heralded as a rare success story.

The sugar milling industry played a critical role in creating the conditions under which subsistence land could be elevated to commercial use. Tsb built its mill in Komati with the express intention of sourcing cane supply from smallholder growers, for whom it provided extension services. A government initiative, the Nkomazi Irrigation Expansion Program (NIEP), provided the necessary infrastructure. For many small-scale growers, sugarcane is the single most – and perhaps only – successful developmental crop in the entire area. These farmers attribute their improved housing, residential supply of electricity, vehicles, education, upward mobility of their children and new business opportunities to the sugar industry. The relative success of these smallholder sugar farmers has secured the industry political goodwill but has also led to increasingly vocal complaints by emerging farmers about the shortage of land and water.

Organizations representing the interests of the smallholder farmers in KaNgwane evolved into organizations with a similar remit operating in the new province of Mpumalanga. Institutional continuity was thus guaranteed; both government land-reform programs and traditional institutions of land governance reinforced relations among the elite rather than distributing land to the very poor. As a result, only some of the conflict over land and water in South Africa is between large-scale, capital-intensive white farmers and their poorer smaller-scale black counterparts; conflict also arises between landed black farmers and their poorer black neighbors. The sugar industry has also seen people moved off the land by traditional authorities who retain control over communal lands. This means that further expansion of the sugar industry is likely to have different effects across households.

The employment generated by large- and small-scale farms has positive and negative aspects. Minimum wage and other labor legislation aimed at bringing South Africa's rural economies in line with international norms has reduced the number of people employed on large-scale commercial farms. The same labor legislation has seen a number of growers switch from more labor-intensive horticultural crops such as citrus into sugar, which has less than a quarter of the per-acre labor requirement. The 1,400 or so people working, mostly informally, on smallholder sugar farms do not enjoy the same legal protection; some are reportedly making one-fifth of the statutory minimum wage.

Poverty Measures

Unfortunately, reliable data at the scale necessary to examine changes in poverty in the Incomati Basin are not available.[11] We summarize here what can be said with some certainty regarding rural poverty in the region. One study (Leibbrandt et al., 2004) estimating national-level changes in poverty between 1996 and 2001 found that poverty rose over the period. Looking specifically at Mpumalanga Province, the study concludes that both poverty headcounts and poverty gaps have risen. Another paper (Hoogeveen and Özler, 2004) suggests that Mpumalanga was one of the few provinces where the poverty headcount fell, though by very little, and that the poverty gap did not change.[12] A more recent study (Van der Berg et al., 2005) produced a set of poverty estimates showing that poverty at the national level rose from 16.2 million in 1993 to 18.5 million in 2000, and then fell to 15.4 million by 2004. These findings have been quite controversial. With merit, the government has challenged findings of increasing poverty and inequality on the grounds that such claims ignore massive government expenditures on free or subsidized goods and services: electricity, water, transport, housing, education, school feeding schemes, sanitation and health care.

A look at the data from the 2001 population census for three Mpumalanga municipalities – Nkomazi, Albert Luthuli and Thembisile – provides a revealing picture of the nature of poverty in Mpumalanga.[13] Together, these municipalities contain 27 percent of the black African population of the province. Illiteracy among the over-20 population approaches 40 percent; unemployment is close to 50 percent; and two-thirds of the population live in households with reported income under R800 per month (US$114). About half the population has piped water. However, attempting to assess the extent to which incomes and distribution of incomes have changed in the years since 2001 is a monumentally difficult task. There are few statistical resources, and all are problematic. Establishing a poverty line as the basis for measuring change is in itself a complicated matter (Lorentzen et al., 2007). See Table 6.1.

Access to Resources

As of 1997, of the total population of 1.1 million covered by the Rural Survey, about half were over age 18 and some 130,300 considered themselves to be farmers. Of the roughly 200,000 households in the former "homeland" areas of Mpumalanga in 1997, about 95,300 had access to land for farming. The bulk of these households were in what is referred to as "true" rural areas rather than denser settlements. Even so, a high proportion of the households in denser settlements had access to land (13,700 out of 16,170). These, however, were probably very small plots. Eighty percent of the land was allocated by local or tribal authorities, with the proportion allocated by these authorities rising as income levels rose. Almost all households below the income level of R1,500 (US$188) per month farmed for subsistence. Commercial farmers are rare. The survey also asked farmers what type of assistance they most needed: among the poorest households, access to land ranked highest; moving up the income scale, access to water became more important; above the level of R1,500 per month, access to land became the main concern again.

Table 6.2 gives an idea of the limited access to water. Only 27,400 of households had a water source on the farm, primarily from piped

Vulnerable places, vulnerable people

Table 6.1   Vital statistics in three Mpumalanga municipalities

		M324	M301	M315
Black Africans				
Number in Mpumalanga (thousands)	2,886			
As proportion of total provincial population	98.9			
In three municipalities		M324	M301	M315
Number of individuals (thousands)	781	334	188	259
Mean household size	4.62	4.66	4.74	4.45
All race groups				
Proportion of households with income <R800/month	66.3	69.2	70.0	60.1
Illiteracy rates of over 20s	39.0	44.3	36.9	33.9
Official unemployment rate	47.0	41.5	52.2	51.2
Proportion of households with piped water	51.2	37.1	46.6	71.7
Proportion of households without adequate sanitation	68.7	59.8	61.4	84.5

Note: Own calculations from data in Stats SA report.

Source: Statistics South Africa Report No. 03-02-21 (2001), 211, 223, and 231.

water. About half of the farms with on-farm water sources experienced a drying up of the source "sometimes" (45 percent) or "often" (5 percent). Households with incomes below R3,000 (US$429) per month were most prone to running out of water. Eighty percent of households with incomes above R3,000 never experienced drying up. A little more than one-third of the households with on-farm water supplies (11,000 out of 27,400) had irrigation systems. The remaining 60,000 households either relied on rain for watering crops (48,000) or fetched water from a source outside the farm (11,400). Broadly speaking, the picture that emerged from this brief analysis above is one of a poor subsistence-farming community, most without reliable water sources, all needing more land.

ENVIRONMENT AND ECOSYSTEM CHANGES

As in other regions of South Africa, population growth accompanied by urbanization has led to an intensification of agriculture, industrialization,

Table 6.2 *Conditions of poverty and resource access in Mpumalanga, 1997*

	R1–200	R201–400	R401–800	R801–1500	R1501–3000	R3001–6000	Total
No. of households with access to farm land	8,000	15,000	34,000	28,800	7,100	2,000	95,300
In "rural" areas	5,100	10,100	30,900	26,900	6,600	2,000	81,600
In "denser" settlements	2,900	4,900	3,100	1,900	500	0	13,700
Water source on farm (Column %)							
River, dam, borehole, rainwater tank, well or fountain	24	0	18	21	22	0	16
Irrigation canal/channel running through farm	30	10	0	8	15	21	9
Piped water to farm & other sources	46	90	82	71	64	79	76
Total (Number)	1,700	5,100	7,600	8,900	3,200	1,200	27,400

Note: Because of rounding, not all totals sum to 100%.

energy and transportation that has altered the natural landscape irrevo-
cably. Even the substantial areas protected as national parks have had
their ecosystems disrupted by upstream cultivation, overgrazing and the
changing climate. Mpumalanga's natural vegetation has been irreparably
damaged, mostly by agriculture. The reduction of terrestrial habitat diversity has gone hand in hand with biodiversity loss. Soil erosion is severe
(Hoffman et al., 1999; MDG, 1997; Peel and Stalmans, 1999). The major
culprit of land degradation is overgrazing, but sugarcane cultivation contributes to the loss of soil fertility through salinization, acidification and
waterlogging. Sugarcane cultivation also contributes to the endangerment
of the region's cycads and the destruction of invertebrate communities that
are crucial to the circulation of nutrients and the maintenance of soil structure (Kotze et al., 1994; Schulz, 2001). The environment of the Incomati
Basin in particular appears to be under great stress, and many species are
threatened. Because all the main rivers are dammed – the Lower Incomati
alone has over 70 weirs and in-stream structures – the hydrological system
has been greatly altered. The Crocodile now periodically stops flowing.
Stagnant in-stream pools cause massive disruption to the local flora and
fauna populations, severely compromising aquatic communities.

Water Use

The sugar industry generates demand for water in the Incomati Basin
for irrigation and as an input to cane milling and processing. Sugarcane
is clearly a water-intensive crop, although the amount of water required
varies even within the relatively narrow geographic and climatic ranges of
the Incomati. The current effect of sugar cultivation and milling on water
demand is used here as the basis for discussing the likely environmental
impact of projected increases in sugar production.

The combination of shallow soils, highly variable long-term average
rainfall and high evapotranspiration makes irrigation necessary in the
Incomati. For the purposes of this study, we drew on the work of evapotranspiration modelers (Penman, 1948; Linacre, 1991; Schulze et al.,
2000) and the irrigation schedules of cane growers, for which substantial data are available, to determine the likely increase in water use. It is
assumed that future expansions of the area under sugarcane will deploy
efficient technology and best management practice and, accordingly, will
raise the sector's average water-use efficiency. It is further assumed that
any contraction of the sector will eliminate the water-profligate growers
and similarly raise the average water efficiency of growers. Based on the
data and assumptions above,[14] a requirement of 5,000 m^3/acre/year of
water to grow sugarcane is assumed, which implies a water requirement of

7,140 m³/acre/year.[15] It is further assumed that future cane cultivations in the Incomati will attain production levels of 36 tons/acre on average and 12 percent recoverable value (RV), with an irrigation requirement of 1,653 m³/ton of RV. Should best practice irrigation and cultivation strategies not be applied, this figure could be as high as 4,609 m³/ton of RV (27,139 m³/ ton of raw cane).

The two Tsb mills in the Incomati require water for boilers used to concentrate the sugar and for cleaning equipment. Together the two mills require over 40 million m³ of water annually to operate, but much of this water is reusable or is returned to the hydrological system. Once all recycling is considered, existing net use is estimated at 6.3 million m³ per year. Based on current use, it is assumed that a ton of cane produced in the future will require 0.75 m³ of water to process; production of a ton of RV will require 6 m³ of processing water. In sum, to grow and process an additional acre of sugarcane will require 714 m³ of water per year. The production of an additional ton of sucrose (RV) will require 1,660 m³ of water. Notably, the sugarcane crushed by the Incomati mills in 2003–04 consumed more water than was reported available for all irrigation in the region and just under one-quarter of the water management area's mean annual runoff (NWRS, 2004).

Environmental Impacts

The Incomati's watercourse ecology is already severely compromised. Abstraction, in-stream dams and siltation have compounded the impact of fertilizer runoff, organic microbes and thermal pollution, resulting in toxicity, eutrophication and encroachment of alien plants into rivers and riparian zones, and have perturbed – and generally reduced – invertebrate and fish populations (SoER, 2001). Fifty-four percent of the threatened bird species, 30 percent of terrestrial mammals and 40 percent of reptiles in the Incomati Basin are wholly or partly dependent on water or riverine habitat (DWAF, 2000). The direct hydrological impacts inflicted by the sugar industry are a threat to these species. Resulting biodiversity losses affect a range of ecosystem services – food, fiber, traditional medicines and tourism – and ecological stability of the region more generally.

Fifty-three million m³ of irrigation water per annum is returned to the rivers of the Incomati in the form of runoff from cultivated land (NWRS, 2004). Sediments suspended in this water bond easily with nitrate and phosphate ions from inorganic fertilizers, creating dangers of unsafe drinking water and eutrophication. The National Water Act (NWA) requires that dam management includes flood-simulating releases aimed at flushing downstream rivers and supporting aquatic and riparian biota.

But even the best regimes affect in-stream flow and alter the sediment and nutrient concentrations that determine the structure of aquatic biota populations. By South African standards, the Incomati is not viewed as a particular water quality risk (Pegram, personal communication, 2005),[16] but this is partly a reflection of the severity of the problem in other catchments. Also, there is a lack of data on non-life-threatening impacts of poor water quality on human health. Clearly, however, the 750,000 people in the region who do not have access to safe water suffer higher rates of disease and higher child mortality rates.

Where sugarcane replaces grassland, the speed of runoff is greatly increased, particularly while the stands are less than 12 inches tall. Accelerated runoff speeds soil erosion and increases peak river flows that contribute to dangerous flooding. Siltation and contamination have also been implicated in the destruction of important aquatic habitats (DWAF, 2000) and the disruption of the Incomati estuarine habitats, with impacts on the shrimp and shellfish populations that support an estimated 3,000 artisan and semi-industrial fishermen (Vas and Van der Zaag, 2003; Monteiro and Mathews, 2003). Moreover, contrary to legislation,[17] sugar cultivation has contributed to alteration of wetlands and riparian habitats. The practice of burning cane prior to harvesting further destroys soil structure and microbes.

High-temperature and sucrose releases, associated with sugar processing, are illegal in South Africa and generally well controlled. However, measurements taken at Malelane show the mill's outlet into the Crocodile River to be 10 °C higher than the ambient water temperature. As a result, algae, tilapia fish – which apparently adjust better to higher temperatures than other species – and crocodiles that feed on them, flourish (Leslie, personal communication, 2005).[18] The danger is that algal blooms may lead to eutrophication. Toxic blue-green algal blooms associated with eutrophication have long been implicated in stock poisonings throughout the Incomati (Steyn, 1945; Falconer and Humpage, 2005). In addition to water for processing, mills are typically flushed once or twice a season. The release of detergents is a problem but causes far less damage than the flushing of large quantities of plant matter into natural watercourses. Decomposing plant material leads to eutrophication of habitats and massive biodiversity loss.

Changes in international trade are likely to exacerbate the existing stress suffered by terrestrial and aquatic ecosystems in the Incomati. With a supply response of between 2 percent and 9 percent to a world sugar price increase of 11 percent, the Incomati mills would produce an additional 84,000–378,000 tons of sugar (RV of 10,080 to 45,360 tons). This would increase water demand by between 16.7 million m^3 and 75 million m^3, depending on efficiency, adding to the 850 million m³ the sector currently consumes. The environmental impacts are, on the whole, unambiguously negative. The issue, then, is whether the benefits of the sugar industry – in its current or expanded capacity – outweigh the environmental costs it entails.

POVERTY AND ENVIRONMENT LINKAGES

The general picture emerging from the Incomati sugar sector is one in which the rural elite, with access to patronage networks, land, water and supply contracts, enjoy the benefits. Growth in the sugar industry, sparked by the EU regime change, is first and foremost likely to benefit these stakeholders. The same growth is likely to generate negative externalities: less land available for the poor, increased water consumption and associated deterioration in the ecosystem services that will disproportionately affect the landless and the poor who are more directly dependent on these services for their livelihoods.

Sugar production consumes more water and delivers fewer jobs and GDP than many of the alternative economic activities in Incomati. Yet, sugar production in the Incomati has expanded by about 42,000 acres since 1996. (Notably, an estimated 60 percent of this expansion is unlicensed and effectively illegal.) These new cultivations have had to rely on the water that was intended for the ecological reserve and Mozambique. To understand why farmers continue to opt to grow sugar rather than taking up more lucrative alternatives, it is important to understand local drivers of land-use decisions. The recent expansion of sugarcane has been driven by the characteristics of sugarcane, the established market and the sunk costs of millers. Sugarcane is attractive because of the resilience of sugar in the face of water insecurity, the low capital requirements (as compared to citrus, for example), the relative ease of marketing, recent price increases, the potential profits accruing to millers who can maintain high levels of throughput and, most fundamentally, the fact that sugar growers do not pay the economic value of the water required to produce cane. Ironically, the variability in rainfall and the relatively low assurance of water supply contributes to growers' preference for sugarcane over other crops. Cane is reasonably drought resistant and tends to recover quickly from short dry spells. Where water supplies are anticipated to become increasingly insecure, sugar represents both an agronomically robust and financially lower-risk investment than many of the alternatives.

So-called "high-value" crops that require less water – such as citrus, mangoes, bananas, nuts and vegetables – are less suitable, particularly for emerging farmers, because they require higher initial investments and a longer maturation time. Because they are more perishable, they are more difficult to market. Moreover, unlike sugar, these crops do not benefit from national pricing support or centralized processing facilities, rendering them subject to a wide range of market fluctuations. Thus, the preference for less profitable, less water-efficient sugar is easily explained. What the recent expansion does not account for, however, are the external costs imposed on non-sugar farmers via ecological impacts.

Although little is known about ecological thresholds and reversibility of environmental damage in Incomati, the ongoing breach of the ecological reserve almost certainly comes at an irreparable cost to the environment. Because the environmental and social costs imposed by sugarcane cultivation are external to the market and to farm- and industry-level decisions driving land and water use, those costs have not been well understood. Nor are these costs factored into decisions about regional growth strategies by officials who are under pressure to deliver immediate results. In this context, little consideration is afforded to the perverse and adverse impacts of seemingly profitable agricultural activities, especially when those profits accrue to emerging black farmers and the environmental impacts are incurred over extensive spatial and temporal scales.

RESPONSES AND INTERVENTIONS

In South Africa, rural livelihoods are under extreme pressure. Commercial agriculture has been shedding employment, and small-scale agriculture, rural small and medium-sized enterprises and direct government development interventions are not picking up the slack. Throughout the country, rural livelihoods are largely survivalist. It is in this context that the Mpumalanga sugar sector, with its many positive income and employment effects, is attractive in spite of the associated problems. The interventions reviewed here are not responses to the EU trade liberalization per se. They respond to two challenges – economic development and water regulation – that will be affected by the trade event but are also important in their own right.

Water Policy

South Africa's political reform and economic transition was underpinned by a process of natural-resource reform intended to redress the highly skewed control of those resources and to comply with international concepts of integrated and sustainable management. New environmental and water management legislation was passed and a program of land redistribution and restitution was initiated. The land-reform program was highly contested but other new legislation was subject to far less scrutiny, allowing for a somewhat opportunistic adoption of international best practice. Notably, the National Water Act (NWA), approved in 1998, drew heavily on the principles agreed at the 1992 International Conference on Water and Environment.

Water policy under apartheid was driven by the need to supply water reliably to mining, industry, agriculture and white residential users. Water access was considered the entitlement of the economically active. In rural areas, abstraction and groundwater rights were linked to land ownership. Water scarcity was addressed through supply-side remedies, particularly dam construction and inter-basin transfers. Significant government investments in water storage and delivery infrastructure were the norm. Quite apart from its inherent injustice, the system promoted financially irrational investments, profligate water use and ecological disruption.

The new NWA seeks to promote more equitable and efficient use of South Africa's limited water resources. It is guided by the basic tenets of Integrated Water Resource Management.[19] Private ownership of water, based on land title and riparian rights, was ended in favor of public ownership. Water is made available within a predefined hierarchy of rights and licenses, at the top of which is the constitutional right of all South Africans to 25 liters per day – referred to as the "human reserve." Equal in status to the human reserve is the "environmental reserve," which requires a critical minimum volume of water to remain in each catchment. The environmental reserve requirement is an acknowledgment that functional ecosystems (as measured by hydrological flows, habitat, water quality and biota) constitute a prerequisite for water availability. Provided these reserves have been satisfied, the next priorities are honoring international treaties and meeting the needs of power stations.

Water-resource planning and development are the responsibility of the DWAF, which is designated as the custodian of this "indivisible national asset." The DWAF must commission catchment management agencies (CMAs) to undertake executive functions at the local level. The DWAF has established 19 CMAs responsible for drafting and implementation of a management strategy in each of the water management areas (WMAs). The Incomati CMA, established March 2004, was the first to be registered. The process of staffing and capacitating this first CMA has been slow and difficult. Because the CMA is expected to pursue a process of consensual decision making, representation on its 14-member committee is highly contested (Pegram and Bofilatos, 2005). Commercial agriculture feels it is under-represented, a situation that may undermine support for the water-pricing mechanisms posited by the CMA (Anderson, 2004).

The biggest challenge in implementing the NWA lies at the local level, where access to water rights by new users must be reconciled with existing patterns of water use. At the same time we redress the use of water across various racial and socioeconomic groups, there is a need, and a mandate in the NWA, to ensure that water is allocated in a manner that supports economic growth. The apartheid policy of free water to agriculture has left a legacy of economically irrational water allocations. Most notably, agriculture, which has demonstrated limited ability to generate revenue or create employment in the past ten years, continues to consume disproportionate volumes of water at the expense of the service sector, manufacturing and mining.

In general, the National Water Resource Strategy (NWRS) does not allocate water for specific activities. Rather, water is allocated for use in an economic sector, such as agriculture, and users within the sector are free to select the crop or activity of their preference. The DWAF has limited capacity to intervene here. Where the DWAF has more reach is in the allocation of water across sectors. It is, in fact, a legislative requirement that the DWAF encourages the reallocation of water from the relatively low yielding agricultural sector to sectors with a greater propensity for employment and revenue generation.

However, there are structural barriers to effecting such changes. The authorization of water use – apart from the human and environmental reserves, international obligations and other limited exceptions – is demand driven. The DWAF relies chiefly on applications from legitimate, generally existing, water users; the problem with this approach is that it entrenches the status quo. Clearly, economically active water users are best placed to launch applications for reissue of water licenses, and expansion of non-agricultural activities is constrained by the historic lack of water resources for these activities. Discrepancies with regard to market access, credit, prices and extension easily translate into influences – some of them perverse – on water-allocation patterns. Notably, the prioritization of allocations to sugarcane plantations has been contentious: although agricultural water use is intended to enjoy a relatively low assurance of supply under the NWA, sugarcane growers in the Incomati have benefited from cheap, secure and, at times, poorly monitored access to water even in times of drought. Certainly, any reform of the sectors making up the Incomati economy, and allocation of water to promote this reform, would have to be a long-term process complete with a full suite of reforms to markets, development support and mind-sets.

The DWAF's response to the Incomati water crisis, in addition to the early establishment of the CMA, has been to schedule the catchment for "compulsory licensing." This approach is reserved for areas where "demands for water are approaching or exceed available supply, where water quality problems are imminent or already exist, or where water quality is under threat or where it is necessary to review prevailing water use to achieve greater equity of access to water" (NWA, Part 8). Incomati will be the first WMA to undergo compulsory licensing, and this process, which is at the heart of the water-allocation reform effort, is expected to test the enforceability of the NWA, the institutional merits of CMAs and the financial sustainability of water-allocation reform. That fact that Incomati sugar is irrigated, and therefore needs to be authorized, provides the entry for legislative intervention in the amount of sugar produced.

Government Institutions

In almost all instances, the institutional framework by which to achieve the necessary interventions is in place. South Africa has appropriate water, land and environmental policies, increasingly high priority is placed on local economic development and, while macroeconomic policy has been conservative, there is an articulation of the intent to redress poverty. The key weakness is in the institutions and capacity to coordinate and implement policy. The three-tiered structure of South Africa's government – national, provincial and local – is top-heavy in the sense that policy making and implementation below the national level suffer severe capacity constraints. This is especially true of the poorer provinces, such as Mpumalanga, and the former "homeland" regions within these provinces, such as KaNgwane. Moreover, since much of the country's regulatory framework is evolving, policy formulation does not always travel all the way to implementation, even where capacity is not an issue. This is the case with water policy. Moreover, a coordinated and rational response to EU trade reforms and other key drivers on the Incomati is, in part, dependent on an SADC-level consensus. As the most powerful SADC member and chief sugar exporter within SADC, South Africa would be required to take an active role in any proposed intervention. But, currently, there appears to be little appetite for this.

On a positive note, the Mpumalanga provincial government, through the provincial Department of Agriculture and Department of Economic Development, has started to consider the questions of appropriate agricultural development strategies, where previously "business as usual" had ruled. In addition, the Incomati CMA finally became fully operational at the end of 2006. Although the CMA, being the first of its kind in the county, will have to find its feet in its new regulatory, consultative and analytic role, the enthusiasm of its staff, board and chief executive agent augur well. Since water is the constraining factor for the economic future of the Incomati area, the CMA has its job cut out and will need all the backing it can muster.

The recent illegal expansion of irrigated sugar cultivation also comes at a cost to the DWAF. The task of establishing effective water-allocation norms is made more complex, more expensive and more disruptive of the status quo by this illegal expansion. Difficult trade-offs will need to be made between the deleterious ecological impacts of sugarcane production, its limited potential to generate income and employment and lock-in to a suboptimal development path on the one hand and, on the other hand, its potential to expand export earnings from sugar as new markets emerge and to improve the livelihoods of sugar-growing farmers, some of whom may be black and previously disadvantaged, via a proven market arrangement.

Sugar Industry

The South African sugar industry is highly organized and, as such, is able to exercise leverage over the evolving and fragmented regulatory environment. Although established commercial and new small-scale farmers do not always see eye to eye, the sector displays a remarkable degree of cohesion. In 2005, the Mpumalanga Cane Growers Association was formed, which represents both smallholders and large-scale farmers from the entire Incomati area. The association deals on behalf of its members with the mills, provincial government and the DWAF.

The Tsb mills have a black economic empowerment strategy that includes, for example, preferential local procurement. It supports small-scale growers through an extension service, including the maintenance of irrigation infrastructure. Tsb favors expansion of the area under cultivation by small-scale growers and the allocation of new water rights to them as a means of increasing its cane throughput. The mill has set up a company to facilitate the graduation of small-scale farmers to commercial farming, and SASA has introduced a Supplementary Payment Fund through which small farmers get more than their "fair" share of the proceeds from sugar and is considering the establishment of a fund for farmers in financial distress.

Political priorities can be expected to prevail over strict economic efficiency criteria in water allocation. Reform may or may not lead to efficiency losses insofar as small farmers shift from inferior irrigation technology to more efficient technologies. The sugar industry could contribute to greater efficiency by providing capital and experience with irrigation.

The exact impacts of the impending water-allocation reform on water-intensive crops such as sugarcane remain to be seen, but clearly there is a tension between the area's current economic specialization on the one hand and the need to provide water to a more diverse constituency and in support of economic diversification on the other. South Africa's obligation to release water across the frontier to Mozambique and the efforts of small-scale sugar farmers in Incomati are likely to receive a high priority in the compulsory licensing process. A measure of strategic and opportunistic positioning around the water reallocation is to be expected, however, as is a drive toward water-saving technologies and increased water-rights trading.

CONCLUSIONS

The most important argument to emerge from this analysis is perhaps that trade does not matter all that much. The reason is not that changes in the trade regime fail to have an effect, but rather that the situation of the rural poor and the environment in Incomati is so serious, even in the absence of trade liberalization, that it would be strange to train one's attention on a European trade reform that may make a bad situation only marginally worse. Yet the point needs to be made that, all things being equal, the reform of the EU sugar regime is likely to lead to a positive supply response in the Incomati. This response is contingent on water being made available to new sugar cultivation, legally or otherwise. On average, every additional ton of sugar produced in the Incomati will require an additional 1,660 m^3 of water to be abstracted from the region's watercourses – an abstraction that is likely to present adverse consequences to the economy, the ecology and poverty alleviation.

Of course, everything else need not be equal. As in many countries, the cost of water that is allocated to agriculture in South Africa fails to reflect its full economic value. The opportunity cost of water required for sugar production in Incomati is high. Whether sugarcane is a rational choice in the Incomati Basin depends on the time horizon one adopts, the scale at which the question is considered and the nature and distribution of the ensuing gains. Someone without much farming experience and capital is well served by the ease of cultivation, support structure and ready market for sugarcane, at least in the short run, provided water is available, legally or otherwise. Similarly, politicians and civil servants desperate to show some success for their commitment to job creation are drawn to the black economic empowerment that is happening, albeit slowly, in the sugar industry. But officials dealing with water allocation, who must grapple with opportunity costs and alternative users making conflicting demands on the same resource, take a different view.

Alternative economic activities with lower water requirements are available but are unlikely to develop without some support and without an increase in water costs that will make them clearly preferable to sugar production. The new CMA can effectively change the allocation of water; however, in the face of the privileged position of the sugar industry, the existing conflicts over land and water and a limited understanding among small farmers about water allocation and price setting, reallocation will be difficult.

NOTES

1. South Africa has a mere 980 m³ of internal freshwater resource per capita as compared with a global average of 14,190 m³ (NWRS, 2004; Falkenmark, 1997).
2. Between 1994 and 2004 the Organisation for Economic Co-operation and Development (OECD) Producer Support Estimate (PSE) for South African agriculture fell from 17 percent to less than 5 percent. Notably, sugar producers and refiners in OECD countries receive an average of 32 percent of their receipts in the form of state support (OECD, 2006).
3. The world price declined from the mid-1990s (US$0.14/kg) to the early 2000s (falling to US$0.06/kg). From 2004 it rose rapidly, but reached only two-thirds of the level of the mid-1990s.
4. Previously Transvaal Suiker Beperk.
5. Botswana, Lesotho, Namibia, Swaziland and South Africa. Zimbabwe accesses the SACU market through bilateral agreements with Namibia and Botswana.
6. South Africa withdrew from the British Commonwealth in 1961, making it ineligible for ACP status. Swaziland, along with the other SADC countries, is an ACP country.
7. In 2001–02 this entailed a tariff quota of 74,185 tons of white sugar equivalent, scheduled to increase to 197,355 before 2008–09 (Huan-Niemi and Kerkela, 2005).
8. The intervention price will be replaced by a reference price and a private storage system as a safety net. The agreement was locked in with no possibility of review until 2014–15.
9. Since demand for sugar is relatively inelastic, what matters most in determining sugar prices is supply elasticity. The supply response of poor countries is likely to vary not just as a result of natural constraints but also as a result of their capacity to marshal the requisite organizational, institutional and financial capital needed to expand sugar cultivation. The response of Brazil, the world's largest and most efficient sugar producer, will be critical in determining the new world price. Brazil's response, in turn, will be driven in part by the price of oil, since much of its sugar production is used for ethanol. A number of sugar market models were reviewed here (CIE, 2002; Elobeid and Beghin, 2005; Koo, 2003; and Wohlgenant, 1999). Estimations of a future world sugar price vary from an increase as low as 10 percent to as high as 63 percent, depending on the liberalization scenario. None of these studies model the events of 2005 explicitly, but it is possible to derive an 11 percent price increase following the 36 percent reduction in the EU intervention price. Other authors arrive at much lower estimates. Wohlgenant suggests an increase of 10 percent following *full* liberalization in all developed countries, something that is clearly very different from a change in the EU regime alone which must logically then have a smaller impact. Since no study reports a higher estimate, it is reasonable to regard an 11 percent increase as the upper boundary. Likewise, since no study reports a zero estimate, the lower boundary is a definite positive price change. With oil price increases, the world price of sugar is likely to rise by more than 11 percent.

10. These estimates are broadly consistent with those of Punt et al. (2004), who estimated that full liberalization of the sugar industry had the potential to increase South Africa's gross domestic product (GDP) by 0.078 percent, and with the findings of an OECD study suggesting that a 50 percent reduction in agricultural tariffs and export subsidies could see net gains of US$250 million for South Africa (OECD, 2006).

11. Lorentzen et al. (2007) provide an extensive review of the available data sets and current state of poverty analysis for the region.

12. This study drew on the IES (Income and Expenditure Survey), LFS (Labour Force Survey) and OHS (October Household Survey) data.

13. Because of the limitations of the existing data, poverty analysis cannot be conducted at anything below the level of municipalities.

14. See Lorentzen et al. (2007) for details.

15. The difference is accounted for by losses from pipes and dams and through evaporation of overhead irrigation (sprinklers) and "wind sweep" of overhead irrigation.

16. Guy Pegram was one of the authors of South Africa's National Water Act and National Water Resource Strategy. He was interviewed as part of this study in 2005.

17. South Africa is a signatory to the Ramsar Convention and has 12 sites protected under the convention. The National Environmental Management Act of 1998 protects wetlands.

18. Bruce Leslie is Senior Ranger in the Malelane Section of Kruger National Park. He was interviewed as part of this study in 2005.

19. These tenets, defined at the Dublin Water Conference in 1992, include the following: (1) the river basin is the most natural unit of management, but effective management integrates the specific strategies of catchments; (2) participatory approaches (with explicit roles for women) are most successful; (3) management should be devolved to the lowest (most local) level possible; (4) water is an economic good and should be valued and managed with economic instruments; and (5) water demand management should be favored over water supply management where possible.

BIBLIOGRAPHY

Anderson, A. (2004), "Engaging disadvantaged communities: lessons from the Incomati CMA establishment. 2004", presented at the International Workshop on *African Water Laws: Plural Legislative Frameworks for Rural Water Management in Africa*, 26–28 January 2005, Gauteng, South Africa.

Centre for International Economics (CIE) (2002), "Targets for OECD sugar market liberalization", mimeo, prepared for the Global Alliance for Sugar Trade Reform and Liberalisation.

Commission of the European Communities (CEC) (2005), *The European Sugar Sector: Its Importance and Its Future*, Brussels: CEC.

Department of Water Affairs and Forestry (DWAF) (2000), "Executive summary: Proposal for the establishment of a Catchment Management Agency for the Incomati Basin, Pretoria", mimeo.

Elobeid, A. and J. Beghin (2005), "Multilateral trade and agricultural policy reforms in sugar markets", Working Paper 04-WP 356, Center for Agricultural and Rural Development, Iowa State University.

Falconer, I. and A. Humpage (2005), "Health risks associated with cynobacterial (blue-green algal) toxins in drinking water", *International Journal of Environmental Research and Public Health*, **29** (1), 43–50.

Falkenmark, M. (1997), "Meeting water requirements of an expanding world population", *Philosophical Transactions of the Royal Society*, **352** (1356), 929–36.

FAO Aquastat (available at: www.fao.org/nr/water/aquastat/main/index.stm).

Hoffman, T., S. Todd, Z. Ntshona and S. Turner (1999), *A National Review of Land Degradation in South Africa*, Pretoria: South African National Botanical Institute.

Hoogeveen, J.G. and B. Özler (2004), "Not separate, not equal: poverty and inequality in post-apartheid South Africa", Draft Paper, World Bank, Washington, DC.

Huan-Niemi, E. and L. Kerkela (2005), "Reform in the EU sugar regime: impact on the global sugar markets", in *Proceedings of the XIth EAAE Congress in Copenhagen, Denmark, 24–27 August, 2005*.

Koo, W.W. (2003), "Alternative United States and EU sugar trade liberalization policies and their implications", *Review of Agricultural Economics*, **24**, 336–52.

Kotze, D., C. Breen and J. Klug (1994), *Wetland-use: A Management Decision Support System for the KwaZulu-Natal Midlands*, WRC Report No. 501/2/94, Pretoria: Water Research Commission.

Leibbrandt, M. L. Poswell, P. Naidoo, M. Welch and I. Woolard (2004), "*Measuring recent changes in South African inequality and poverty using 1996 and 2001 census data*", CSSR Working Paper No. 84, South African Labour and Development Research Unit (SALDRU), University of Cape Town.

Linacre, E. (1991) Unpublished manuscript. School of Earth Sciences, University of Sydney, Australia.

Lorentzen, J., A. Cartwright and C. Meth (2007), "*The impact of trade liberalization on rural livelihoods and the environment – Land governance, asset control, and water access and use in the Incomati River Basin in Mpumalanga, South Africa: a case study of sugarcane production past, present and future*", Final Report, WWF/World Bank

Low, A. and A. Rebelo (eds) (1996), *Vegetation of South Africa, Lesotho and Swaziland*, Pretoria: DEAT.

Millennium Development Goals (MDG) (1997), *United Nations Development Program*, New York: United Nations.

Monteiro, P.M.S. and S. Mathews (2003), "Catchment2Coast: making the link between coastal resource variability and river inputs", *South African Journal of Sciences*, **99**, 299–30

National Water Act (NWA) (1998), Pretoria: Department of Water Affairs and Forestry.

National Water Resource Strategy (NWRS) (2004), Pretoria: Department of Water Affairs and Forestry, available at: www.dwaf.gov.za/Documents/Policies/NWRS/Default.htm.

Organisation for Economic Co-operation and Development (OECD) (2006), (see www.oecd.org).

Pauw, K., C. Punt and M. van Schoor (2005), "*A profile of Mpumalanga: Demographics, poverty, inequality and unemployment*", PROVIDE (Provincial Decision-making Enabling) Project Background Paper 2005:1(8), Elsenburg, Western Cape.

Peel, M. and M. Stalmans (1999), "The Systematic Reconnaissance Flight (SRF) as a tool in assessing the ecological impact of a rural development programme in an extensive area of the Lowveld of South Africa", *African Journal of Ecology*, **37**, 449–56.

Pegram, G. and E. Bofilatos (2005), *"Consideration on the composition of governing boards to achieve representation"*, presented at the International Workshop on African Water Laws: Plural Legislative Frameworks for Rural Water, Management in Africa, Gauteng, South Africa, 26–28 January.

Penman, H.L. (1948), "Natural evaporation from open water, bare soil, and grass", *Proceedings of the Royal Society of London*, **A193**, 120–46.

Punt, C., K. Pauw and M. van Schoor (2004), "Trade liberalisation efficiency and South Africa's sugar industry", Working Paper 2004 (1), Elsenburg Agricultural College, South Africa, available at: www.elsenburg.com/provide.

Sachs, J. (2005), "Can extreme poverty be alleviated?", *Scientific American*, **293**, 56–65.

Schulz, G. (2001), "Aspects of length, mass, fecundity, feeding habits and some parasites of the shortfin minnow, *Barbus brevipinnis* (Cyprinidae) from the Marite River, Mpumalanga, South Africa", available at: www.dwaf.gov.za/sfra/sea/usutu-mhlathuze%20wma/Biophysical%20Component/Mpumalanga%20Biobase.pdf.

Schulze, R.E., M.J. Horan and E.J. Schmidt (2000), "Hydrological complexities in assigning rainfed sugarcane a 'stream flow reduction activity'", in *Proceedings of the South African Sugar Technology Association*, 74, pp. 140–50.

State of the Environment Report (SoER) (2001), Pretoria: Department of Environmental Affairs and Tourism.

Statistics South Africa (2001), *Key Municipal Data*, Report No. 03-02-21 (2001), Pretoria.

Statistics South Africa (StatsSA) (2003), "Census 2001, investigation into appropriate definitions of urban and rural areas for South Africa: discussion document", 15 July, Report No. 03-02-20 (2001), Pretoria.

Steyn, D. (1945), "Poisoning of animals and human beings by algae", *South African Journal of Science*, **41**, 243–44.

Van der Berg, S., Ronelle Burger, Rulof Burger, M. Louw and D. Yu (2005), "Trends in poverty and inequality since the political transition", Stellenbosch Economic Working Papers, No. 1.

Vas, A. and P. Van der Zaag (2003), "Sharing the Incomati waters: co-operation and competition in the balance", *UNESCO Technical Documents in Hydrology*, **14**, available at: http://unesdoc.unesco.org/images/0013/001332/133297e.pdf.

Wohlgenant, M. (1999), *Effects of Trade Liberalisation on the World Sugar Market*, Prepared for the Sugar and Beverages Group, Rome: FAO.

7. Expansion of shrimp farming in Ca Mau, Vietnam

**Mai Trong Thong, with Hoang Xuan Thanh,
Ha Thi Phuong Tien, Nguyen Thu Huong,
Tran Tuyet Hanh, Ngo Van Hai,
Vu Ngoc Huyen, Le Dang Trung,
Le Phu Cuong, Le Van Hung, Cao Chi Hung,
Tham Thi Ngoc Diep and Jacques Marcille**

Vietnam has dramatically reorganized its economy over the last two decades, moving from a centrally planned, state-dominated model toward a market-based, open economy. The economic and social results have been remarkable: production of new export crops has soared and poverty levels have dropped substantially. The results for the environment have been more problematic, as changes in production have often moved ahead of environmental understanding and regulation. This study looks at the very rapid expansion of shrimp farming in Ca Mau Province in southern Vietnam, an expansion that occurred first spontaneously and then with government support in the wake of liberalization of trade and new farmer autonomy in production decisions. The growth of shrimp exports transformed the socioeconomic structure of Ca Mau. New economic opportunities were created for both landowners and landless in the region, and poverty levels have fallen. The sustainability of these improvements, however, depends on the adoption of appropriate shrimp-farming models and protection of the region's remaining natural mangroves and freshwater systems. The authors of this chapter carried out detailed studies in three different sites in Ca Mau, representative of the three most common shrimp-farming models. Research focused on how trade liberalization and the resulting changes in production affected people's livelihoods, with a particular emphasis on poverty alleviation and environmental conditions, and on the interrelationship among these changes.

SITE DESCRIPTION

Ca Mau Province forms a peninsula between the South China Sea and the Gulf of Thailand. With an area of 1.3 million acres, it accounts for over 13 percent of the Mekong River Delta region. The region has a sub-tropical climate, shaped by monsoons. A complex river and canal system creates connections to both the South China Sea and the Gulf of Thailand through 20 estuaries that are affected by two different tidal regimes. Mangroves predominated in the past, but a system of dikes now protects over 70 percent of the total area that would otherwise be flooded during high tides. Nevertheless, Ca Mau's mangrove forest remains the largest in Vietnam.

The population of Ca Mau is about 1.2 million.[1] People in the province have traditionally worked in the agriculture and forestry sectors, which still employed 60 percent of the population as of 1997. The population has been poor, their livelihoods depending on the production and sale of rice along with some fruits, vegetables and livestock. In mangrove and forest areas, collection of wood and firewood provided additional income and, in coastal areas, fisheries products were an important source of nutrition and income.

Until the early 1990s, the local authorities and people of Ca Mau followed the central government's push to invest in infrastructure for rice production. Many saline regions were converted to freshwater for rice farming, thanks in part to a major irrigation project. The rice crop of the region increased to about 1 million tons, providing not only food security but also surplus for export. However, productivity in the new rice fields was low, and freshwater irrigation was not possible in the dry season, limiting production to one crop. Poverty levels remained high; the provincial poverty rate as of 1996 was 33.2 percent, with higher rates in the rural areas. During the 1980s, a few farmers ventured into shrimp farming, which offered promise of higher incomes and a source of protein. By 1988, about 71,700 acres were in use for shrimp farming, primarily in the southern and coastal parts of the province where brackish water and natural shrimp seeds were easily accessible.

During this period, mangrove forests – which had already been severely degraded during wartime – were further cleared, primarily for new rice production. Of the 345,900 acres of mangroves recorded in 1943, only 202,600 acres remained in 1975. Another 76,600 acres were lost to expansion of rice cultivation in the ensuing years. When the forests were still intact, the region supported a high level of biodiversity in different ecosystems, including a great variety of birds, reptiles and amphibians in the *Rhizophora* mangrove forests, which support a tropical intertidal forest community primarily in the eastern portion of Ca Mau, and in the *Melaleuca* forests, which predominate in seasonally flooded freshwater areas in northwestern Ca Mau. Valuable species of mollusks (hard clam, blood cockle) and crustaceans (mud crabs, white and greasy-black shrimp, giant prawns) were collected in mangrove areas, as well as honey, fuelwood and timber. Forests also provided protection against coastal erosion and served as a nursery for marine organisms, including many exploited by fishermen.

ECONOMIC LIBERALIZATION

Beginning in 1986, the government of Vietnam began to implement a reform process, known as Doi Moi, to address the inefficiencies of its centrally planned economy through a shift to a market-based economy. Economic liberalization, particularly the liberalization of trade policy, brought major changes that created the impetus for rapid development. The first phase of Doi Moi focused on currency devaluation, liberalization of foreign investment, banking reforms and the elimination of the monopoly of agricultural cooperatives. Agricultural development still focused on intensification of rice production for food security. The second phase, initiated in 1989, focused on trade liberalization and support of export-led growth. The Trade Law of 1999 granted all economic actors the right to participate in import and export activities. Changes in land-use policies, giving greater rights and decision-making powers to farmers, also encouraged production. Vietnam signed more than 80 multilateral and bilateral trade agreements that have benefited exports, including the fisheries sector, culminating with accession to the WTO at the end of 2006. After more than 20 years of reform, Vietnam's economy has made great progress toward regional and global integration.

Prior to the 1990s, aquaculture was not a priority for the central government. The fisheries sector, based exclusively on wild catch, accounted for only 7.5 percent of agricultural production and a smaller share of agricultural exports. In 1994, however, the central government issued a key policy decision that triggered the expansion of aquaculture through a program of infrastructure construction. By 2001, the program had mobilized US$25 million to develop 211 projects around the country. Following the initial success of aquaculture exports, more vigorous policies were adopted in 1999, including a program for development of aquaculture in the Mekong Delta that set a target of 1.7 million acres of water surface and US$1.5 billion in export earnings.

Under these policies, farmers were allowed to convert rice paddies for aquaculture production. A system of shrimp hatcheries, irrigation infrastructure, research programs and extension services was established to support the sector. Within a short period of time, 1999–2002, aquaculture production expanded by 80 percent in area and doubled in volume. This expansion was particularly pronounced in the Mekong Delta, where shrimp production reached 159,700 tons, triple the 1995 volume.

In addition to the impetus from domestic policies, access to growing export markets has been critical for the expansion of shrimp production. Traditionally, Vietnam exported wild shrimp to Japan. With the introduction of aquaculture, exports to Japan have risen. However, exports to the United States account for the bulk of the new production. The US trade agreement concluded in 2000 granting "most favored nation" status was probably the most important international factor affecting shrimp expansion in Vietnam. Aquaculture exports to the United States increased dramatically, beginning to rise even during the negotiation of the agreement. Shrimp products exported to the United States rose fivefold in terms of value and 6.5-fold in terms of volume between 1999 and 2002. By 2004, exports to the United States reached 60,000 tons.

As a result of economic liberalization, shrimp prices are now determined by international markets and can fluctuate wildly. In 2001 and 2002, the European Union (EU) refused Vietnam's shrimp products because of excessive antibiotic levels and applied a tax of 10 percent, which led to a fall in farm-gate prices. In 2004, after an anti-dumping suit brought by US companies against Vietnamese shrimp, US Customs required that Vietnamese firms post bond for an anti-dumping tax on shrimp products imported to the United States equal to one year of exports. This led to a drop in exports to the United States and a further fall in farm-gate prices of some 20 percent. Given these variations in the international market, revenues to producers and processors can fluctuate widely from year to year. Nevertheless, demand is high because of the high quality of Vietnam's shrimp raised using extensive methods without chemical additives.

SHRIMP-FARM DEVELOPMENT IN CA MAU

In Ca Mau Province, major changes were sparked by the central government's decision to support aquaculture. Through the 1990s, the authorities of Ca Mau Province, known as the Provincial People's Committee (PPC), implemented the central government's policies to prioritize rice farming. Nevertheless, a switch to shrimp farming was gradually taking place. In 2000, in response to the change in central government policy, the local authorities began to officially support the conversion of low-productivity rice fields to shrimp farms. Within three years, the livelihoods of most of the population had changed – their incomes, which had been tied to rice production, came to depend nearly exclusively on shrimp.

This rapid change was possible because of the 15 years of economic reform that preceded the push for aquaculture exports. Liberalization of the economy gave a positive signal to all links in the market chain – from farmers to processing factories to traders. Producers changed the use of available land, primarily rice fields and mangroves, adopting a variety of shrimp-farming models. The labor structure of the province changed as many new service activities developed related to the shrimp industry. And the new farming techniques soon began to affect the environment and the socioeconomic characteristics of the rural communities of Ca Mau.

Shrimp Production

As shrimp prices rose in the 1980s and 1990s, Ca Mau farmers increasingly realized that they could make more money with less effort by switching from rice to extensive shrimp farming. The area under shrimp production reached 222,400 acres by 1999. Productivity under the extensive model of production without additional seeding was low, averaging about 40–60 kg/acre/year. With the introduction of improved techniques and additional seeding, productivity rose to 80 kg/acre/year. Production shifted from white and greasy-black shrimp to black tiger shrimp as farmed seeds began to be used. Rising prices pushed producers to invest in more productive technologies.

Once authorities began to promote the conversion of low-productivity rice fields to shrimp farming, change was much more rapid. More than 167,086 acres (67,619 hectares) were converted to monoculture shrimp production between 2000 and 2004, bringing the total area of shrimp aquaculture to 672,112 acres (272,000 hectares). Since seed production was developing rapidly as well, more farms were able to adopt technological improvements, including semi-intensive and intensive farming methods for black tiger shrimp. The result was a sharp increase in production from 20,000 tons in 1999 to 86,000 tons in 2004. Shrimp production from Ca Mau multiplied fourfold between 1999 and 2004, and export value grew threefold, from US$150 million to US$450 million (see Figure 7.1). Most of the shrimp produced in the province is processed for export in the 21 local factories; these include cooperative, state-owned enterprises, private enterprises and joint-venture enterprises.

The district of Cai Nuoc affords a good example of the rapid transformation from rice to shrimp in Ca Mau. In 1997 there were only 18,600

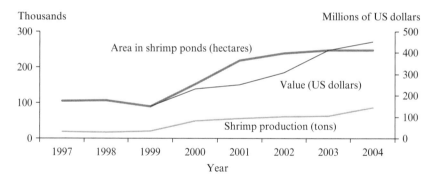

*Figure 7.1   Change in area, production and export value of shrimp in Ca
Mau, Vietnam*

acres of shrimp farms in Cai Nuoc, producing 1,800 tons of shrimp. Five
years later, shrimp farms occupied 158,100 acres and produced 11,485
tons. Rice farmers reacted quickly to the new market demand for shrimp
and, once in shrimp production, moved quickly toward improved methods
of extensive production. This transformation took place in response
to short-term profits, without consideration of long-term sustainability
issues. The conversion did not follow the long-term master plan proposed
by the authorities, nor did it address the conflicting production requirements of rice (a freshwater crop) and shrimp (a brackish water crop).
Infrastructure, such as channels to direct salt water into fields or sewage
out, was not modified to accommodate shrimp production. In some
places, households destroyed dikes and anti-salt drainage systems built to
support rice production in order to get saltwater for shrimp production.
This has led to conflict among villagers and to higher salinity levels in the
soil, causing loss of rice crops.

Labor

The labor structure in Ca Mau has changed dramatically as a result of
the development of aquaculture. While jobs in forestry and agriculture
declined substantially, from 290,000 in 1997 to 194,000 in 2003, jobs in the
aquaculture sector increased from 85,000 to 312,000. Aquaculture has not
only absorbed all the jobs lost in the other sectors but also the increase in
the labor force.[2] The jobs created are primarily low-skilled jobs in all segments of the shrimp production and processing chain and related services.
By 2003, more than half of all households in Ca Mau were directly or indirectly involved in the shrimp industry.

Thousands of hectares

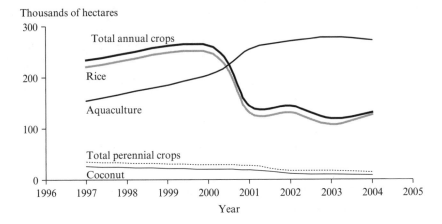

Source: *Ca Mau Statistics Bulletin 2003* (DARD, 2004).

Figure 7.2   Area of agriculture and fisheries production in Ca Mau, 1997–2004

Change in Land Use

Given the high population density in Ca Mau (one person for every 1.22 acres), for a population living primarily from agriculture, finding new land has always been a challenge. Land for aquaculture could come only at the expense of existing rice fields and mangrove forests. Rice areas have been massively transformed into shrimp ponds. The area in rice declined from 612,800 acres (248,241 hectares) in 2000 to 311,400 acres (126,517 hectares) in 2004 (see Figure 7.2), with a consequent drop in rice production from 850,000 tons to 400,000 tons, a level still sufficient to supply the province. In Cai Nuoc District, one-crop rice farming, which had covered 51,900 acres, disappeared completely.

Technology and Farming Models

Farmers adopted different aquaculture models depending on the environmental characteristics of the area where they were living. The shrimp-farming models in use in Ca Mau include shrimp monoculture, forest-shrimp, rice-shrimp and organic or ecological shrimp. Farmers living in mangrove areas cleared forest and adopted a forest-shrimp model of extensive aquaculture; those living among rice fields adopted monoculture or rice-shrimp models. Each of these can be implemented in a purely extensive mode, where seeding density is low, or in an improved extensive mode, where seeding density is higher. The extensive model requires little investment in pond building or technology and has been adopted by many households, including the poorest. This system depends on the tide for water and combines natural shrimp larvae with a low density of farmed larvae; the food source likewise is mostly natural, with few or no chemicals used to prepare the ponds. With rising shrimp prices, many extensive models have been upgraded to improved extensive models. This has been the case with most monoculture shrimp farming in former rice fields. The improved model requires greater funds for seed purchases and to cover the costs of pond preparation.

All extensive models are operated in an open system, with shared sluices letting water in and out, where outflow from one farm becomes inflow for another farm. Although the level of harmful pollutants is low in extensive farming, particularly in the forest-shrimp model, any pollution source can easily affect the entire system. In particular, the risk of epidemic is high. Research has shown that the rice-shrimp rotation model creates less pollution than shrimp monoculture and also better stabilizes the ecosystem. This holds true even if the rice crop is small or fails.

Depending on the model used, dredging of shrimp-pond sludge must be done once or twice a year, contributing to a variety of pollution problems. For example, in Nam Can District, about 20 percent of the sludge is discarded directly into the public drainage system, creating water pollution, raising the level of suspended solids and clogging the drainage system. Since the improved models require dredging twice a year, they contribute more to the problem than extensive models. Solving the pollution problem and reducing the high risk of epidemics would require a total revamping of the drainage system to separate water inflow and outflow.

Under the organic or ecological model, shrimp receive only the food naturally provided by the mangrove ecosystem, and existing canals in the forest are used, without new clearing. Productivity levels are low (averaging 60 kg/acre). However, the quality and size of the shrimp meet high export standards and, with an organic certificate, they can be sold at a 20 percent higher price. Canals are flushed regularly, and pollution levels are low.

The intensive model, which has productivity levels as high as 1–2 tons/acre, still covers only a small area (1,400 acres in 2004). Because it requires much greater investment in technical knowledge for soil preparation, water treatment, seeds, food supply, water quality control and oxygenation of ponds, only very rich households or enterprises with borrowing capacity have been able to implement this model. It does create many job opportunities for unskilled workers in soil preparation, removal of sludge, feeding of shrimp and other activities. Intensive models use a closed system, which reduces the risk of epidemics. While, with competent technical management, intensive models can be very water efficient, harmful sludge accumulates rapidly. In Ca Mau, technical capacity in aquaculture is insufficient to manage this model, increasing the risk that disease or pollutants will affect the surrounding extensive shrimp farms.

Managing Risk

After the transition is made into shrimp farming, its risky nature becomes evident. The productivity of ponds has shown a regular decline, and many producers have lost all their harvest. In general, however, households involved in extensive farming intend to stay in the business. Given their low investment in technology and labor, one good harvest can compensate for some crop losses. Most, however, are seeking ways to diversify their sources of income, without abandoning shrimp farming.

In former rice areas, where the most technologically improved models have been developed but losses have become more frequent, farmers have endeavored to diversify through mixed farming with other species such as crab, oysters and fish. In mangrove areas, losses are less frequent and households continue to try to extend their farms at the expense of the mangroves; this often occurs in violation of a local regulation requiring that 70 percent of mangroves be kept intact on allocated land.

Rising market demand and price fluctuations have led to a gradual increase in capital and technology investment in shrimp farming, in order to increase efficiency. Farmers have moved increasingly into improved models when they can afford them. Since improved extensive farming requires funding for seed purchase and pond preparation, most poor households are unable to make this change. Those poor households that do shift to the improved extensive model often cannot purchase high-quality seeds, which puts them at greater risk of losing their harvest. Aquaculture risks may lead to bankruptcy, forcing poor households to sell their land.

According to interviews, only a few rich households have started, after some initial success in extensive farming, to adopt intensive models. About half these attempts have been successful; half have lost everything, and some have had to sell their land. Similarly, some companies have succeeded with this model, but others have failed.

Provincial guidelines emphasize diversification and encourage farmers to combine shrimp with other agriculture products. Although from the outset local authorities promoted use of a rice-shrimp model, in the initial phase of the transformation, many farmers opted for monoculture shrimp cultivation. Later, as farmers realized (in part because of government training efforts[3]) that the rice-shrimp model can improve shrimp harvests, and as salt-resistant rice seeds were introduced, the mixed model has become more common (reaching the government target of 106,300 acres). However, shrimp farming, combined with a lengthening drought, has increased soil salinity over a large area, leading to reduced rice productivity and crop failure rates of 50 percent.

In the case of the shrimp-forest model, an average of 40 percent is in mangroves. Government plans are to increase this forest area to 70 percent, with a consequent reduction in shrimp area from 84,000 acres to 74,100 acres by 2010. In the case of shrimp monoculture, the policy push is to shift to rice shrimp, which yields demonstrably better shrimp crops, as well as mixed-shrimp models where shrimp is associated with crab or fish. Organic shrimp farming offers good potential for production in the mangrove forests. This model has been used almost solely by one enterprise (about 12,400 acres in 2005), but it is planned for an additional 24,700 acres to be run by other enterprises. An increase in intensive shrimp farming is also planned, with a target of 17,300 acres to 18,500 acres of industrial aquaculture in concentrated zones and an additional 7,400 acres to 8,600 acres in household-scale intensive production.

LIVELIHOOD CHANGES

The new opportunities offered by shrimp farming have increased incomes, reduced poverty and generated new jobs in Ca Mau. These positive changes, however, are tempered by an increasing income gap between rich and poor and between landowners and landless, as well as by the risks inherent in the shrimp export business.

Income and Poverty

Shrimp farming has increased average incomes in Ca Mau. While the rich have been best placed to take advantage of this new opportunity, shrimp farming has also lifted many families out of poverty. Income from shrimp farming accounts for 25 percent of household income (as compared with only 8 percent from rice) in the province. Incomes in Ca Mau, as of 2002, were 8.5 percent above the average level for the Mekong Delta region and 20 percent above the national average. Poverty has decreased substantially. Between 2001 and 2004, the number of poor families fell by more than 17,000, and the poverty rate fell from 15.5 percent to 7.8 percent.[4]

Analysis of the poverty rate in different districts within Ca Mau confirms the importance of shrimp farming in reducing poverty. Districts that do not have significant shrimp farms, because of a lack of brackish water, have a higher poverty rate than those with brackish water areas. Moreover, the areas using the rice-shrimp model (namely Cai Nuoc) have a higher poverty rate than those using the forest-shrimp model. This is explained by the fact that the rice-shrimp model is more risky and that landholdings are, on average, smaller in Cai Nuoc than in the coastal regions. The forest-shrimp areas, in turn, have a higher poverty rate than the coastal areas; this is because of the relatively high number of low-skilled immigrants in low-paying jobs in the forest-shrimp areas.

Looking at the differences between shrimp-farming and non-shrimp-farming households likewise confirms the importance of shrimp farming to poverty alleviation. As of 2002,[5] the poverty rate among shrimp-farming households was 28.6 percent compared with 34.7 percent for non-shrimp-farming households. Moreover, between 2000 and 2004, the rate of poor households participating in aquaculture increased sharply, from one-half to two-thirds. Shrimp farming clearly offers some households a chance to escape from poverty.

Non-shrimp-farming households have also experienced livelihood changes. Poor households with little or no land can benefit from shrimp farming by providing direct or indirect services, such as working as hired labor (dredging and maintaining ponds), working for seafood process-ing companies, running small businesses such as shrimp-collection services, and running boats. The number of poor households hiring out labor has increased sharply. In Ca Mau there are now 25 seafood processing enterprises (21 for shrimp alone) employing 20,000 full-time and seasonal workers, of whom 60 percent are women. There are many small businesses importing materials, chemicals and food for shrimp and collecting raw shrimp for delivery to processing plants. Shrimp hatcheries in the province now meet 50 percent of local demand for shrimp seed and employ a network of distribution agents. When asked about changes in income sources over the last five years, more than half of poor households said that income from wage labor has become more important.

Income Distribution and Equity

While shrimp farming offers a chance to escape from poverty for some, the gap between rich and poor households is significant. The average per capita income of poor households is only 40 percent that of non-poor households. The average income of non-shrimp-farming households is one-third that of shrimp-farming households. Even among shrimp-farming households there are significant differences: the income from shrimp aqua-culture for poor households is one-third that of non-poor households.

Poor households also generate a smaller proportion of their income (44 percent) from shrimp farming than do rich households (68 percent).

The primary reason for the gap in income between rich and poor is the difference in size of landholdings. While more than 35 percent of households in Ca Mau are landless,[6] 25 percent have more than 4.9 acres. Generally, non-shrimp-farming households have no land, or very little. Shrimp farmers, on the other hand, have been able to accumulate land in recent years and land prices have increased sharply. Unused land is very limited, leaving little opportunity for land-poor and landless families.

The second reason for the income gap lies in differences in loan accessibility. Households with little or no land do not have access to bank loans. Shrimp farmers, however, make substantial use of bank loans. Some 70 percent of shrimp farmers, as compared to 7 percent of non-shrimp farmers, have taken out bank loans. This borrowing is crucial for the switch from freshwater production (with low investments, profits and risks) to saltwater or brackish water production (with high investments, profits and risks). Most shrimp producers report that they rely on future shrimp harvests to pay off their loans; however, the increasing risks associated with shrimp production are making debt riskier.

And third, rich households are better able to cope with the risks of shrimp farming. Losses from shrimp farming were common across all surveyed sites. After one or two profitable seasons, shrimp productivity declined and losses became more frequent. Surveys showed that losses in both the rice-shrimp model and the forest-shrimp model were higher in 2004 than they had been in 2000. Because of the instability of shrimp prices and the risk from pollution and diseases, people have begun to diversify their income, often combining shrimp with crabs, fish and other products. The poorest households are most likely to diversify production and do more hired work. Surveys carried out in Ca Mau for this project found that diversification of aquaculture improves the livelihoods of both rich and poor farmers.

Recent migration to Ca Mau is closely linked to shrimp production. On average, 2,000 migrants arrive annually, primarily in the coastal districts. Migrants are mainly men, looking for hired work in the shrimp industry or related small businesses. Most are poor and landless; some stay and become residents. Although the unemployment rate has dropped slightly since the mid-1990s,[7] the total number of unemployed in Ca Mau has risen because of the growing population. Shrimp aquaculture has created many jobs for women, primarily in processing plants. However, many women still do not work outside the home. The shift from rice farming to shrimp farming had the effect of greatly reducing the workload of many women, since shrimp require little intervention, leaving many of them underemployed. Diversification of products has the benefit, in addition to reducing risks, of improving the utilization of labor for both men and women.

ENVIRONMENT AND ECOSYSTEM CHANGES

In the first years of shrimp-farming expansion in Ca Mau, thousands of acres of mangrove forest were cleared, with significant impacts on the ecosystem. In the subsequent years, the initial profitability of shrimp production induced many farmers to convert rice fields to shrimp. This conversion of coastal mangrove forests and rice fields has had serious consequences for the natural environment, degrading ecosystems and reducing biodiversity, which in turn has reduced the opportunities for many of the poorest people to maintain their traditional activities. At the same time, the pollution and salinization associated with shrimp farming are both increasing the risks of shrimp-crop loss and reducing the viability of crop diversification.

Between 1975 and 1983, about 49,400 acres of mangrove forest were cleared for rice farming. Shrimp development in subsequent years led to the destruction of an additional 29,700 acres in Ca Mau. In response, the province applied a forest allocation policy in 1991. Under this policy, local households were each assigned 7.4 to 24.7 acres of forest in which to build a shrimp pond, with the obligation to leave 70 percent of the mangrove intact. This policy had positive impacts in terms of reducing deforestation and forest fires. It was complemented by a resettlement program and a replanting effort that increased the mangrove area by 39,500 acres. However, the forest cover rule is not strictly applied, and the actual proportion of forest cover left intact is often below 60 percent. In addition, by allowing each shrimp farm to select an area for mangrove protection, the policy has resulted in the fragmentation of the remaining forest into small blocks, with negative impacts on biodiversity.

The reductions in the surface and density of Ca Mau's mangrove forest have severely restricted the available natural habitat. Biodiversity has declined measurably in the forests. The diversity of trees has been reduced, and five species of plants and 10 species of birds have vanished.[8] Moreover, since coastal mangrove forests are a critical ecosystem for the reproduction and development of many marine species, their degradation may lead to lower marine populations and diversity and consequently lower productivity of traditional fishing activities.

In the areas transformed from rice paddies to shrimp farming, aquatic communities have changed as a result of the inflow of brackish water.

A number of irrigation systems built to prevent salt invasion have been destroyed in order to facilitate shrimp cultivation. Salinization now occurs far inland during the dry season, and brackish water fauna is likewise invading further inland, at the expense of many valuable fresh-water species. Migrant species requiring freshwater have also died or have moved further inland because of the increasing salt levels.

Compounding the problems of salinization is the increasing amount of pollutants being released into the Ca Mau water system.[9] Shrimp produc-tion generates waste – composed of shrimp, food and toxic chemicals – that accumulates in the form of sediment or sludge in shrimp ponds. The greater the intensity of the farming system, the more sludge is produced. The total volume of waste from shrimp aquaculture in Ca Mau in 2003 was 248 million m^3. Producers usually dispose of this waste in rivers and chan-nels without proper treatment, spreading pollutants to surrounding areas and increasing the risk of an epidemic. The level of dissolved oxygen in the waterways, a good indicator of pollution levels, is below the environmental standard, especially during the dry season. This can affect shrimp produc-tion. During the rainy season, shrimp-pond health is also affected by falling pH levels that are the result of alum soil being washed into shrimp ponds lacking erosion barriers. This likewise can reduce shrimp production.

These ecosystem changes affect local livelihood options. In addition to increasing the risk associated with shrimp farming and lowering pro-ductivity, these changes have affected other resource-based activities. Collection activities – for timber, firewood, fish, crabs, honey, and so on – have declined substantially. Some freshwater grasses used for feeding cattle have been lost. Most coconut plantations have disappeared, and salinization has reduced the productivity of vegetable gardens by as much as 25 percent. This decline in environmental provisioning and supporting services has affected poor households more than others, since they rely most heavily on non-shrimp sources of income.

RESPONSES AND INTERVENTIONS

Successes in aquaculture in the 1990s, especially in the Mekong Delta and in Ca Mau in particular, led to the formulation of stronger aquaculture policies by the central government. With the aim of boosting aquacul-ture exports, a series of policies were issued that supported investment in hatcheries, research and development for technology and aquaculture extension by both private and state entities. The results of these policies – in the context of liberalization of trade and the domestic economy – were spectacular.

In the early stage of aquaculture development, which was largely spontaneous, local authorities were unable to anticipate problems. However, they have reacted quickly to sensitive issues such as the destruction of mangroves. As early as 1991, the Provincial People's Committee (PPC) of Ca Mau issued a policy on allocation of land for forestry and aquaculture, for individuals and state-owned enterprises. This policy reduced the indiscriminate cutting of mangroves and offered people improved livelihoods through shrimp farming. However, the policy had the unintended impact of fragmenting the mangrove forest.

The rapid transformation of rice fields to shrimp farming, like the cutting of mangroves, was also largely uncontrolled, and the scale of pollution was unanticipated. However, the Ca Mau PPC responded in the late 1990s with a decision to support an economic model mixing aquaculture, agriculture and forestry and to prioritize the conversion of low-productivity rice fields to a rice-shrimp model. Implementation of this model was not initially widespread, but it has gradually been more widely adopted as its advantages become apparent.

In response to growing environmental pollution, the Ca Mau PPC has issued a number of directives assigning the tasks of environmental management and monitoring to provincial agencies, and setting guidelines for imposing fines on organizations and individuals violating environmental protection regulations. One of the problems in environmental management of aquaculture is that conditions are quite diverse across the province. Planning must be adapted to specific local conditions. A possible step toward improved efficiency of regulations could be the adoption of an "open" planning system for each sub-region. The development of models, production systems and cooperative mechanisms would then be based on the participation of stakeholders. Planning and building irrigation systems at the sub-regional level would help to promote this cooperation.

The Ca Mau administration has taken various steps to increase the benefits of shrimp farming. Plans have been established for promoting ecological or organic shrimp-farming models, the government has banned the use of many antibiotics and toxic chemicals and processing plants have been upgraded to improve the quality of exported products. Other measures have been taken to facilitate access to credit for farmers, including poor households, and special funds have been allocated for the poorest. However, farmers still see a need for better access to finance; most would prefer to borrow directly from banks rather than being obliged to go through forest or fisheries enterprises.

Many other organizations played important roles in the development of shrimp production and the consequent economic restructuring of the province. Because of the limited capacity of the Ca Mau administration, state-owned companies, in coordination with the districts and communes, were given a leading role in implementing various changes, particularly in the allocation and preservation of natural forest and mangrove areas. Unions and cooperatives have played an important role in providing loans to the poorest households. In some places, people have formed cooperatives that have taken on additional activities. Given the high risks involved in shrimp production, cooperatives could play an important role in reducing risk through improved quality control and irrigation systems; however, they generally have not taken on this role.

Since the shrimp business is almost exclusively directed to exports, foreign importers are playing an increasing role in the ongoing transformation of the industry. To ensure quality products, some importers have directly promoted changes in processing technology as well as certain farming practices, such as organic or ecological farming, through labeling or bans on the use of particular chemicals. This pressure has led the government to adopt a number of production standards and has led shrimp farmers to think in terms of improving practices and participating in certification programs. Besides the benefits from reduction in production risk and market losses, certification can help address major environmental concerns related to shrimp aquaculture.

Shrimp farmers are well aware of the need for increased control over seed quality and of the need for measures to reduce pollution. They would like to see further study of the various farming models, particularly with regard to their environmental impacts. There is increasing concern that shrimp farming, particularly as practiced in the monoculture model, is not sustainable over the long term.

CONCLUSIONS

Trade liberalization has brought positive change to Ca Mau Province in terms of increased incomes, improved livelihoods for most people and better employment opportunities for the landless and land-poor. However the rapid shift from rice farming to shrimp farming has affected the environment in ways that are detrimental for both shrimp farmers and other users of natural resources in the province. Moreover, the opportunities afforded by shrimp farming are not equally distributed. Rich farmers, particularly land-rich farmers, have been best able to develop successful operations and to shoulder the risk of shrimp farming. The poor and landless face more difficult trade-offs between the new economic opportunities and social and environmental change.

Shrimp farming is associated with various risks. The region has become heavily dependent on shrimp exports, putting the local economy at risk if prices or international quality control regulations change quickly. There is also a high risk that shrimp harvests will be lost because of epidemics or water contamination. Some of the problems now appearing in Ca Mau have been observed in neighboring countries. In Thailand, for example, shrimp productivity generally falls after just one or two years of production, and intensive farming leads to the accumulation of so much sludge that farmers often have to move to new lands after just three to four years. Clearly, before moving wholesale into a new monoculture such as shrimp, in-depth environmental studies should be carried out to understand whether and how the activity can be made sustainable. This is particularly important for a country such as Vietnam, where demographic pressures are strong and land is scarce.

The long-term outcome of many of the environmental changes that are being induced in Ca Mau remains uncertain. Little is known, for example, about the long-term impacts of soil salinization or the capacity of the ecosystem to absorb pollutants. The recent decision to develop intensive farming models should be carried out only with careful study that takes into account all the social and environmental aspects, not just the short-term boost to exports.

Despite the clear economic benefits associated with the shift to shrimp farming, some of the impacts on livelihoods have been negative. In addition to the economic and environmental risks of shrimp farming, poor people in Ca Mau face increasing disparities in wealth and declining availability of natural resources and options for crop diversification. Losses of forests and of productive rice and garden land are most critical for the poor. While the government has responded fairly rapidly to both socio-economic and environmental issues as they have arisen, the issues of forest degradation, reduced food security and long-term sustainability have not been adequately addressed.

NOTES

1. Statistics given in this report are taken from the *Ca Mau Statistics Bulletin 2003* (DARD, 2004), unless otherwise noted.
2. The total labor force in the province rose from 660,000 to 767,000 between 1997 and 2003.
3. In 2004 the provincial agriculture agencies held training in the rice-shrimp model for 73,400 households.
4. These data are from the Vietnam Household Living Standards Survey (VHLSS 2002), which used a sample size of 670 households.
5. Again, using VHLSS 2002 data on poverty rates, which uses an expenditure poverty standard.

6. Notably, over 64 percent of Khmer ethnic households have no land; 39 percent of Khmer households were classified as poor in 2001. This rate had fallen to 30 percent by 2003, in part because of government efforts to provide special support through loans and land allocation.
7. The rate fell from 5.9 percent in 1997 to 5.4 percent in 2003.
8. These include some rare birds such as *Plancanus onocrolatus*, *Ibis leucocephalus* and *Leptopilos dabius.*
9. This is particularly problematic in the northern districts, where the density of canals and rivers is lower. In the southern districts, the higher density of waterways affords the system a higher self-cleaning capacity.

BIBLIOGRAPHY

Ca Mau Department of Agriculture and Rural Development (DARD) (2002a), *Progress Report on the Implementation of Annual Agriculture and Rural Development Plan in 2001, 2002*, Ca Mau: DARD.

Ca Mau Department of Agriculture and Rural Development (DARD) (2002b), *Progress Report on Transformation of Economic Structure in Agriculture and Rural Sectors in Ca Mau*, Ca Mau: DARD.

Ca Mau Department of Agriculture and Rural Development (2004), *Ca Mau Statistics Bulletin 2003*, Ca Mau: DARD.

Ca Mau Department of Fisheries (DoF) (2003), *Progress Reports on Implementation of Annual Sectoral Plan in 2001, 2002 and First 6 Months of 2003*, Ca Mau: DoF.

Ca Mau Department of Science, Technology, and Environment (DOSTE) (2000), (2001), (2002), *Ca Mau State of the Environment Report*, Ca Mau: DOSTE.

Ca Mau Provincial People's Committee (PPC) (2002), *Draft of Organizational Renovation of Forest Management and Forestry Land in Ca Mau Province*, Ca Mau: PPC.

Ca Mau Provincial People's Committee (2003a), *The Synthetic Report on Amendment of the General Planning in Socio-economic Development in Ca Mau Province up to 2010*, Ca Mau: PPC.

Ca Mau Provincial People's Committee (2003b), *Socio-economic Development in Ca Mau – Progress Reports in 2001, 2002 and First 6 Months of 2003*, Ca Mau: PPC.

Ca Mau Provincial People's Committee (2004), *Aquaculture Development Plan for Nam Can and Ngoc Hien Districts in 2005–2010*, Project supported by SUMA component, FSPS, Ca Mau: PPC.

Le Sam (2003), "Issues in transformation of production patterns in Mekong Delta", *Magazine of Agriculture and Rural Development*.

Phan Nguyen Hong (1997), *Characteristics of Viet Nam's Mangrove Forest – Recovery and Sustainable Use*, Hanoi: Center for Natural Resources and Environmental Studies.

Thieu Lu and Mai Sy Tuan (2004), *Environment Status of Aquaculture Area in Ca Mau Province and Technical Solutions for Sustainable Shrimp Aquaculture Development*, Proceedings of Workshop on Sustainable Aquaculture in Mekong Delta, Kien Giang: Department of Fisheries, Kien Giang Province.

Tran Thanh Be (2002), "Assessment of rice-shrimp farming system in brackish water of Mekong Delta", *Science Magazine*, Can Tho University.

Truong Hoang Minh et al. (2002), "Assessment of forestry–fishery method development in buffer zone of Ca Mau Province", *Science Magazine*, Can Tho University.

Truong Quoc Phu et al. (2002), "Current state of the application of forestry–fishery mixed farming practice in Ngoc Hien and Dam Doi districts, Ca Mau Province", Scientific research newsletter, Can Tho University.

VIE/01/021 Project: Formulation and Implementation of Viet Nam's National Agenda 21 (2002), *Impacts of Policies on Agriculture and Forestry Extension and Processing Industry on Environment and Natural Resource*, Hanoi: Ministry of Planning and Investment.

8. Lessons from the case studies: 1

Pamela Stedman-Edwards, Jonathan A. Cook and Owen Cylke

WWF came to this project out of concern that the impacts of trade liberalization on biodiversity and on the long-term sustainability of the earth's ecosystems were being ignored, largely because they were not well understood. Neither the crafters of trade policy nor most academic efforts to examine its role had given much consideration to the local impacts of trade liberalization – particularly to those impacts on the ground in places of concern for conservation. WWF's long experience working in these unique places has made us well aware of their vulnerability to change from outside. This experience has also created a keen awareness of the complex relationships between the rural people who inhabit these places and the survival of critical ecosystems. These people are often impoverished and directly dependent on the resources and services provided by the ecosystems where they live. Successful conservation requires us to address the needs of these vulnerable people in order to protect vulnerable places, and vice versa. Existing methodologies for analyzing the changes engendered by trade and the package of growth-oriented development policies of which trade forms an integral part had failed to capture important, place-specific impacts on poverty and the sustainability of ecosystem services. Thus, WWF entered into this project with the goal of developing a more comprehensive approach to understanding the complex relationship between trade, poverty and environment at all levels, but with a strong focus on the local – on the specific places where environmental damage is occurring.

The six case studies in this book look at the opportunities and problems generated by trade liberalization for vulnerable people and ecosystems. Vulnerable ecosystems are ecosystems considered to be of high ecological importance – generally because of their rarity, the species they harbor or the essential services they provide – that are either threatened or experiencing pressure or degradation from human activities. Vulnerable people are the rural poor, indigenous populations and other groups who face a number of constraints – including economic poverty, limited control over resources (such as uncertain land tenure), limited access to political power, limited opportunities (such as low levels of education, poor health care and little access to capital) and economic insecurity – and whose liveli-hoods are often directly dependent on local natural resources. Each case study examines not only the individual effects on poverty and ecosystems, but also changes that occur in the relationship between a vulnerable group and the vulnerable ecosystem upon which they depend. This chapter seeks to analyze the case studies using a lens that focuses directly on these rela-tionships between people and ecosystems.

TRADE, POVERTY AND ENVIRONMENT THROUGH A NEW LENS

Examining trade, poverty and environment from different perspectives – or through the lenses of different methodologies – leads to different ways of understanding their inter-relationship. In the debate over trade and environment, briefly described in Chapter 1, the traditional economic lens has focused overwhelmingly on the aggregate effects of trade, on midterm results of liberalization and on rational choices about use of resources, without consideration of local short-term or long-term impacts. The conservation lens has brought into focus the damage done to the environ-ment in particular places in the short term and to the planet as a whole over the long term. But it has often failed to make a clear link between environmental changes and specific trade-related policies and institutions. The substantial differences between these lenses – between these alternate ways of seeing the issue – have created two divergent pictures of the role of trade in fostering socioeconomic and environmental change in developing countries.

Use of the economic lens, with its focus on the aggregate, has led to a conflation of the trade and development agendas in which trade expan-sion, national and even global economic growth and development have been viewed as a single package. The predominant school of economic thought, sometimes labeled the Washington consensus, has argued in favor of trade expansion as a fundamental tool for reducing overall poverty, largely through its capacity to create export-sector jobs and increase the efficiency of domestic production. Economists are still debat-ing the strength of the supposed relationship between trade and poverty reduction;[1] however, regardless of what the final evaluation may be, policy makers around the world have largely adopted trade liberalization as one of the key tools for promoting development. Donor institutions are putting substantial funds into "aid for trade," largely to facilitate exports as a means to development. And, indeed, in many countries, trade liberalization is an important catalyst of economic growth and job creation at the national level.

But trade-generated income and new job opportunities have not been evenly distributed. While the aggregate figures have improved, many people in developing countries have not enjoyed these benefits;[2] in fact, too many of them have actually suffered declining incomes and job losses as fundamental structural changes have occurred in these economies. In addition to the uneven distribution of benefits from trade and economic growth, changes in trade patterns often cause short-term economic disruptions, dramatic changes in the scale or composition of production and changes in methods of production, which may all have negative consequences for particular people and places. These consequences become apparent only when we adopt a more local or micro level perspective, rather than looking exclusively at aggregate outcomes. Of course, these structural changes are the result not only of trade but also of broader macroeconomic and development policies and, as this chapter will argue, the particular set of conditions and institutions affecting each place.

Classic economic theory, drawing on the law of comparative advantage, has also presented trade as a tool for improving environmental outcomes. This argument is made on the grounds that trade liberalization will shift production based on comparative advantage (so that a country's most abundant resources will be exploited) and will improve the efficiency of resource use through competition. Given the factor endowment of developing countries, their exports often have a major natural-resource component, such as food, fiber or minerals. Increases in exports are therefore likely to increase competition for the use of natural resources. Yet, from an ecological perspective, these resources are not discrete economic goods, but are products of functioning ecosystems that provide the fundamental services on which human life depends. Thus, while national incomes may improve in the medium term as resource-based exports increase, the accompanying drawdown of natural resources may cause irreversible damage to these ecosystems and the people who depend on them.

Inevitably, trade-offs are made among the possible uses of ecosystems, among the beneficiaries of ecosystem services and between current economic growth and the long-term sustainability of ecosystems. These trade-offs are usually made without full information about the long-term economic or environmental consequences and without the participation of the most vulnerable stakeholders. Conservationists believe that both the short-term and long-term environmental trade-offs – particularly loss of biodiversity – are too rarely factored into decisions about economic activity, with sometimes disastrous results for ecosystem services and biodiversity. Thus, conservationists who are familiar with these place-specific outcomes have taken a much less sanguine view of trade and trade-centered development than many economists, though generally without offering better alternatives for development.

The more nuanced view taken in this set of case studies, and that shapes our analysis in this chapter, gives primacy to ecosystems, ecosystem services, their underlying processes and the livelihoods of the people who depend on them. This view differs from the traditional economics-centered approach in some critical ways, notably in its understanding that human livelihoods and well-being are fundamentally dependent on the sustainable use of ecosystem services. At the same time, it differs from traditional conservation perspectives in taking a broad view of the factors shaping human use of environmental services and in recognizing the critical role of human institutions, markets and behavior in shaping environmental outcomes.

OUR ANALYTIC FRAMEWORK

The lens or approach taken by our analysis of these case studies has been most clearly articulated in the Millennium Ecosystem Assessment framework (2003). At the heart of the Millennium Ecosystem Assessment (MA) effort was the development of an interdisciplinary framework for looking at the interplay between human activities and the ecosystems in which they are conducted. It was undertaken at multiple scales, local to global. Because the MA was carried out concurrently with this study, and did not have a fully developed methodology, our researchers were able to make only limited use of its early products. However, we draw on it for our analysis here because it clearly reflects how analytic thinking has evolved in recent years regarding the relationship between humans and the environment.

The Millennium Ecosystem Assessment framework emphasizes the fundamental link between the natural environment and human well-being, and the centrality of this relationship to the effect of policies. The framework places human well-being at the center of analysis, recognizing that the purpose of economic growth is to increase well-being (rather than simply to reduce economic poverty). Human well-being is a function of access to environmental services, material goods, health, good social relations, security, freedom and choice. Lack of access to these is largely equivalent to vulnerability. Because the poor are particularly dependent on environmental services and natural resources, poverty cannot be addressed without ensuring access to these resources. Environmental services are defined as the benefits that people obtain from ecosystems, including food, water, flood and disease control, cultural services and the fundamental supporting services – nutrient cycling, soil formation, primary production – that are essential for maintaining life on earth. Biodiversity is the source of many of the goods that people draw from ecosystems; changes in biodiversity can affect the supply of ecosystem services, and vice versa.

Changes in the provision or functioning of environmental services are explained in terms of direct and indirect drivers. Direct drivers are those that directly affect ecosystems, such as planting of agricultural crops or extraction of firewood. The MA framework includes in this category changes in local land use and land cover; species introductions and removals; technology adaptation and use; external inputs (e.g., fertilizer use, pest control, irrigation); harvest and resource consumption; climate change and natural physical changes (e.g., volcanoes, drought). These drivers can affect human well-being directly – for example, by generating an increase in the food supply or a decrease in the fuelwood supply. They also shape changes in ecosystem services that in turn affect human well-being, such as a reduction in soil erosion as a result of improved agricultural practices, or increased flooding caused by deforestation.

Indirect drivers shape the direct drivers. This broad category includes trade, our primary focus here, along with other economic drivers, demographic change, sociopolitical drivers, science and technology, and cultural and religious drivers. Interactions between these indirect drivers and human well-being are numerous. Indirect drivers affect the decisions made at the local level by individuals and small groups who directly use environmental services; by public and private decision makers at the regional and national levels; and by public and private decision makers at the global level through international corporations and international conventions.

Although there is substantial variety among the methods used by the case studies in this book, broadly speaking, the studies are based on this global view. At the heart of each study is an effort to understand the dynamic between human well-being and environment as it is affected by trade liberalization. The case studies explore a variety of direct drivers of changes in land and water use in specific places: changes in crops, changes in the scale of production and changes in technology. These changes are generally explained in terms of a combination of indirect drivers, including trade policies and opportunities, that shape many of the local decisions about what crops to produce, where to produce them and the technology to be used. These drivers are found at the local, regional and global levels.

To sort out the impacts of this range of indirect drivers, we rely here on an approach developed over the course of several case study projects. This approach is known as 3×M because it is focused on the role of indirect drivers at three levels – the micro, meso and macro levels – that shape local outcomes of macroeconomic change. WWF has been analyzing the impacts of macroeconomic policies on the environment for two decades. A large number of case studies[3] have contributed to the development of a broad analytical approach that draws on a number of disciplines and delves into processes of local environmental change as driven by economic policies. Designed to analyze the political economy of poverty and ecological disruption, the approach emphasizes understanding direct drivers of environmental change in terms of the indirect drivers across all scales, from micro (local) to meso (national or regional) to macro (international), and their interactions. The capacity of the poor to make sustainable use of natural resources and improve their own well-being depends on the whole range of indirect drivers. Analysis of the opportunities and constraints created by these drivers starts with the results on the ground – in the case of these studies, the impacts on land and water use – and examines the role of indirect drivers at all levels in shaping local decisions. Given the focus here on trade, we examine the ways in which international markets and national development frameworks interact with, or work their way through, different institutional, social, political and economic configurations to reach the point of environmental and economic consequence in very different ecosystems and socioeconomic communities.

Particular attention is given to the role of institutions and governance structures at different levels, which shape the way in which international and national policies filter down to affect real people and places. Analysis of the role of institutions has shown clearly that the type and quality of institutions at various scales makes a great difference in how the poor participate in economic growth, trade opportunities and management of natural resources.[4] Trade liberalization that opens international markets to developing country products generally increases overall economic opportunities. But the structures and processes of governance are critical to determining how trade-offs are made regarding income distribution, equity and environmental impacts, present and future.

The developing countries in these studies have essentially two things to offer on the international market: labor and natural resources. The studies examine how returns to labor and use of natural resources changed with a particular trade event. All of the countries have relatively cheap labor to offer, but their endowment of natural resources varies, and so do the conditions and institutions that govern the use of those resources by the poor. The question we ask, in looking at these studies, is to what extent these countries were able to harness trade to create jobs and returns to labor, in particular places, without drawing unsustainably on their natural resources. In other words, to what extent did trade contribute to genuinely sustainable development? In the context of trade liberalization, we need to look at which drivers – conditions, institutions, policies – worked positively and which did not in terms of:

1. Alleviating poverty, including increasing incomes and improving other measures of well-being such as health, access to resources and educational opportunities.
2. Protecting the environment, including both locally important environmental services, such as clean water, and global public goods, such as the climate and biodiversity.
3. Improving the relationship between the poor and the environment so the former can benefit from natural resources while managing them sustainably.
4. Promoting more equitable and inclusive resolution of trade-offs among objectives of economic growth, poverty alleviation and environmental protection.

LESSONS FROM THE CASE STUDIES

The project focused on the impacts of trade liberalization, defined here in terms of countrywide measures that facilitated the expansion of trade, as well as policy changes in other countries affecting national producers in the case study country. These measures included reduction in import and export tariffs; reductions or elimination of non-tariff barriers to imports and exports; liberalization or dismantling of foreign exchange controls and reduction or dismantling of commodity or market regulations that hinder imports and exports of goods and services. In some cases these reforms were enacted unilaterally by the national governments of the case study countries; in other cases, they were a result of multilateral (World Trade Organization, or WTO) or regional negotiations (e.g., South African Customs Union) and in still other cases, they were enacted by other countries, such as European Union (EU) reforms, with important impacts on the international markets in which the case study countries participate.

Neither the environmental nor the social impacts of these trade "events" could be isolated from other socioeconomic changes occurring in the case study countries. Trade liberalization is part and parcel of a package of economic reforms enacted in many developing countries in recent years, and it relates directly to the broader impacts of globalization. Likewise, trade liberalization is always part of a tapestry of economic, institutional, social and ecological changes within a given country, such as demographic trends, democratization, changing balance of government supports for agriculture and industry, and expanding environmental regulations. These surrounding events as well as the particular economic, social and environmental institutions and conditions in each place substantially shape the outcomes of trade liberalization.

The 3×M approach, in conjunction with the MA framework, provides a useful tool for teasing out the role played by these various indirect drivers at different levels in shaping the outcomes of specific trade policies. The local effects of a particular trade policy may be shaped by intervening factors at various levels – for example, the investments of an international company, national policies on irrigation and local land-distribution rules. Cascading impacts are common, meaning that results on the ground may be quite distant from the initial driver and that similar trade events can have very different impacts in different places, depending on the other indirect drivers at work. For example, rapid economic growth in the coastal regions of China, largely driven by exports, has led to beneficial changes in agricultural production patterns in the remote, mountainous regions of Yunnan Province, which has begun to provide agricultural goods to the coast and to neighboring countries. In Madagascar's spiny forest, changing markets for corn led to migration and the opening of new lands for agriculture. In Chile the expansion of the export salmon industry, sparked by initial government investments in research, has displaced some artisanal fisheries but provided many new jobs. In each of these cases, a cascading series of events had impacts on poverty and sustainability that were not adequately anticipated as trade liberalization went forward.

Although it is difficult to isolate the impacts of trade liberalization, given its interactions with other policies and socioeconomic changes and the cascading nature of effects, there are some valuable observations we can make based on these six case studies. The next three sections examine the role of trade as a direct driver in shaping environmental and poverty outcomes and in shaping the relationship between the environment and poverty. The following sections examine the role of trade policy as an indirect driver, in conjunction with other indirect drivers, in shaping opportunities and constraints on the poor, and in terms of efforts to protect vulnerable places and ecosystem services.

TRADE AND ENVIRONMENT

Trade liberalization, whether rooted in national policy or imposed by changes in international markets, induces changes in rural production patterns. Changes in trade policy, along with accompanying economic changes, were generally successful in sparking the growth of natural-resource-based export sectors in the case study countries. The resulting changes in productive activities, all of which have implications for the environment, can be categorized as changes in the scale of production and the speed of change in production patterns, in the composition or structure of production and in production technology. These all entail effects on the sustainability of ecosystem services, both locally and at an aggregate level. The changes affect ecosystems through the intensification of resource use, conversion of ecosystems and abandonment of managed lands. In many of the cases, expanding commercial sectors replaced traditional resource-based activities; in others, new economic activities drew on a new set of natural resources. The following paragraphs discuss examples from the case studies.

Scale and Speed of Change

Large areas of existing agricultural land and natural habitat were converted to new crops as market opportunities arose, often at a remarkable pace. The speed and scale of change were particularly notable, since in all these cases growth was driven by small producers. In Vietnam, shrimp production expanded very rapidly, with exports to the United States increasing fivefold in just three years. Much of the land devoted to shrimp ponds was converted from rice paddies (which were previously converted from mangrove forests). Thus, despite a great increase in the scale of production, the direct conversion of mangrove ecosystems was fairly limited. However, the scale of shrimp production now makes the Ca Mau region vulnerable to shrimp epidemics. Moreover, the land may now be useless for other agricultural production because of salinization and contamination from the shrimp ponds, meaning should the shrimp market collapse, the land could not be converted back to rice paddies. In southwestern Madagascar, rapid conversion of large areas of spiny forest to corn production contributed substantially to the loss of that unique ecosystem.

In both cases the speed with which change took place left little time for environmental monitoring, adaptation or management for sustainability. In Vietnam, shrimp production techniques have now been largely adapted to local conditions, but only after failed experimentation with more intensive methods. In Madagascar, the corn boom-and-bust cycle was over before an effort could be made to protect the forest. Thus, changes in trade policy have been important because of the extent to which natural landscapes were affected and because they caused such rapid changes that environmental policy could not keep pace.

Composition of Production

Changes in the composition of production driven by trade liberalization also have important environmental implications. In South Africa, changing global sugar markets are expected to drive an expansion of sugar, a crop that draws unsustainably on the Incomati Basin's very limited water supplies. In Vietnam, government-mandated rice production has been replaced by production of shrimp for export. As demand for paddy land has decreased, efforts are being made to combine production of shrimp with restoration of the mangrove forests. In Chile, forest plantations replaced annual crops with some positive implications for soil erosion. And in China, trade has brought a beneficial diversification away from land-intensive crops, reducing pressure on natural habitats. Because such changes in the composition of production alter the environmental impacts of production, they can contribute to the conservation of important places or hasten their degradation.

Production Technology

The technology used for production of natural-resource-based products affects the efficiency of resource use, the extent of pollution and other impacts on natural resources and environmental services. Technology is differentially available to different people. The cases examined here largely dealt with smallholders with only limited access to modern technologies. In some cases this had few environmental impacts and, in others, aggravated them. While the shift from rice to shrimp farming in India, as in Vietnam, did not destroy additional mangroves, the technology used has been problematic. Collection of wild shrimp larvae in the Sundarbans is reducing local biodiversity levels through substantial bycatch of other species. But in Madagascar, contract farmers producing green beans have learned about composting, which has positive effects for all their crops and may reduce pressure to open new agricultural lands.

Multiple Environmental Impacts

These production changes have both discrete, or local, environmental impacts as well as aggregate environmental implications because of the scale on which change is occurring in places of environmental importance. A couple of examples follow.

The rapid development of the Chilean salmon industry does not appear to have had serious environmental consequences as yet, in part because the area directly affected is still small. Nevertheless, the deposition of food, feces and antibiotics in the immediate area of the "cage shadow" has been associated with a 50 percent drop in biodiversity. Regionally, escaped salmon may compete with other predator species and reduce stocks of local fish. And at a global level, the expansion of the salmon industry contributes to the over-exploitation of pelagic fish used for the fishmeal and fish oil needed to support salmon production.

The development of the Chilean forestry industry has had mixed environmental results. Plantations established on degraded agricultural land may reduce local erosion, provide some habitat for biodiversity (though clearly not comparable to the natural forest) and, at an aggregate level, contribute to carbon dioxide sequestration. Yet, where natural forest has been replaced by exotic plantations, there is a major loss in biodiversity and perhaps other environmental services. The impacts of intensive plantation management, including watershed impacts from road construction and harvesting as well as the application of pesticides, are still being debated.

These changes in scale, speed, composition and technology have in some cases been associated with improved management of resource use and in others are clearly unsustainable. Most often, the changes bring some environmental degradation but with some clear benefits in terms of increased production and income. These trade-offs are being made, however, with very limited knowledge of the environmental implications. The key question is thus whether trade-offs among economic growth, poverty alleviation and environmental sustainability are being made with adequate information about long-term sustainability and with equitable participation by potentially affected stakeholders.

TRADE AND POVERTY

Poverty was understood in these case studies as a broad range of conditions that reduce human well-being and lead to greater vulnerability, including lack of income, health care, education and political voice. Data restrictions, however, limited most of the analysis to considering basic measures of income, income equality and employment. While these are not the only poverty or vulnerability measures that could be used, they are usually indicative of other measures of well-being. Trade liberalization is associated in these six cases with both increases and decreases in income among the poor, with positive and negative changes in income inequality and security of income, and likewise with both new employment opportunities and loss of traditional livelihoods. Unfortunately, analysis of the health, social, cultural and vulnerability effects is more limited and purely qualitative in these studies.

Incomes and Equality

In terms of income changes, South Africa offers a representative case. Expansion of the market for sugar has created economic opportunities for some small-scale black farmers who, under apartheid, had none. However, the poorest among the black population remain landless, benefiting only marginally from increases in the use of hired labor. The result is an increase in inequality, a problem that is common to a number of these case studies. Likewise, in Chile, the expansion of the forestry sector has created new jobs for skilled labor but has left indigenous communities out of economic growth as the viability of subsistence agriculture decreases. The Chilean salmon industry, in contrast, has created a number of unskilled jobs. This has attracted more people to the region, with the result that local unemployment has actually increased even as jobs were created. In India, small landowners have profited greatly from the expansion of shrimp exports; and the landless poor have participated through the collection of shrimp larvae. But this opportunity has hardly offered the poorest an escape from economic poverty and has worsened health conditions.

Vietnam presents a more dramatic case. In the Ca Mau region of Vietnam, local incomes are now 20 percent above the national average and 8.5 percent above the average for the Mekong Delta region. New jobs have been created not only on shrimp farms but also in seafood processing plants, hatcheries and a number of associated small businesses involved with shrimp collection and transport, including many jobs for women and unskilled laborers. Similarly, in the Pingbian region of China the poverty incidence has fallen by some 10 percent in recent years as new markets have opened, and equity has increased even as it has worsened in the rest of the country.

Instability

The changes induced by trade liberalization have in many cases increased both economic and social instability for the poor – that is, increased their vulnerability, even as new opportunities are created. Increased exposure to markets can lead to higher economic risk if there are insufficient safety nets and appropriate policies and institutions are lacking. This trade-off between stability and higher incomes may be considered politically acceptable, but the risk must be recognized and given due consideration. The case of corn production in Madagascar – which expanded rapidly in response to an opportunity to export to Ile de la Réunion and collapsed equally rapidly – clearly illustrates the volatility that can afflict export markets. In Vietnam the remarkable expansion of shrimp production, based on exports to the United States, has been threatened by US trade sanctions. On the other hand, new opportunities can increase stability. Contract farmers producing green beans in Madagascar appreciate the stable income that their relationship with Lecofruit affords them.

Rapid economic change is also associated with social instability, which can lead to environmental degradation. In the case of corn production in Madagascar, the large number of migrants to the spiny forest region probably contributed to the breakdown of traditional resource management systems and thus to the loss of the forest. In Chile, new land uses have put pressure on the Mapuche people's traditional resource uses.

Economic Opportunities

Trade has afforded new opportunities to the poor by giving the natural resources to which they have access a new or increased value. In India, the expansion of shrimp production has turned wild shrimp larvae into a valuable resource that is accessible to the poorest. In Vietnam, small land-holdings formerly under rice became much more profitable under shrimp. And in China, the opening of new markets allowed a shift in production to more profitable and labor-intensive crops, increasing the productive value of land and labor, even in remote Pingbian. However, the value of the resources held by the poor likewise may decline in the face of new markets. In Chile, the growth of the forestry industry has reduced the viability of subsistence farming. Most commonly, vulnerable people do not have access to the resources necessary to take advantage of new opportunities – including natural resources, capital, market access, education, and so on. This issue is considered in greater detail below.

LINKS BETWEEN TRADE, POVERTY AND ENVIRONMENT

By affecting economic opportunities for the poor and their access to natural resources, trade affects the relationship between poverty and environment, sometimes for better, sometimes for worse. There are "win–win" situations in which trade has created new opportunities for the poor that have also contributed to more sustainable use of environmental resources. But in many of the cases, trade has heightened pressure on vulnerable people and places. Vulnerable people have no control over the national and global policies that shape their world and few options in terms of how they earn their livelihoods. In the face of a trade-off between providing for basic needs today and protecting resources for the future, there is no real choice.

The cases illustrate a variety of trade-offs made between economic growth and long-term sustainability in the face of changing trade policies, ranging from "win–win" to "lose–lose" situations. In China, the shift from land-intensive to labor-intensive crops among the Miao people clearly had positive impacts for both the environment and incomes. More common were "win–lose" situations. In the Sundarbans, the shrimp industry greatly improved economic prospects for those with access to land and, for the poorest people, created a more stable source of income through shrimp-larvae collection – but at a substantial cost to biodiversity in the region. In South Africa, some small farmers are benefiting. Yet the poorest have not only been left out of sugar production but also are likely to suffer from the worsening water shortage as the sugar industry increases its demand for water. Farmers downstream in Mozambique are also likely to suffer.

The Madagascar case offers two polar examples. Corn production led to extensive environmental damage, as the poor rushed to take advantage of an apparent opportunity – but it created few long-term benefits for the poor. In the case of green beans, on the other hand, producers have ben-efited not only from steady incomes but increased production of all crops as a result of improved environmental management. Chile also offers two different examples. Growth of the salmon industry created new jobs and added considerably to national income. The forestry industry, however, did not create jobs for the poor and contributed to the decline of subsist-ence agriculture; but it has provided some, perhaps limited, environmental benefits as well as national income. Finally, shrimp production in Vietnam provided substantial income improvements for the poor, but at the cost of greater vulnerability and risk, including environmental risk.

In most of these cases, the country faced a trade-off between participa-tion in new markets and sustainable management of natural resources. Not surprisingly, the trade-off was usually made in favor of national economic growth, only sometimes with the benefit of improving local socioeconomic conditions, and usually at the expense of vulnerable ecosystems.

Whether the relationship between the poor and the environment improved or worsened – whether the poorest contributed more or less to the sustainability of the ecosystem – depended on indirect drivers at the local (micro), national (meso) and global (macro) scales.

Local to Local

Local decisions were shaped by local institutions governing access to natural resources, such as the *panchayats* and tribal authorities who granted land in the Sundarbans and Incomati River Basin, respectively. Local decisions were also shaped by the intervention of private firms, as in the case of green beans in Madagascar, the development of which depended entirely on the role of the Lecofruit company with its access to knowledge and markets.

National to Local

Local decisions were shaped by national programs and institutions, such as government investments in aquaculture research in Chile that demonstrated the feasibility of salmon farming and provided a model for local enterprises; extension work in India that encouraged local shrimp production; and, conversely, the withdrawal of government rice production mandates in Vietnam that opened the way for shrimp production. Local decisions are also shaped by other national changes, such as the end of apartheid in South Africa that led to new opportunities and programs for small farmers; democratization in Chile that increased the voice of local people in resource-use decisions; and the broad opening of the Vietnamese economy that led to a fundamental expansion of the rights of communities to make decisions about resource use.

Global to Local

Local decisions were shaped by global trends and changes in markets and institutions governing trade, such as competition from Argentina that contributed to the collapse of Madagascar's corn exports; the growth of shrimp consumption in developed countries that drove production expansion in India and Vietnam; and changes in European Union sugar policies potentially affecting South Africa's sugar production.

The outcome of interactions among these layers of drivers for the environment and the poor depends in large part on the poor's access to and control over the natural resources that are essential for them to participate in new opportunities in global or regional markets. Their ability to improve their incomes and general well-being, without seriously increasing the risks they face, depends on their ability to manage their resources. This includes employing their resources in new ways and selling their products in new or existing markets in order to support local development. The factors affecting this ability are explored below.

DEVELOPMENT PATHWAYS: CRITICAL FACTORS SHAPING TRADE–POVERTY–ENVIRONMENT LINKS

The studies explore a great variety of indirect drivers that affect the ability of vulnerable people to benefit from natural resources and to maintain essential environmental services in the face of changes in the trade regime. The outcomes depend not on trade policy alone, but on how trade policy combines with many other indirect drivers. Together, these determine who uses environmental services, for what purposes, what the results are for the poor and the environment, and the relationship between the two. These are the factors that determine whether a development path is chosen – for a country or a particular place – that balances economic growth with environmental sustainability and social equity. Of these, three important factors, all of which shape the ability of the poor to take advantage of new economic opportunities while protecting environmental services, are explored here. They are (1) the nature of different economic sectors; (2) resource governance; and (3) resources of the poor. These factors are of particular importance because they can be shaped by government policies and by the development of institutions designed to improve the opportunities created by trade and reduce damage by improving the decisions made about trade-offs.

NATURE OF THE ECONOMIC SECTOR

The nature of the export sector is important to shaping resource use, sustainability and job creation and thus the poverty–environment impacts of trade. Thus, the choice of exported product matters immensely.

Natural Resource Requirements of the Export Product

The particular resource requirements of each product dictate, to an extent, its environmental impacts. For example, production of sugar requires relatively large quantities of water. In South Africa, where water is scarce in many places, the use of water for sugar production limits the amount available not only for other productive activities but also for human consumption and for the maintenance of environmental services. Likewise, shrimp production requires saline ponds. In Vietnam and India the conversion of rice paddies to shrimp ponds is believed to limit the future possibility of producing agricultural crops on those lands. In Madagascar, the simple demand for increased agricultural land drove destruction of the spiny forest. But in Chile, some tree plantations have restored degraded land, although not to its original state. And in China, a shift to horticultural crops has reduced the overall demand for agricultural land.

Labor Requirements of the Export Product

Different products have different labor requirements, depending in part on the choice of technology. In Chile the forestry and salmon sectors, which both expanded under liberalization, had very different consequences for job creation. While forestry created relatively few jobs, and those were largely for skilled laborers, the salmon sector created relatively more jobs, including many for women and unskilled laborers. Moreover, the salmon sector created other opportunities through a variety of linkages with the local economy, which began to supply food and other inputs. The Mapuche indigenous people who live in the forestry region have not bene-fited from the forest sector's expansion; in contrast, the salmon-producing regions have supported substantial in-migration, in part because of the development of associated economic activities, although the livelihoods of artisanal fishermen have been affected. The creation of local eco-nomic linkages was very important in several other cases. In India, the shrimp-seed-harvesting sector provided incomes to many poor people. In Vietnam, local linkages also developed well, creating many associated jobs for the landless and land-poor. Other export sectors fail to develop local linkages, instead forming part of an international value chain, with ancil-lary jobs created elsewhere. This was the case with corn in Madagascar as well as Chilean forestry.

International Market Characteristics

The nature of the international market for a product is also important in shaping local poverty–environment outcomes, although it may seem far removed from them. The rapid growth of the world market for shrimp has supported a dramatic expansion of production in India and Vietnam. International demand for high-quality horticulture products has sup-ported the growth of a labor-intensive industry in Madagascar and China. The distorted nature of the international sugar market has allowed South Africa to maintain a substantial market share despite world oversupply. The boom-and-bust cycle of corn production in the spiny forest region of Madagascar – disastrous for both the environment and the producers – was driven in part by Madagascar's inability to compete internationally in terms of volume and transport costs.

Capital, Technology and Standards

This last case –Madagascar – illustrates the ways in which capital and technology investments shape a country's ability to compete in the global marketplace. Participation in international markets often favors or even requires certain forms of production. Increasingly, these tend to be capital and technology intensive, which is not what developing countries have to offer. The effect is to make participation difficult, and when countries do successfully participate, thanks to investments in technology, they are likely to draw on their natural resources without creating many jobs or opportunities for the poor. Such is the case in the Chilean forestry sector.

International market requirements and foreign direct investment, however, can have positive impacts. The standards for such products as shrimp and green beans exported from India and Madagascar can improve the sustainability of production practices. However, these standards tend to favor wealthier countries and larger producers that can invest in the necessary technology. And they can exclude participation by small producers and even small countries unable to make the necessary investments, thus reducing the possibilities of poverty reduction and aggravating inequality.[5] Many producers in these studies portrayed these standards as barriers to market entry, particularly when they change frequently, although the overall impact was unclear.

Competitive Advantage

As a result of these various requirements of the international market, the export sector chosen for expansion depends on a variety of factors that may or may not relate to labor or natural resource availability, but rather to installed infrastructure, existing access to markets, capital and technology requirements and support from the government or private sector. In other words, the choice depends on competitive advantage (the relative ability to compete) rather than comparative advantage (the relative endowment of resources). In China, the shift to horticulture was driven not only by national growth but also by proximity to the border with Vietnam. In South Africa, established markets for sugar, existing infrastructure, the failure to price water rationally and government price supports all contributed to the choice of a crop that is environmentally irrational. In Madagascar, corn production expanded in reaction to perceived access to Ile de la Réunion markets, access that proved to be elusive because of the lack of appropriate infrastructure and capital investment. Green bean production succeeded, however, in large part because the company owner had contacts in the European market. Finally, in Chile, government support for forestry development and for basic research on salmon production fostered the growth of two industries with very different social and environmental impacts.

RESOURCE GOVERNANCE

Governance occurs at different levels and with different objectives and concerns as a result. Institutions – including both formal institutions such as government agencies and informal institutions such as markets – create constraints and opportunities for different groups of people. National, regional and local institutions play a fundamental role in shaping the trade-offs between growth and sustainability, growth and equity and between different environmental services, trade-offs that almost inevitably accompany changes in the scale, composition or structure of production. Equitable and participatory institutions allow stakeholders with a shared interest in the use or conservation of ecosystem services to recognize and negotiate the trade-offs. But many institutions simply mirror societal patterns of political and economic power and privilege, leaving vulnerable ecosystems and the poor, who most directly depend on the maintenance of environmental services, out of the decision-making process. It may be national or local public institutions or private firms that determine who has access to resources, for what purposes and within what limitations. Market institutions play a key role, as discussed above, but so do traditional institutions and governments.

Institutions and Access to Resources

Many of the factors that shape the development of export sectors and their environmental impacts are rooted in the institutions that govern natural resources (land, water, biodiversity, fisheries and forests). Control over distribution of land was important in many of the cases. In South Africa, India and Vietnam, the poor with some access to land were able to improve their lot, while the landless were largely unable to reap the benefits of economic growth. Institutions responsible for distribution of land tended to reinforce or even aggravate existing inequalities in these countries, as in India where *panchayats* favored existing landowners, and South Africa, where a new class of black small farmers was favored over the landless. But this need not be the case. In China, the government relocated families from steep mountain slopes to more productive lands closer to transport and other services.

Traditional institutional arrangements for resource access and management have tended to break down as new economic opportunities arose, heightening pressures on resources. In Madagascar's spiny forest, deforestation was lowest where there were traditional community management systems in place; but the influx of migrants appears to have led to the breakdown of these systems. Moreover, some of the traditional informal institutions for control of resource use, such as the establishment of ownership through clearing, probably aggravated deforestation. Some efforts to reconstitute community management, such as the Gelose[6] program in Madagascar, have had some success.

Governments and Environmental Regulations

Government institutions clearly play a key role in shaping access to resources, providing incentives for different uses, determining which stakeholders have a voice and creating and enforcing environmental controls. In a number of the cases, governments actively intervened to support the development of natural-resource-based export sectors. In Vietnam, rules on land use were changed to support the expansion of the shrimp industry. The Indian government also backed shrimp producers, for example, through the provision of nets. The Chilean government supported some of the initial research on salmon production that fostered growth of the industry. While these interventions were not primarily aimed at the poor, they did contribute to the expansion of these new industries and the associated employment.

Most governmental efforts to support sustainability have come in reaction to rapid or acute degradation of resources. Environmental regulations were enacted once a problem became severe, rather than in anticipation of degradation of environmental services. The National Water Act in South Africa is a promising example of institutional response to resource scarcity. The act offers a very comprehensive regulatory framework to allocate water-use rights. In the context of democratization it proposes to limit the role of the large sugar millers while giving small farmers an important voice and providing for the sustainability of environmental services. However, implementation of this exemplary act may be stymied by entrenched interests in the sugar industry. In India, for lack of appropriate environmental institutions, the high court intervened to outlaw highly intensive shrimp production when the environmental costs became evident. In China, decentralization has allowed local governing bodies and individuals to make more appropriate decisions about resource use. At the same time, environmental laws designed to protect watersheds, such as the Grain for Green program, have limited forest clearance and supported participating farmers. But in Vietnam, environmental regulations on the percentage of land to be kept in mangroves have not been enforced and, moreover, are not well designed to protect biodiversity, since they promote forest fragmentation.

Non-governmental institutions may also play an important role. In Madagascar, in the absence of adequate government agricultural extension services, a private firm has played a critical role in improving the lot of small farmers by providing training and financial support. And in Vietnam, again in the absence of appropriate enforcement of existing laws and policies, international market requirements combined with local experience have driven the use of more environmentally sound techniques, though only after substantial economic and environmental losses.

In some of these cases, it might have been possible to anticipate new pressures on the environment that were likely to accompany the trade events. (In fact, the South African case study is intended to be predictive.) But a lack of environmental impact assessments and, more generally, a lack of monitoring have meant that institutions have responded only when pressures became severe. Likewise, incremental, long-term environmental damage in the places studied is largely unmonitored. This is true, to a greater or lesser extent, in every case: in Madagascar where outside trade events dramatically affected a rare ecosystem; in India, where there are no viable alternatives to collection of shrimp larvae from the wild; and in Chile, where expansion of the salmon industry is contributing to a global drawdown of ocean resources.

RESOURCES OF THE POOR

The poor's access to and control over natural resources is a key factor in their ability to take advantage of new economic opportunities. Their access to other types of resources, such as education, training and finance, is also relevant. Too often, the poorest are not able to take advantage of opportunities and, having lost out to those who can, find themselves with even more restricted options. Notably, the most vulnerable people are generally those without access to land, especially productive land – and the development of successful export sectors in no way solved this problem. In Vietnam and India, access to land was critical for participation in shrimp production. Moreover, those with more land did substantially better. In the case of Vietnam, the reason was clearly that they were better able to tolerate the risk of a lost harvest. Those with only a small amount of land were more likely to diversify their production, which reduced risk but also lowered incomes. In South Africa, the shortages of available land and water are reported by farmers across the board as problems; however, the poorest report lack of land as their primary problem.

Population pressures played a role in several of the cases, notably China, where the government played an active role in reallocating natural resources; India, where the poorest have no access to land; and Madagascar, where migration has led to the opening of new agricultural land. Successful development of new opportunities, as in Chile's salmon sector, inevitably led to an influx of migrants looking for work. Cultural factors, however, tend to prevent or at least slow this type of migration. The Mapuche in Chile, for example, remain tied to their traditional lands despite the worsening prospects for subsistence agriculture. Likewise, in China, despite the relocation of upland communities, local ethnic ties are strong and prevent large-scale migration to the coastal regions. These community ties can play a positive role in fostering sustainable resource use. However, in Madagascar, where local traditions were disrupted by an influx of migrants, traditional resource management systems broke down.

Not only access to the necessary resources for production, but also access to markets is critical for the poor. The difficulty of participating in international markets is illustrated by the case of corn production in Madagascar. There, corn exports ultimately failed because poor farmers could not produce on the necessary scale or provide the transport needed to compete with more developed countries. The success story of green beans illustrates the rare conditions in which these vulnerable places can participate in international markets. Green bean exports have succeeded because Lecofruit was able to negotiate the international market requirements (standards, transport, contacts) on behalf of the farmers and has provided direct support to them to develop production.

For many small farmers, local and regional markets may be more important, and are often more accessible, than international export markets. The South African study points out that the best opportunities for local sugar exports are likely to be with other African countries through regional trade agreements. In China, the development of new local and regional markets accessible to the poor has boosted local incomes and improved the use of environmental services.

The very poor and indigenous or ethnic groups are often left out of political and economic processes – further reinforcing their vulnerability. Consequently they are unable to govern the resources they depend on or take advantage of new opportunities. Trade-offs are made between human well-being and the use of resources for economic growth without the participation of some of the most affected people. Yet these people live in some of the most valuable places in the world, when we consider the biodiversity and environmental services there.

CONCLUSIONS AND RECOMMENDATIONS

In our analysis of these studies, a focus on the effects of trade liberalization on vulnerable people and places has clearly shown that important trade-offs are being made without knowledge or consideration of the needs of the poor or of the capacity of the environment to support particular paths of development. Trade can provide a strong impetus to economic growth and can therefore play a positive role in development. But the local impacts vary considerably from the aggregate impacts. Debate about the impacts of trade must shift away from a focus on aggregates and on incomes to look at the effects on particular people and places. Like most spurs to economic growth, trade does not necessarily create the kind of targeted or managed growth that addresses the needs of the poor or that incorporates the true cost of environmental services. The people most detrimentally affected are among the poorest of the poor, many of whom rely heavily on natural resources – traditional agriculture and fisheries, forest products, wildlife – for their livelihoods.

Trade liberalization sits squarely at the center of the current development paradigm and is a recurring component in poverty reduction programs of both national governments and the international development community in recent years. For many developing countries, trade liberalization has been equated with a push for agricultural and other resource-based exports. This is evident in the prominence of export-driven trade approaches in development assistance packages – even as many developing countries have begun to question the presumed pathway from trade liberalization to development. Agricultural exports in particular have been expected to play a key role in poverty reduction. Yet an expansion of agricultural exports most often requires large-scale production, capital investments and technology that prohibit participation by the most vulnerable populations and that put heavy pressures on the environment. This approach to development fails to recognize the limitations faced by smallholders and the importance of safeguarding environmental services, in part because of their direct contribution to existing livelihoods.

We have seen also from these studies that trade liberalization, by increasing the role of non-local markets, can profoundly affect relationships between the poor and the environment. The viability of local markets and of existing economic relationships among the rural poor may be affected. To better understand what is happening, greater attention must be paid to the role of outside investment, including foreign direct investment, and vertical supply chains, which may undercut local markets while also further limiting the ability of smallholders to participate in international markets. While many recommendations about reform of the trade system focus on the need to bring smallholders further into international markets, it must be recognized that many of the rural poor have little competitive advantage in this market. Their opportunities lie more often in local or regional markets where scale and technology are less important. Thus, greater attention should be paid to the role of these markets and to the ability of the rural poor to participate in them, rather than to the expansion of international exports. A focus on local markets should allow for greater development of backward and forward linkages, a necessary component of development that was achieved in only a few of our case studies. A local focus should also promote local capital accumulation and investment, rather than just an increase in some incomes, as a way to support local development and improved well-being. It should also promote the creation of new off-farm and urban employment, eventually moving people off marginal lands and reducing environmental pressures.

Addressing the needs of vulnerable people and places will require a rethinking of today's development paradigm, which has been largely built on premises about the role of economic growth that have not held true for many people and that have made growth a goal in itself at the expense of development. Human well-being – rather than rising exports, national economic growth or even higher incomes – must be the primary goal of development strategies. Increasingly, we are coming to understand the fundamental role that biodiversity and environmental services play in supporting human well-being. This role makes it essential that sustainable development become standard practice and not just a buzzword. It is time for an open discussion of better ways to address the needs of smallholders and other vulnerable rural people, and consideration of a new development paradigm, in the context of our interaction with the environment.

Our recommendations here focus on some particular interventions and changes that global actors, multilateral and bilateral donors, national governments and conservation organizations can make that would support more beneficial outcomes from trade liberalization, and from globalization more generally, for the poor and the environment. These changes should help refocus the goal of development from economic growth to sustainable improvements in human well-being through increases in the resources of the poor, improvements in resource governance and greater attention to development paths.

Global Actors

International trade negotiations have bogged down in recent years in part because of the perceived lack of adequate "policy space" for developing countries. Policy space is described as the ability of developing countries to make domestic policy as they see best, without being unnecessarily restricted by the rules of international trade agreements. The concern about policy space implies that the developing countries have lacked power in the trade negotiating process. This understanding of the problem is rooted in the widespread perception that trade is not solving the problems of poverty or environmental degradation in developing countries in part because the rich countries have had control of the process. Based on what we have learned from these studies about the effects of trade liberalization, giving the developing countries policy space as well as a stronger role in the negotiations should mean more than special tariff treatment or giving them the power to "say no" to free trade. It must mean ensuring that the negotiations are transparent and that the participating countries are well informed not only about the macro-level benefits of trade liberalization but also about the likely local impacts on the poor and on the environment – on vulnerable places and peoples. This information would allow developing countries to decide to what extent, and at what speed, they want to participate in liberalization in order to best promote sustainable development under the particular conditions they face.

Development assistance in recent years has emphasized "aid for trade," mostly as a way to increase and facilitate exports. In these studies, we have seen that a variety of factors affect the ability of vulnerable places to participate effectively in international and regional markets. Given the importance of investing in appropriate productive sectors, in providing for resource governance and in building up the resources of the poor, we recommend broadening the definition of aid for trade and the scope of aid-for-trade initiatives. To more effectively ensure that trade expansion leads to positive results, aid for trade should focus on the possibilities of trade to generate jobs and reduce poverty, address the needs of smallholders and other vulnerable people and support investment in public goods, including environmental services. For example, it could include research and investment into sectors that have good sustainable development possibilities; support creation of the competitive advantage that these places need, for example, through education and market links; and support expanded participation in local and regional markets, rather than focusing exclusively on international markets. Aid for trade could also support early analysis of impacts and the development of appropriate social and environmental institutions and safeguards, as well as assisting with ex post facto analysis of environmental and social change.

Governments

This chapter has discussed three factors of great importance in shaping the way in which trade liberalization affects poverty and environmental outcomes: the nature of the economic sector, resource governance and the resources of the poor. Addressing these areas through government policy can improve the results of trade liberalization. First, by better

understanding the nature of different economic sectors and their requirements in terms of natural resources, labor and investment and the ability
of a country to successfully compete in international markets, donors and
governments can choose to invest in research, infrastructure, training or
other needs for the most appropriate sectors. Second, the way in which
natural resources are governed will determine not only whether they are
used sustainably, but also who will benefit from their use. By ensuring that
appropriate governance mechanisms are in place – not only from the point
of view of environmental sustainability but also equitable development –
donors and governments can improve the results of the trade-offs made
as new economic opportunities arise. And third, addressing the needs of
poor rural communities that go beyond income, such as health, education,
access to markets and involvement with national institutions, will allow
communities to make better long-term decisions about resource use and
contribute to a shift toward more sustainable development paths.

While some of these cases illustrated win–win situations in which both
the environment and the poor benefited under trade liberalization, in
most cases trade-offs were made without due consideration of the needs of
the poor or the environment. There is a clear need for strong institutions
linking local stakeholders to national institutions and for formal institutions that will act as a voice for the environment. South Africa's National
Water Act provides a good model for designing an institution that gives
due consideration to the requirements of development and environmental sustainability. Such institutions would allow for the identification
of options that will better address development needs though ongoing
adjustments and responses to trade-induced change, as well as direct
engagement with the trade policy regime. Responses and adjustments that
could support sustainable development would include changes in government policies and regulations, land-use planning, improvements in private
sector practices and capacity building.

Policy makers will need to look at the nesting of local, regional, national
and international factors affecting policy outcomes when designing trade
policies and other policies that may affect vulnerable places and peoples.
These studies have shown clearly that these outcomes are the result of
complex interactions among a great variety of social, economic and environmental factors. Solving the problems that occur at the local level can
only be achieved by understanding and addressing those problems in the
larger context in which they occur. The 3×M methodology used in this
chapter provides an initial tool for moving toward this comprehensive
approach.

Finally, given the limited information available about ecosystem
requirements for sustainability, and even basic data on the current status

of ecosystems, the precautionary principle should play a central role in the design of policies that are likely to affect local and global environmental services. This includes trade policies, development policies and agricultural policies, among others, as well as natural resource policies. Environmental impact assessments and strategic vulnerability assessments can provide an important tool in this regard (Stedman-Edwards, 2005). Early warning of possible negative impacts and early recognition of potential opportunities could allow countries (with targeted support from international institutions and donors) to put in place the necessary social and environmental institutions and safeguards to ensure that policy changes promote sustainable development and protect vulnerable places and peoples. The existing literature provides the necessary tools for anticipating most changes, but this is done formally in very few cases. Governments and civil society should expect use of the precautionary principle and early assessments to ensure that policies, planning and development decisions recognize the full value of environmental services and the role that vulnerable peoples play in protecting them.

Conservation Community

While the conservation community has been working extensively in vulnerable places for many years, these studies strongly reinforce the fact that we need to work with the vulnerable people in those places for long-term protection of ecosystems. Smallholders and indigenous communities (whether poor or not) own, manage or have access to many of these places, and the pressures they face and the decisions they make in the face of changing economic opportunities greatly affect the environmental outcomes. Many model projects related to rural livelihoods, sustainable agriculture and natural resource management have been developed, but too many of these failed to recognize that the outcomes in vulnerable places are shaped by events and policies at the regional, national and international levels. As a result, these projects have not often been economically sustainable or successfully expanded. Intervening to solve problems in vulnerable places must be done with the cognizance that, while problems occur locally and are often specific to place, they are often driven by regional and global forces. Solutions will need to be found at all levels, from local to global, in order to remove the obstacles to sustainable development.

Some environmental organizations have recently shifted the focus of their work around agriculture issues toward large-scale, commercial operations, particularly multinational operations. This approach is an important component of an integrated approach to reducing the environmental impacts of agriculture, but it does not take account of the continued importance of smallholders. Small farmers still account for the majority of agricultural activity in many of the world's most important and threatened ecosystems. Their impacts, when aggregated across a critical landscape, can be significant. Thus, they can be a major contributor to environmental problems or a powerful ally in reducing them. Conservation groups should take this into account when designing programs and partnerships.

These studies looked specifically at the impacts of trade liberalization, but the basic issues that they reveal are relevant to many other events affecting vulnerable places and peoples today. The need for transparency about impacts can only be met with greater information. The need to give the poor and the environment a voice in the decisions that determine development paths applies not only to trade policy but also to other economic and social changes. Ensuring that the environment and the poor are given due consideration, and recognizing that trade-offs are an inevitable part of development, are fundamental to the support of more sustainable development paths that will allow these vulnerable places, along with the people who depend on their diverse resources, to thrive as the world continues to change.

NOTES

1. See Ackerman (2005); Wise and Gallagher (2007); Polaski (2006); and World Bank (2005).
2. It is important to recognize that benefits have not only been unevenly distributed within countries, but also among developing countries. The lion's share of trade benefits has gone to a small set of developing countries, namely China, India, Mexico, Russia, South Africa and South Korea (UNCTAD, 2008). While developing countries increased their share of world trade threefold between 1995 and 2005, almost all this growth was accounted for by China and the newly industrializing countries; the export share of the 50 least-developed countries, primarily commodity-dependent countries of sub-Saharan Africa, fell from 2.5 percent in 1960 to just 0.8 percent by 2006 (UNCTAD, 2008).
3. See Reed (1996, 2004, 2006a, 2006b); and Wood et al. (2000).
4. See Sen (2002); Winters et al. (2004); and Ostrom (2005).
5. IMF (2007).
6. Gelose stands for Gestion local securisée des resources renouvelables.

REFERENCES

Ackerman, F. (2005), "The shrinking gains from trade: a critical assessment of Doha Round projections", Working Paper 5-01, Global Development and Environment Institute, Tufts University.

International Monetary Fund (IMF) (2007), *World Economic Outlook, October 2007: Globalization and Inequality*, Washington, DC: IMF.

Millennium Ecosystem Assessment (2003), *Ecosystems and Human Well-being: A Framework for Assessment*, Washington, DC: Island Press.

Ostrom, E. (2005), *Understanding Institutional Diversity*, Princeton, NJ: Princeton University Press.

Polaski, S. (2006), *Winners and Losers: Impact of the Doha Round on Developing Countries*, Washington, DC: Carnegie Endowment for International Peace.

Reed, D. (1996), *Structural Adjustment, the Environment and Sustainable Development*, London: Earthscan.

Reed, D. (2004), *Analyzing the Political Economy of Poverty and Ecological Disruption*, Washington, DC: WWF-MPO.

Reed, D. (2006a), *Escaping Poverty's Grasp: The Environmental Foundations of Poverty Reduction*, London: Earthscan.

Reed, D. (2006b), *The 3×M Approach: Bringing Change across Micro, Meso and Macro Levels*, Washington, DC: WWF-MPO.

Sen, A. (2002), "Globalization, inequality and global protest", *Development*, **45** (2), 11–16.

Stedman-Edwards, P. (2005), *Strategic Vulnerabilities Assessment: Framework Paper*, Washington, DC: WWF-MPO.

UNCTAD (2008), *Globalization for Development: The International Trade Perspective*, New York: UNCTAD.

Winters, L., N. McCulloch and A. McKay (2004), "Trade liberalization and poverty: the evidence so far", *Journal of Economic Literature*, **XLII**, 72–115.

Wise, T. and K. Gallagher (2007), "No fast track to global poverty reduction", Policy Brief 07-02, Global Development and Environment Institute, Tufts University.

Wood, A., P. Stedman-Edwards and J. Mang (eds) (2000), *The Root Causes of Biodiversity Loss*, London: Earthscan.

World Bank (2005), *World Development Report 2006: Equity and Development*, New York: Oxford University Press.

9.   Lessons from the case studies: 2

John D. Nash and Donald F. Larson

INTRODUCTION

The lowering of trade barriers is a visible point of policy change that is often associated with broader changes in the economy and a deeper set of policy reforms. In general, poor countries undertake trade reform because it carries the potential to lessen poverty through the increased opportunities that come with open markets and economic growth. Even so, when changes in trade policy have impact, they are likely to enhance the value of some activities and diminish the value of others. This, in turn, can have important consequences for how natural resources are used and the livelihoods of the poor.

For this reason, trade policies and trade agreements are controversial and have rightly received a good deal of attention from policy makers, advocates, scientists and social scientists. As discussed in Chapter 1, the scale of research devoted to the topic across a range of disciplines is large. At the same time, outcomes from trade reforms are varied, and practical lessons found in the literature are elusive. Collectively, evidence put forward by advocates in support of particular policies often seems inconsistent and contradictory. With this as background, the studies in this volume are motivated by a desire to move the debate forward by bringing together a set of accessible, tangible examples of the relationships between global markets, local economic activity and local ecology.

The studies in this volume suggest that the reason why generalizations about how trade, poverty and the environment relate are difficult to obtain lies in the very specific and local conditions affected by trade. The individual studies from Africa, Asia and Latin America are set in places where the poor live in close proximity to important and valuable natural resources and focus on the cascading consequences that trade has on the way people interact with the environment to earn their livelihood. The studies illustrate the significance of global markets for important ecologies and the poor who depend on them. They provide insights into how people can act collectively as stewards of natural resources.

For a number of reasons, the once-remote areas in the case studies have become more closely tied with the global economy, and there are good reasons to expect that trade policies, acting through these strengthened links, will play an increasingly important role in environmental outcomes. At the same time, incentives from global markets filtered through national trade policies are one of several determinants of how people interact with the environment. A key lesson from the case studies is that this relationship between global markets and local action is complex and that outcomes are difficult to anticipate, at least partially because of the location and situation specific nature of the relations. As evidence, the studies include examples where evolving economic practices work to mitigate the pressure of growing rural populations on limited soil, water and forest resources and also provide examples of how new export-tied demands can arise along with incentives to rapidly diminish important environmental resources, sometimes in irreversible ways. More to the point, the case studies in this volume suggest that important natural resources are often undervalued and poorly safeguarded. Consequently, how these resources are used is subject to shifting incentives that often go unchecked. One implication for policy is that restrictions on trade will rarely adequately safeguard important ecologies. Moreover, in some cases, trade restrictions can speed the degradation of natural resources.

A second key finding from the studies is that the local poor often depend heavily on natural resources and sometimes exploit them in unsustainable ways. They exploit them in part because access by individuals to forest, land, water and marine resources is difficult to police, which in the aggregate contributes to overuse. More fundamentally, however, the studies suggest that the problem is rooted in the condition that poor households are drawn to and become dependent on common-pool resources because they lack the private resources needed to support better livelihoods. For policy, finding equitable ways to protect vulnerable people who rely on vulnerable habitats poses a difficult challenge.

A third major finding from the studies is that differing ecologies give rise to distinctive sets of interdependent livelihoods and markets. As a practical consequence, decisions taken locally play an important role in how natural resources are used, which in turn has ramifications for income and for the environment. For this reason, policy solutions that address the preservation of important natural resources as well as the needs of the local poor must have a component that reflects local conditions and practices. This can be problematic, since the institutions needed to do so may be weak or altogether missing.

WHAT CONSTITUTES A TRADE EVENT?

It was recognized from the beginning of this research that, with such an eclectic mix of country case studies, the definition of the trade event would need to be fairly broad. Indeed, the authors recognized that it is seldom possible to identify a single event and that what we call in shorthand "the event" is usually a sequence of policy decisions, sometimes stretching over several years, or is in some cases a whole collection of (more or less) simultaneous actions. By way of example, while World Trade Organization (WTO) membership might be viewed as the driving trade event in both China and Vietnam, the case studies point out that reform in China began with a partial liberalization of agriculture in 1978 and that the Doi Moi policies of Vietnam began in 1986.

For purposes of the discussion here, it is possible to use a two-way taxonomy of the cases, which constitutes (1) general trade liberalization of the country under study: Chile, China, India, Madagascar (horticulture), Vietnam; and (2) a trade event affecting mainly one product market: sugar in South Africa and maize in Madagascar. One could conceptually categorize the cases in other ways. One way to divide them would be into those dealing with effects of external trade events on the country under study: Madagascar (maize) and South Africa; and those dealing with the effect of a country's own trade policy decisions: all others. Yet another way to categorize the cases would be according to the drivers of the trade policy event: multilateral (WTO) agreements: China and Vietnam; unilateral policy decisions: Chile, India and Madagascar (horticulture); and policy actions external to the country under study: Madagascar (maize) and South Africa.

The latter way of looking at things may yield some interesting insights into the political economy of trade policy. But to a trade economist, the first classification scheme mentioned above is the most economically meaningful, since it basically differentiates those cases whose effects are on a general equilibrium (economy-wide) level from those whose effects are mainly partial equilibrium. Of course, in making this distinction we have to recognize that, in the real world, the division between these two classes of cases is not black and white. For example, even though new opportunities to export cash crops were direct trade-related drivers of change in China's Pingbian County, internal migration and the emergence of new domestic markets brought about by broader changes in the Chinese economy deeply affected livelihoods. And, as is suggested by the other ways of cutting the pie, each of the two categories includes examples of cases that differ in many ways from others in that category.

The trade events affecting mainly one product market are the most straightforward to conceptualize, since the linkages between the event and the specific market being studied are more direct. For example, the Madagascar maize study focuses on the effects of an external policy program in Europe – an event that opened specific opportunities for maize exports while Madagascar was undergoing a more general process of trade policy reforms, the effects of which conditioned the impact of the market-specific policies. And the South Africa study modeled the potential impact on the sugar industry of a rise in sugar prices that would result from external trade liberalization. In these cases, the link between the event and the product market being studied is direct and linear: the event causes an increase or reduction in the demand and price of the product, without significantly affecting other markets.

In cases in which the trade event was general trade liberalization, the link with the market under study is more subtle. By "general trade liber-alization" we mean a process of reducing barriers to trade more or less across the board, including import tariffs and non-tariff barriers as well as export taxes and controls. This includes dismantling or at least relaxing foreign exchange controls. Trade reform of this kind was the cornerstone of reforms in Latin America in the 1980s and 1990s, as illustrated by the case study on Chile, and in developing transition economies following the break-up of the Soviet Union (Thomas et al., 1991). The policy objec-tives of this kind of reform are to increase the degree of competition and improve the efficiency of resource use in the economy (thereby raising the average level of income), and ultimately to increase the rate of growth and reduce poverty.

It is easy to see the connection between some of these policy actions and some of the intermediate objectives. Reducing import barriers obviously increases competition for domestic producers, reducing any monopolistic power they might have and putting pressure on them to become more efficient. Opening channels for imports of productive inputs and capital goods expands the set of available production technology for local indus-tries, and liberalization that reduces domestic prices on consumer goods clearly benefits consumers directly.

Other links are less obvious, though no less important. Reducing import barriers encourages exports, but it does so indirectly. To the extent that increasing imports causes a reduction in the use of labor, capital and other resources by import-competing industries (either because the industries contract or because they are forced to become more efficient in resource use), these resources are released to be used by exporting industries and non-trade sectors. Another way to look at the process is that increased demand for imports causes an increase in the demand for foreign currency (which is necessary to buy imports), which bids up its price or domestic purchasing power – the "real exchange rate." Since export industries generate foreign exchange, this real exchange rate effect benefits them. Of course, a country's ability to take advantage of improved incentives and opportunities that may be opened by trade reform is conditioned by many other factors – some external, some under the government's control and some a mixture. This will be discussed in more detail below.

All the cases identified here as general trade reforms are ones in which the government has consciously adopted a policy of fostering increased integration with the global economy and export-led growth through reduction of import barriers. China and Vietnam did this in anticipation of accession to the WTO, Madagascar accomplished it as part of a structural adjustment program, and Chile and India took unilateral actions. In some cases, the policy measures also entailed explicit policies to support exports. For example, Madagascar allowed exporters to operate under a special policy regime that exempted them from certain regulatory restrictions and local taxes. Chile, on the other hand, relied very little on special treatment for exporters (other than some very general and small-scale support), relying instead on the impetus coming from reducing government interventions (including import barriers and tariffs) to boost exports. Since all case studies focus on specific products, they begin from the implicit assumption that the general equilibrium effects of these overall reforms work their way through the system and eventually have an impact on these particular markets.

As noted above, the macroeconomic real exchange rate effect of general trade liberalization also tempers the impact of product-specific liberalization. When foreign exchange in effect becomes more expensive, this raises the price of imports, all other things being constant, and benefits import-competing productive sectors. But, of course, in a general trade reform, all other things are not constant; tariffs are being reduced and non-tariff barriers relaxed, which tends to increase competitive pressure on producers of these products. In the face of these two offsetting effects, not all import-competing producers will feel an equal reduction in their incentives, and some may even benefit, if their sector is liberalized much less than others. So it is expected, for example, that a reduction of 40 percent in tariffs on corn as part of a general trade reform will not reduce the real domestic price of corn by 40 percent, but rather by something less, since some of the tariff reduction is counterbalanced by the real exchange rate effect. If, on the other hand, the tariff is reduced by 40 percent with no liberalization in other products, then one would expect that corn producers would indeed see prices decline by the full 40 percent.

The potential linkages between trade on the one hand and growth and poverty reduction on the other are many and complex, but the underlying intuition rests on two concepts fundamental to the modern theory of inter-national trade – comparative advantage and factor price equalization. The first of these is the idea that when two countries trade freely, each will be relatively more efficient in producing the kinds of goods that intensively use the factors (e.g., labor, land, capital) that are relatively abundant (and therefore cheaper) in that country. Trade will therefore lead each to specialize in doing what it does best. The second concept follows from the first. Because the intensive use of a factor increases demand for it, and so also increases its price, increased trade will cause the relative price of each factor to rise in the country in which it is most abundant. So, to take the simplest example, a country with a lot of labor and little land might produce vegetables – which require labor-intensive cultivation – most efficiently, while a country with a lot of land and not many people might specialize in wheat. Trade between the two would increase the demand for labor in the first (where labor is cheaper), raising its price relative to the price of land. Conversely, in the second country (where land is cheaper), the price of land relative to labor would rise. The factor prices would therefore tend to "equalize."

Transfer of technology through foreign direct investment (FDI) or imported inputs can also be a channel through which trade liberalization improves productive efficiency, as was the case in our studies of Chile, Madagascar, Vietnam and China. Other studies have also found this effect to be important. Transfer of agricultural technology "imbedded" in inputs has sometimes been blocked by regulatory requirements on seed, fertilizer or machinery imports, with adverse effects on farmers (Gisselquist et al., 2002). Applying these concepts to developing countries, one would expect that since labor – especially unskilled labor – is abundant and cheap, these countries would tend to specialize in products that use a lot of this labor, which in the end would raise incomes of low-wage laborers and thereby reduce poverty. In the real world, of course, things are not so simple, and there are many intermediate steps between changes in the incentive structure triggered by trade policy reform and the consequent effects on growth and poverty reduction. Many of the most important lessons from this project and other research on the effects of trade reform concern the institutional and legal framework necessary to make sure that this trade–poverty linkage works well. It should also be recognized that the labor intensity of a product is not measured only by the labor use on the farm, but also by labor required to distribute inputs, process the primary product and bring it to market. This was underscored by several of our case studies (more below).

Similar considerations apply to the linkage between trade and environ-ment. Traditional trade theory would predict that countries that have a relative abundance of natural resources – true of many developing countries – would specialize in goods that use these intensively. The problem, however, is that often natural resources and environmental services are free goods with uncontrolled access. With no pricing mechanism to guide decisions, overexploitation is the likely result. In some cases this may be done by the poor, creating a trade-off (in the short run at least) between poverty reduction and environmental damage. In the long run, at least some of these short-term win–lose trade-offs may turn into lose–lose situations, as environmental degradation kills the goose that temporarily laid golden eggs, leaving the poor even poorer. Again, many of the lessons of the project concern how to use institutions to prevent or mitigate this kind of adverse outcome.

For a trade event to result in behavioral changes in the markets for particular products, two basic requirements are that: (1) the event be translated into changes in incentives for producers and consumers in that market; and (2) conditions exist that allow these producers and consumers to respond. This study was not designed to examine in detail the transmission of trade policy reforms to changes in domestic prices, but it can be inferred from the fact that most case studies found significant producer response that the transmission mechanism generally functioned as expected.[1] The case studies focused on the second link in the chain; that is, from changes in incentives to economic response.

OUTCOMES FROM THE CASE STUDIES

The cases studies presented in this volume were chosen partially because there appeared to be an ex ante relationship between trade-tied industries and resources drawn from vulnerable habitats. For this reason there is an emphasis on areas that have experienced export-led growth. Not surprisingly then, there is a tendency among the case studies to find that the trade events have worked to reduce poverty, while at the same time have placed additional demands on the resources that support fragile ecologies. Because of this selection process, the case studies are not in any sense a random sample of trade reform episodes, and do not offer a balanced view of whether the environmental impact of trade on poverty or on the environment is generally positive or negative. They do, however, highlight instances where the need to find sustainable solutions is most pressing and illustrate the ways in which trade effects may manifest themselves and the factors that influence this.

At this point it is also useful to say something about how outcomes are measured in the case studies. At the outset of the project, the study teams sought to develop comprehensive quantitative measures for trade, human welfare and the environment. For trade, emblematic measures included border tariffs and equivalents for subsidies or quantitative restrictions; for the environment, efforts were made to document the full and varied types of services provided by the studied ecology and to measure changes over time; and human welfare measures were sought that would supplement evidence on income. As a practical matter, the study teams often had to settle for more circumscribed measures. As will be discussed later, this speaks to the need for more comprehensive measures of important ecologies and the people who depend on them for their livelihoods.

ENVIRONMENT

The case studies illustrate two primary reasons why the fragile ecologies studied are undervalued and overused. The first has to do with externalities – benefits or costs that accrue to those who do not manage the resources. In most of the case studies, the studied ecologies generate non-market services that benefit local communities and, in some cases, provide global public goods. At the same time, mechanisms for valuing core resources and paying for their preservation are often lacking. Instead, market incentives, based on a partial valuing of the resource, determine use. A second, related issue has to do with difficulties associated with policing the use of natural resources. As a practical matter, firms and households were able to exploit many of the natural resources identified in the case studies, with minimal restrictions. This tendency for unfettered access to common resources to give rise to overuse is often referred to as the "tragedy of the commons."[2]

As discussed, many of the case studies focus on places that environmental scientists and the broader environmental community consider valuable and at risk. In several instances these environments provide the habitat for rare and diverse plant and animal populations and contribute significantly to the planet's biodiversity. The Da Wei Shan Nature Reserve, the setting for the China study, is home to 3,619 plant species and 555 animal species. The Sundarbans National Park in India was declared a United Nations Educational, Scientific and Cultural Organization (UNESCO) World Heritage Site in 1989 and provides a sanctuary for wild tigers, Gangetic dolphins, wild boar and estuarine crocodiles. The reserves provide ancillary services as well. The reserves in Da Wei Shan serve as catchments for drinking water supplied to nearby municipalities, and the forests there stabilize steep slopes that are prone to erosion. And the estuaries of the

Sundarbans provide natural hatcheries for shrimp and other harvested sea life.

Still, as will be discussed later, the costs of maintaining the core environmental resources on which global and local public benefits depend are not broadly shared. For example, farmers or fishermen operating in the mangrove forests of Vietnam or India are not directly rewarded for adopting approaches that preserve the rich biodiversity of the regions. Of course, were the full range of environmental services well known and their relationships with livelihood choices understood, it might be possible to devise resource management schemes that provide incentives for farmers and local communities to manage and maintain common-pool resources such as forests and estuaries at appropriate levels.

In practice, the resources at the center of the case studies are undervalued and underprotected and their overuse is well documented. The studies from Chile, China, and Madagascar all provide examples of how easy access to untitled forest lands leads to diminished ecologies. In the studies from India and Vietnam, commonly owned mangrove estuaries were converted over time for private use. In the South Africa case, the common property relevant to the study is water. Sugar is a thirsty crop that requires irrigation in the Incomati region. The authors suggest that, were water priced at its opportunity cost (i.e., its value to other users), it is doubtful that sugar would be grown in this area at all. And if it were, more water-efficient cultivation techniques would be employed. As a virtually free good, large quantities of water are used on a low-value crop, to the great detriment of the ecosystem and downstream users.

In most of the case studies, the problem of common resources is a longstanding one, and fundamental problems exist separately from the studied trade events. For example, the steady decline in the spiny forests of Madagascar or the loss of native forests in Chile occurred over time in response to growing demographic pressures and shifting cultivation.

Even so, because access to these common resources in largely unfettered, additional demands to serve export markets can accelerate their depletion. This is well illustrated in the case study from Madagascar, where land ownership is informal and use rights are conveyed by clearing or otherwise using the land. The authors of the study suggest that 10 percent of deforestation in the study area could be attributed to a temporary demand for maize exports. Additional examples include an overharvesting of traditional plants and animals for domestic and export markets in Pingbian, China; bycatch losses of larval fishes and shellfish associated with the harvesting of wild prawn seed in the Sundarbans of West Bengal, India; the loss and fragmentation of mangrove habitat in Ca Mau, Vietnam, also partly associated with shrimp exports; and the potential loss of habitat from reduced river flows in the Incomati River Basin of South Africa, should sugar exports increase.

A similar problem arises when common resources can be polluted without penalty or cost. As in the earlier examples, trade does not lie at the root of the pollution problem; however, trade can give rise to incentives that result in increased pollution. Examples include the spread of disease through shared water resources in Ca Mau and the consequences of accumulated waste from caged salmon in Chile.

While trade liberalization can increase incentives for unsustainable exploitation of the resource base, the worst examples uncovered in the studies were caused by policies that created incentives against trade, generally in the cause of food self-sufficiency. The severest losses of the Madagascar spiny forest were in the anti-trade period of the 1970s and 1980s and were caused by the government's encouragement of slash-and-burn cultivation of rice.[3] Likewise, in Vietnam, particularly in the south, much of the lost mangrove area was initially cleared for rice cultivation or clear-cut for charcoal, firewood and building materials by forestry agencies. After the removal of the mangroves, some of the areas were leased to farmers for shrimp farming (30 percent of the area), with the balance for mangrove replanting that was to be done by the shrimp farmers, in most instances at their own cost. Similarly, in Pingbian, longstanding incentives to grow land-intensive crops on marginal and steeply sloped lands, which created severe erosion problems, were reversed as internal trade and external trade with Vietnam and Laos developed. Instead, farmers shifted their production to supply emerging markets for fruit and vegetables.

Protection may also be largely responsible for the overuse of water for sugar production in the Incomati region, since it is doubtful that, without a protected domestic market, sugar would be grown there. It is nonetheless true, however, that global liberalization could exacerbate this problem by raising world sugar prices. Regional trade liberalization, which would grant more access to South Africa's market for lower-cost producers in neighboring countries, would reduce domestic prices and discourage sugar production.

Importantly, even as the case studies focused on direct links between trade and resource use, several authors note that some of the most significant impacts were secondary effects tied to a shifting of labor resources from agriculture to other sectors. As is discussed next, such general equilibrium effects are closely tied to economic growth and poverty reduction; however, important effects on the environment were noted as well. For example, in China, an out-migration of labor helped ease pressures to convert additional lands and harvest fuel from public forests. In contrast, migrants were attracted to study areas in Madagascar and Vietnam, placing additional strains on those ecologies. Moreover, the authors predict that the entry of new industrial activity in Pingbian will give rise to problems associated with water and air pollution.

POVERTY

As the previous discussion indicates, the case studies provided several examples of how trade policy, in combination with other policies and events, can increase employment opportunities locally and in other parts of the economy. Consistent with this, most case studies reported general national declines in poverty levels during the study periods as well as local improvements. For example, rapid economic growth across China was matched in Pingbian, where economic growth led to significant declines in poverty. Similarly, economic growth in Vietnam was matched with improved incomes and declining poverty in Ca Mau. In the maize-growing areas of southwest Madagascar, declines in poverty were less pronounced, but evidence suggests that poverty fell more rapidly there than in other parts of the province.

Even so, the studies suggest that not everyone benefited from economic growth. In Chile, significant reductions in rural poverty nationwide mask remaining regional differences. Moreover, even where poverty reductions have been significant, absolute poverty levels remain high. For example, the authors note that poverty levels in Pingbian and southwest Madagascar remain at 61 percent and 73 percent, respectively.

Generally, the studies suggest that differences in household access to assets, such as capital and land, partly determined the degree to which families were able to take advantage of economic opportunities. For example, the studies from India and Vietnam found that farmers with access to land benefited directly from new shrimp export markets. Moreover, those with better access to capital were able to take advantage of more profitable production technologies. In contrast, benefits for unskilled landless workers were less direct and came from employment in soil preparation for ponds, sludge removal, caring for shrimp, processing companies and transportation. Nevertheless, the Vietnam study noted that more than half the households in a survey of the region said this kind of aquaculture-related income was increasingly important to them. In Madagascar, a select group of households with landholdings near the Export Processing Zone were the primary beneficiaries of farm contracts linked to exports.

Importantly, the studies suggest that access to natural resources mattered as well. For example, in Pingbian, rainfall and soil conditions determined the extent to which households could convert to more profitable crops. In South Africa, the authors note that access to land and water resources largely determines livelihood strategies and income among the poor in Incomati. The case studies also suggest that, to a degree, poor households were able to supplement incomes limited by access to private assets by drawing on natural common-pool assets. For example, in India, a large number of poor landless households generated income by harvesting wild prawn larvae. In Pingbian, some households earned a portion of their livelihood from harvesting herbal plants from surrounding forests. In Vietnam, households with limited access to capital relied more heavily on tidal flows and natural food sources to raise shrimp for sale into export markets.

The study on Chile, which covered a much longer time period, illustrates how the links between trade and income can also evolve with time. The Chile study found that growth was at first driven by export-oriented primary production, but over time it became increasingly driven by resource-based manufacturing, processing and upstream service and input supply, with increased value added. This is consistent with a study of agricultural growth in Chile, which found that the biggest poverty impacts came not from farming itself, but from the development of these related upstream and downstream activities (Valdés and Foster, 2003).

TRADE, LOCAL LIVELIHOOD CHOICES AND ENVIRONMENTAL CONSEQUENCES

As already mentioned, the case studies in this volume feature uncommon ecologies that support diverse habitats. As the case study authors emphasize, these same ecologies, in combination with a variety of factors, including markets for traded goods, give rise to local livelihoods. Importantly, the case studies suggest that it is the interaction between the local ecology and livelihood choices that largely determines how broad changes in trade or other policies translate into a given set of outcomes for vulnerable ecologies and households. Said differently, the case studies suggest that trade events shape poverty and environmental outcomes by influencing production decisions and livelihood choices.

In particular, as suggested in the previous section, many households that live in close proximity to important ecologies craft livelihoods by drawing on the same resources that support valuable habitats and other local environmental services. They do so in combination with other private and public assets, such as household labor, capital and public infrastructure. Because households differ in their range of accessible assets, different livelihood strategies and different production choices will emerge, even in the same community. In turn, different livelihood choices will have different consequences for income and will also place differing demands on local ecologies.

A good example is found in the Vietnam study, alluded to above. The authors point out that a variety of farming methods are used to raise shrimp in Ca Mau, but note that many poor farmers, who lack the capital to build shrimp ponds, choose an extensive farming method that relies partly on food sources and tidal flows provided by local estuaries. In contrast, many wealthier farmers with better access to credit employ more input-intensive production methods that are also more profitable. Just as each approach has different economic consequences, each approach places different strains on the local ecology. For example, the extensive systems operate using open sluices and shared water systems. Consequently, pollution sources, while generally low, are shared among all producers and local estuaries. The same is true of disease, and so the risk of epidemic is high. In contrast, more intensive production systems provide better contamination controls but also employ higher chemical concentrations that can spill into local estuaries. Moreover, pond sludge accumulates more quickly when intensive methods are used, resulting in problems related to blocked drainage systems and higher levels of water pollution.

The other side of the same coin is that, because household and firm dependence on natural resources differ, policy changes that limit access to overused natural resources will have greater effect on some firms and households than others. This can create a quandary for policy makers when a large number of dependent households are poor. In such cases, even though in the long run it is in the interest of the poor who depend on ecological services to preserve them, taking steps to better safeguard natural resources can, in the short run, adversely impact the livelihoods of those least able to adjust. By way of example, the authors of the South Africa study argue that, while sugar firms are geographically diversified in South Africa, smallholder producers are not, and they would be hard hit by a policy that more appropriately prices scarce water resources in the Incomati River Basin. Similarly, the study from India notes that the poor without land and resources who harvest wild shrimp larvae in the Sundarbans also depend most on access to estuarine resources.

HOW CAN POLICY CONDITION OUTCOMES?

As discussed, the consequences of trade reform for specific ecologies and for the poor can be driven by a combination of international and national market outcomes and also by decisions taken by local communities, firms and households. Indeed, it is this large set of determinants and the complex way in which they interact that makes the outcomes hard to predict. Even so, lessons drawn from the case studies suggest that predicting the outcomes from trade policy changes is less crucial than putting in place safeguards that protect vulnerable ecologies and households from a wide range of adverse outcomes and finding policies that broaden participation in economic opportunities.

As the previous discussion suggests, understanding how the physical features of the studies' ecologies combine with market incentives and local livelihoods to affect poverty and the environment is crucial for the formulation of policy. At the same time, not all determinants are mutable and responsive to the instruments available to policy makers. In this section we focus on four areas suggested by the case studies whereby policy can influence poverty and environmental outcomes related to trade. These are (1) how market institutions determine the range of new economic opportunities stemming from trade reform; (2) how government programs that provide public goods can complement economic opportunities arising from trade and lower the hurdles that preclude participation by the poor; (3) the role institutions can play in building knowledge about important natural resources, the services they provide and their relationship with the livelihoods of the poor; and (4) resource management approaches and the role institutions play in safeguarding vulnerable ecologies and people.

MARKET INSTITUTIONS

Overall, the case studies suggest that factor market institutions seem to be especially important in transforming the potentially beneficial economic impacts of trade reform into actual growth and poverty reduction on the ground.[4] In turn, governments play an important role in establishing the legal framework on which markets depend. Governments and informal institutions can also introduce programs to help markets work better. The case studies provide several examples.

Good legal frameworks for labor and land markets underpinned Chile's growth. This case emphasized the "importance of migration to translate economic growth into poverty reduction" and found that those without mobility were at a significant disadvantage. Chile's legal framework facilitated the movement of labor and land resources, which allowed the smooth transfer of resources from contracting to expanding industries and areas. Labor mobility is particularly important to help equilibrate wages and ensure that benefits are not confined to areas or activities that are direct beneficiaries of trade reform. Fluid labor markets are also important to enable industrial restructuring that is necessitated by reform. Chile's forestry industry, for example, was a heavily protected, inefficient producer before the reforms, but with some restructuring it was able to transform itself into a competitive exporter.

In China, ancillary policies also improved labor market mobility. The government helped organize migrant workers and enacted policies to retain property rights for migrants, so they could leave their villages temporarily without fear that their property would be taken away. This encouraged off-farm employment and diversification of income sources, helping to spread the benefits of trade reforms even to very remote areas, and reducing income inequality. India's shrimp farming development, which brought large economic benefits to one of the poorest areas in India, was facilitated by a fluid land-rental market. Failed market institutions were noted as well; in South Africa, researchers conclude that ongoing weakness in the land tenure system there creates uncertainty and thereby reduces farmers' ability to invest and diversify out of sugar. The Chile study reports that the failure to resolve land-use disputes in the forestry sector led to conflicts among indigenous people.

The studies also noted the importance of traditional and informal market institutions. For example, in India, traditional middlemen, known as *aratdars*, helped organize and finance dispersed markets for wild prawn seed. In a similar way, informal cultural ties between the Miao people of Pingbian and the Hmong people of Laos and Vietnam facilitated the creation of new markets once trade barriers had been removed.

The case studies suggest that international institutions and their influence on international markets are important as well – for better or worse. Some of the positive drivers have already been mentioned. International consumer pressure transmitted to Chilean producers through global value chains was instrumental in upgrading environmental standards for exports. Free trade agreements also had this effect. Contract farming arrangements set up through direct investment provided both capital and technology, and were environmentally friendly and effective in reducing poverty in Madagascar and China. Contracts to deliver vegetables to European supermarkets from Madagascar addressed employment practices and hygiene standards. Foreign direct investment also played a key role in Chile. Other drivers have been part of the problem, rather than the solution. High and changing standards (sanitary and phytosanitary, labeling requirements) present challenges for shrimp producers in India and farmers in China. US anti-dumping duties have heavily penalized Vietnamese shrimp farmers. One lesson coming out of recent research (Jaffee, 2005) is that while standards are sometimes used by governments as protectionist non-tariff trade barriers (in principle subject to challenge under WTO rules), relatively strict standards in global markets related to quality, labor or environmental standards are often driven by the private sector (not subject to challenge under WTO rules). These can serve as constructive catalysts for change, although producers faced with standards-related barriers should weigh up the costs and benefits associated with participating in different market segments before embarking on programs to upgrade production standards. In some cases, producers may have profitable opportunities to service the domestic market, the regional market or market segments in industrialized countries that impose less stringent standards or allow more time to implement certain measures. Similar considerations should apply to governments' decisions to make necessary public sector investments. But, in any case, experience demonstrates that it is much better to actively plan ahead than to respond to crises.

TARGETED PROGRAMS AND PUBLIC INVESTMENT

As discussed, the case studies suggest that general institutions and the markets they support play crucial roles in creating new economic opportunities. The case studies show that this is also the case for more tailored programs that target particular types of economic activity. Generally, the programs focused on information and technology dissemination, or on the provision of public infrastructure. The case studies suggest that governments and other agencies can help develop an understanding of the consequences that new opportunities will have for the poor and provide public services that lower hurdles to a broader participation in economic growth.

The case studies from Chile, China, India and Vietnam illustrate how private entrepreneurs are often the first to identify new economic opportunities, making use of informal networks for information and investment capital. At the same time, state and local governments quickly recognized the potential of the new opportunities as a vehicle for growth and moved to disseminate information about markets and about production technologies. For example, in the case of Chile, the government trade group, ProChile, helped with market identification and product promotion overseas. In India and Vietnam, the provincial government sponsored technical research programs and provided extension services. In some cases, private firms provided information on production technologies and other extension services through contracts. The already-mentioned case of vegetable exports in Madagascar is one example; another example from the

South African study is services provided to smallholder sugar producers by the Tsb sugar mill.

In other cases, state or local governments also invested in transportation or irrigation systems. For example, the Vietnam case study explains that the decision to ease restrictions on converting rice land was coupled with investments in irrigation systems and hatcheries as well as extension services. In South Africa, the Nkomati Irrigation Expansion Program provided irrigation infrastructure investment for smallholder farmers. In India, the state government established a development agency specifically charged with assisting shrimp farmers. The agency not only invested in public services, such as irrigation and road systems, training and extension, but also took on additional tasks such as distributing fishing nets and providing housing, which might have best been left to private markets.

INSTITUTIONS AND KNOWLEDGE BUILDING

As discussed, natural resources of the type covered by the case studies provide a range of environmental services. In cases where the benefits of these services accrue exclusively to individuals or cohesive groups, markets can be relied on to properly value and preserve the underlying resources. In other instances, when natural resources provide benefits to a larger community, markets alone are insufficient, and alternative methods for preserving core resources must be devised. Doing so, however, requires an understanding of the full range of services provided by the resources and how they can be sustained. At an international level, this entails identifying the role that local resource plays in the global ecology. Locally, an understanding is needed of services provided to local communities as well as the ways in which the welfare of the local households and firms depends on the local ecology. This effort includes understanding especially the incentives and constraints that households face and the consequences of household choices for incomes and for the local environment.

The case studies suggest that many national and international groups play a role in the creation of basic knowledge. One aspect of this is identifying priority areas for the purpose of directing global efforts and providing special protection at a national level. For example, the World Conservation Monitoring Centre, an agency of the United Nations Environment Program, includes China, India, Madagascar and South Africa in its list of 17 mega-diverse countries, and the geographic focus of many of the case studies is in or near national wildlife preserves. Similarly, the case studies illustrate how national groups and governments take steps to identify important ecologies. As already discussed, the study areas in

China, Chile, India and South Africa include national forests or wildlife preserves. For this reason, these areas have attracted national and international attention and have been the focus of study by scientists and social scientists. A case in point is the selection of areas for study in this volume, which were intended to highlight ecologies that are considered vulnerable and important by conservationists.

Another aspect of knowledge creation has to do with building basic measures that can be used to quantify existing conditions, changes over time and relationships between policy and outcomes. As discussed, the case studies suggest that this type of knowledge creation is uneven and sometimes weak, especially with regard to environmental measures over time. For this reason, many of the research teams found it difficult to fully quantify changes in core natural resources over time or in the services that they provide. For the same reason, the research teams found that broader measures of human welfare that take into account the consequences of air or water pollution were hard to determine. Very broadly, the researchers were generally able to document changes in income and poverty over time by drawing on national and regional surveys. Moreover, data on local production and income sources were available; for example, available time-series data in China.

Less readily available was information that would allow the researchers to quantify the types of provisioning services provided by the studied ecologies and to measure changes in those services over time and their impact on human welfare. For example, while environmental services such as the provision of drinking water or biodiversity from the Da Wei Shan Nature Reserve in Pingbian are noted, baseline measures from which the authors could draw comparisons are lacking. In India and Madagascar, for example, focus groups and surveys were used to provide broader measures of human welfare, but comparisons over time were based on recall and subject to error. For this reason, many of the conclusions about environmental degradation over time are based on deforestation maps. The research team from South Africa concluded, as they tried to evaluate the consequences of potential increases in sugar production, that "little is known about ecological thresholds and reversibility of environmental damage in Incomati."

MANAGING VULNERABLE ECOLOGIES

The case studies present several mechanisms for managing natural resources. At a fundamental level, these systems are intended to properly value the broad range of services that ecologies provide and to preserve the core resources that provide those services. As discussed, one key aspect of preserving those resources is to limit access to common-pool resources in a way that precludes a tragedy of the commons. In principle, one way to do this is to charge an appropriate price for the use of the resource to "internalize the externality," but examples of this in developing countries are rare in practice. The authors of the India case study mention this possibility but conclude that it would be impractical given current institutional shortcomings.

Another approach to managing natural resources is to grant some form of ownership over a common-property resource – thereby creating an incentive for the owner to conserve it. In the traditional systems identified by the case studies, group ownership is implied and group leaders are obligated to ensure that resources are used in a sustainable way. Examples from the studies include the role of traditional authorities in Madagascar and India. Still, the case studies suggest that these informal arrangements can be fragile. In particular, evidence from Madagascar suggests that some types of internal migration can result in reduced social cohesion that undermines traditional institutions.

A more common approach is to create formal institutions that provide title or other use rights. Conceptually, such rights could be granted to groups rather than individuals; this was the idea behind the Gelose program in Madagascar. More commonly, resource management approaches identified in the case studies involved private use rights, usually in connection with restrictions on how the resources can be used. In the case of some natural resources, private ownership can go a long way to solve the problem of overuse. An example is the contract-farming case study from Madagascar, which illustrates how private ownership creates incentives for farmers to adopt practices that preserve soil fertility. More generally, positive or negative externalities are sometimes associated with the private use of natural resources, which has motivated restrictions on their use. Often, regulations are intended to stem specific pollution problems. For example, the study from South Africa notes that sugar mills are required to cool water used in processing before returning it to rivers in order to stem thermal pollution in natural habitats; in India, the supreme court intervened to limit particular technical approaches to shrimp farming because of adverse environmental consequences. In Ca Mau, the government stepped in to ban the use of certain types of antibiotics in shrimp production.

However, because ecological systems of the type studied in this volume are complex, their preservation usually requires more than restricting certain forms of private use. One approach, well illustrated by the case studies, is to establish a mix of private use areas combined with public areas held in reserve. This method of juxtaposing wildlife preserves and buffer areas is illustrated in the case studies from India. In Vietnam, households were assigned 7.4 to 24.7 acres of mangrove forestland under the condition that 70 percent of the forest was to remain intact. The studies suggest that the success of mixed-use strategies depends significantly on the institutions, formal and informal, charged with policing differentiated use. For example, the authors of the study in Vietnam suggest that restrictions on use were not well designed or fully enforced.

As discussed, when the poor have come to depend on natural resources, tightening access to common resources can impose a cost on already vulnerable households. One solution illustrated by the case studies is to couple restrictions on use with compensation combined with efforts to provide an alternative livelihood. For example, the China case study documents two programs designed to reforest slopes through cash buyouts and resettlement programs; the case study from Chile also examines incentives for private firms to plant trees on new lands or lands that were formerly forested. Similarly, the Vietnam study notes that a resettlement program was used to reclaim 39,500 acres of mangrove forest.

As the examples above illustrate, resource management strategies rely heavily on a combination of social norms and formal rules and on organizations charged with enforcing them. In many instances, it falls to national and local governments to create and support these institutions, and the case studies provide examples of practical difficulties that frequently arise.

For one, institutional arrangements of all types tend to lag behind economic and environmental events. For example, in Chile a general legal framework for fisheries and aquaculture did not appear until 1991, despite rapid growth in the subsector during the previous 10 years; significant environment regulations were not in place until 1996. Once in place, the institutions have operated fairly effectively, so Chile's forestry and salmon sectors have had relatively neutral environmental impacts. The institutional arrangements have developed along different models – more self-regulation in the salmon industry, for example – and some of the institutions (CONAF, the forestry regulator, is mentioned) still need further development, but in general they are performing their intended role. Likewise, programs to protect fragile soils and the rehabilitation of degraded land in Chile were enacted in 1998. Similarly, the authors of the Vietnam study note that mangrove forests in Ca Mau were afforded protection only after significant loss had already occurred. Moreover, they note that while governments of various levels provided early assistance to expand shrimp production, the pollution consequences were largely unanticipated, and relevant regulations have been introduced in a catch-up manner.

In other cases, the institutions charged with enforcement or implementation have been underfunded, weak or missing. For example, the Madagascar team notes governance problems with the Gelose program. Moreover, the team notes that only 3 percent of Madagascar's spiny forest is protected, despite its importance as a habitat for endangered plants and fauna.

More fundamentally, however, most of the management systems described in the case studies are partial and reactive. This is not surprising, since lessons from the case studies suggest that the tasks required to put in place a comprehensive system are challenging. For one, the previous discussion suggests that the job of measuring the full range of services and the role they play in the lives of vulnerable households is incomplete, as is the job of building quantitative baselines to measure progress. Moreover, the case studies suggest that the number of stakeholders is large for the type of ecologies studied in this volume. Resolving competing objectives and implementing any resolution is likely to involve a large number of local and non-local institutions, some of which must be built up from scratch. Consequently, the potential for coordination failures is high.

The case study from the Incomati River Basin in South Africa illustrates the large set of stakeholders that are often associated with important natural resources and the complex task of consultation, policy formulation and implementation. To start, national policies formulated in a 1998 National Water Act drew on an international statement of principles embodied in the 1992 International Conference on Water and Environment. Accordingly, the national legislation created a hierarchy of users that included an environmental reserve. In parallel, a set of 19 catchment management agencies was created to reach consensus on how water resources from each catchment should be used. In practice, the authors suggest that representation on key advisory committees largely drives licensing decisions, and the authors argue that this favors old outcomes that were both inefficient and inequitable. In particular, they argue that South Africa's three-tiered structure of national, provincial and local policy making and implementation is impractical because of weak institutions and agencies below the national level.

WHAT STANDS IN THE WAY OF BETTER POLICY?

The case studies provide additional evidence that key ecologies that are rich in biodiversity are being used in unsustainable ways. Further, the studies suggest the reason for this has to do with a range of non-marketed services provided by ecologies that make natural resources difficult to properly value and to secure. When trade events occur, the weakness of existing protections is often revealed as new demands for market-related services are added. In the same way, the weak protections have given rise to livelihoods that rely on ecologies in unsustainable ways. For the poor, this dependency is especially crucial because, lacking private assets, they depend more on common-pool assets. At the same time, the case studies suggest that broad policies related to trade or to poverty reduction are unlikely to realign incentives or adequately safeguard vulnerable ecologies. Instead, the studies suggest that strong institutions that operate locally and that find support across a wide range of stakeholders are needed to manage fragile ecologies and the livelihoods that depend on them. This task of building such institutions is challenging, but the studies suggest two tasks that should be priorities for policy makers and the broader sustainable development community.

Most pressing is the task of building and disseminating a better understanding of the services natural resources provide and what is required to sustain them. Especially important is the need to improve measurements of ecological services that do not enter markets, including such services as water purification or the provision of biologically diverse habitats. This is a first step in arriving at sensible resource management solutions; it is also essential when assessing the success or failure of current and future policies. As the case studies point out, it is important to develop location-specific information about livelihood choices and their consequences for incomes and for the environment. In particular, the case studies point out the value of understanding the consequences of alternative production technologies and barriers the poor might face in choosing among them.[5]

A second task, which builds on the first, is to create and strengthen institutions that match the range of global and local market and non-market services. In terms of market services, the case studies point out the value to the poor of general institutions that support private markets as well as ad hoc programs that help the poor to participate in new opportunities. For non-market services, the case studies do provide several examples of how partial steps, such as certification or land-titling programs or regulations on specific production technologies, can be useful and important. Even so, the case studies suggest that in many instances holistic resource management schemes are needed to adequately protect core resources. The case studies suggest that the challenge of doing so comprehensively is great; however, they also give an indication of where action is most needed. One frequently noted obstacle is a weakness in types of local institutions required for an integrated management scheme. Such institutions are especially important, since some of the trade-offs among management and production choices play out contentiously at the local levels. Moreover, some of the most costly and difficult tasks, such as policing and monitoring, often fall to local governments and organizations. For this reason, the successful implementation of policy is often crucially linked to the strength of local institutions.

This suggests a third key task: to find ways to share the costs of creating and disseminating knowledge, of building institutions and of providing safety nets for vulnerable households that are hurt by changes in trade or resource management policies. As the case studies explain, local ecologies often benefit the global ecology in many ways and also benefit local communities. Still, to a large degree, the costs of institution building and policy implementation fall to local governments and organizations. Moreover, misaligned incentives arising from under-valued ecological services encourage households to take up livelihood choices that degrade local ecologies. The case studies provide examples of programs and policies that help households transition to sustainable practices; however, these programs cannot be maintained without financing from central governments or the international community. Finding and financing ways to align local incentives that take into account non-market consequences offers the potential to address the vulnerability of households and ecologies.

NOTES

1. The transmission mechanism has been examined in previous studies, such as Mundlak and Larson (1992), or Baffes and Gardner (2003).
2. The term was popularized by a 1968 essay by Garrett Hardin.
3. Citing earlier research by the World Bank (2003), Minten et al. (2006, p. 10) note: "It is estimated that Madagascar lost about 12 million ha of forest between 1960 and 2000, effectively reducing forest cover by 50% in just 40 years . . ... The severest losses took place during the 1970s and early 1980s during the height of the socialist revolution when the practice of slash-and-burn agriculture was actively encouraged in order to produce more rice to feed the growing urban population. Since the mid 1980s, Madagascar has therefore been the focus of international conservation efforts with international development organizations providing loan and assistance programs explicitly aimed at environmental objectives.
4. By institutions, we mean the formal and informal economic rules of the game (North, 1990). Institutions that permit broad economic participation, enforce contracts, protect property and speed the dissemination of information are expected to be particularly important.
5. A good example of how international expertise can be drawn on to consolidate and advance knowledge gains is the recently published Millennium Ecosystem Assessment (2005).

BIBLIOGRAPHY

Baffes, J. and B. Gardner (2003), "The transmission of world commodity prices to domestic markets under policy reforms in developing countries", *Journal of Policy Reform*, **6**(3), 159–80.

Gisselquist, D., C. Pray and J. Nash (2002), "Deregulating technology transfer in agriculture: impact on technical change, productivity, and incomes", *World Bank Research Observer*, **17**(2), 237–65.

Grossman, G.M. and E. Helpman (1991), *Innovation and Growth in the Global Economy*, Cambridge and London: MIT Press.

Hardin, G. (1968), "The tragedy of the commons", *Science*, **162**(3859), 1243–48.

Jaffee, S. (2005), "Food safety and agricultural health standards and developing country exports: rethinking the impacts and the policy agenda", Trade Note 25, 14 September, World Bank International Trade Department.

Millennium Ecosystem Assessment (2005), *Ecosystems and Human Well-being: Synthesis*, Washington, DC: Island Press.

Minten, B., P. Méral, L. Randrianarison and J. Swinnen (2006), "Trade liberalization, rural poverty and the environment: the case of Madagascar", Mimeo.

Mundlak, Y. and D.F. Larson (1992), "On the transmission of world agricultural prices", *World Bank Economic Review*, **6**(3), 399–422.

North, D.C. (1990), *Institutions, Institutional Change and Economic Performance*, The Political Economy of Institutions and Decisions Series, Cambridge, New York and Melbourne: Cambridge University Press.

Thomas, V., A. Chhibber, M. Dailami and J. de Melo (1991), *Restructuring Economies in Distress: Policy Reform and the World Bank*, Oxford: Oxford University Press for the World Bank.

Valdés, A. and W. Foster (2003), "The positive externalities of Chilean agriculture: the significance of its growth and export orientation, a synthesis of the roles of agriculture Chile case study", 18 December, Food and Agriculture Organization of the United Nations, Rome.

Winters, L. A., N. McCulloch and A. McKay (2004), "Trade liberalization and poverty: the evidence so far", *Journal of Economic Literature*, **XLII** (March), 72–115.

World Bank (2003), "Madagascar rural and environmental sector review", (Two Volumes), *Volume I: Main Report*, Report No. 26106-MG, Washington, DC: World Bank.

10. Beyond trade: economic transition in the globalization era and prospects for poverty and environment[1]

Bruno Losch

When WWF and the World Bank decided to join together in 2003 to investigate linkages between trade, rural poverty and the environment, the main objective was to improve the understanding of the complex relationships between these three issues and to throw light on vulnerable places and people facing the consequences of trade liberalization. The project was logically shaped by an international debate that was deeply focused on the trade issue. At that time, a successful ministerial meeting in Cancún was expected to show some progress in the WTO Doha Round that had begun in 2001. The so-called Doha "development round" emphasized the potential contribution of trade liberalization to poverty reduction; it was a direct reply to WTO critics echoing both ideological positions and national interests, dramatically expressed by the Seattle ministerial meeting protests in 1999, and also a more indirect response to the tragic events of September 2001.

However, Cancún was a failure, as was the Hong Kong ministerial (2005), and three years later, in 2008, additional attempts to conclude the Doha Round were unsuccessful.

Nevertheless, since then, the international debate has clearly evolved. The trade issue itself has faded in importance, notably because estimates of the gains from trade liberalization have been reduced and also because these estimates have provided a more nuanced view of the potential winners and losers, with many developing countries (particularly the least developed economies) in the second group. Discussions progressively shifted to the implementation of bilateral or regional free trade agreements (FTAs), which received increasing attention and also segmented the debate dynamics. But, above all, the international discussions have been progressively captured by other emerging issues.

First, global climate change clearly became an increasing concern. The *Stern Review on The Economics of Climate Change* (Stern, 2006) and later the Intergovernmental Panel on Climate Change (IPCC) report showed that climate change is expected to have various adverse effects with great impacts on livelihoods, particularly in rural areas, including direct consequences for agriculture and natural resources (increased rainfall variability, long-term drought trends, reductions in cultivable land and length of the growing season, etc.).

Second and more recently, a significant increase in global food prices in early 2008 has completely renewed the discussion on agriculture, on the prospects for food production under the constraints of climate change, and on the linkages between food access and poverty. The price increase is a burden for consumers but can be an opportunity for net producers when their connection to markets is effective and efficient. It can also obviously translate into increasing pressure on natural resources, particularly with the extension of cultivable land and over-exploitation. These new issues have broadened the scope of the debate and what was the early reference point for this project. While the initial goal was to assess the consequences of "trade events" for poverty and the environment, the concern has widened. The consequences of trade liberalization remain absolutely relevant, but they are embedded in issues like the impacts of the world growth regime on global change (e.g. climate, the stock of fossil materials) and other dimensions of globalization, particularly the new market dynamics related to the interconnection of places, spectacularly shown by the food-price and financial crises of 2008–09.

The case studies presented in this book have brilliantly illustrated the complexity of the processes of change and the need to position the trade events in their context, which determines both their impacts and the opportunity for maneuver and action by local stakeholders. My objective with this final chapter is to position the trade, poverty and environment debate in historical perspective and to emphasize the fact that places, and the people who live in them, do not share the same stage in the process of structural transformation that characterizes the evolution of economies and societies. This difference matters because it broadly determines the options when dealing with the opportunities and constraints related to globalization, and it clearly impacts on the poverty and environment issues.

I will adopt a three-step articulated perspective that should facilitate the final interpretation of the stories provided by the case studies, both by giving historical guidelines and by reducing divergence thanks to a broader scope for interpretation. First, I will discuss the ongoing processes with reference to the structural transformation characterized by the transition from natural resource-based activities to secondary and tertiary activities, and of labor and people from country to city. Second, I will reposition trade liberalization in the broader trend of globalization, which is today's main driver of change and induces deep processes of restructuring to which trade contributes. And, third, I will reconnect the discussion to the global challenges of demography and climate change. Population growth is often missing in the debate, even though it will deeply affect the future of people and places. Many developing regions will face the unique challenge of managing both their demographic and economic transitions in the context of globalization and under the constraint of growing resource scarcity. I will conclude with some guidelines for policymaking and an insistence on the importance of development strategies as a way to deal with the complexity of the current challenges.

THE NEED FOR A HISTORICAL PERSPECTIVE

Trade events or trade reforms are part of the trajectories of economic and social change followed by people, places, and countries and directly associated with the modalities of their insertion into the global economy. These trajectories of change are characterized by a progressive structural transformation of economies and societies, which has been a core issue in development studies since the early works of Lewis (1955) and Rostow (1960). The historical record and the statistical evidence (Timmer and Akkus, 2008) clearly confirm a progressive switch from agriculture to industry and then services, which appears as a powerful pathway toward economic development. The well-known underlying dynamics of this structural change – or "economic transition" from one configuration to the other – is an increase in agricultural productivity, based on innovation fostering technical change, that allows labor and capital transfers towards other economic activities (Mundlak et al., 1998). This process is accompanied by a progressive spatial restructuring from scattered activities (typically agriculture) to more concentrated ones (typically industry), with a growing urbanization that characterizes industrialized and post-industrialized countries. The world is very close today to the tipping point of 50 percent of global population living in cities, and this trend is deeply transforming the linkages between societies and nature.

With various paths and paces, this global process of structural change has been followed by various regions, starting with the closely related agricultural and industrial revolutions in Western Europe at the end of the eighteenth and early nineteenth centuries, and followed by the USA, other parts of Europe, most of Latin America and various regions of Asia. The result of these processes is a clearly differentiated picture emphasized by a recent World Development Report, which was dedicated to agriculture and development (World Bank, 2007). It presents "three developing worlds" characterized by their level of economic diversification: at one pole, "agriculture-based" countries (where agriculture plays the major role in terms of economic growth and employment), mainly Africa; at the other pole, urbanized countries (where industry and services have the largest shares and allow higher levels of income), typically Latin America; and an intermediate situation of "transforming" countries, which still have high levels of rural population and where there is broader diversification of the economic structure, such as South and East Asia.

However, one of the main analytical challenges today is to keep track of the historical processes. These three worlds have to be interpreted in light of their different modalities and sequences of integration within the world economy, and one major risk would be to adopt a mechanical and evolutionist vision disconnected from the world history, as if history could repeat itself.

The economic transformation of Western Europe and then the USA in the nineteenth and twentieth centuries was clearly embedded in their long-lasting political hegemony, notably marked by colonization and "influence" zones. This hegemony directly facilitated their structural transformation, thanks to attractive situations of both supply and demand, with captive markets (the competition being broadly eliminated) that boosted specialization toward industry, competitiveness, and profitability of businesses. The economic transition was also eased by a huge flow of international emigration, which was a clear exit option for the increasing pressure related to rural depopulation (in Europe) and the insufficient pace of job creation despite a strong process of industrialization. Between 1850 and 1930, nearly 60 million Europeans migrated to the New World, of which 35 million went to the United States alone. This population transfer was, of course, a consequence of a unique situation of political domination through the development of settlers' countries. For cases in both Latin America and Asia, which today host the main portion of the so-called "emerging economies" (so frequently recalled to confirm the evolutionist vision), the structural change was engaged during the very specific period of self-centered development that was the world international regime between the 1929 crisis and the current new globalization era dated to the end of the 1970s. Everywhere in the world, nation states adhered to import substitution and protection, strong state intervention, and national development projects (often strengthened by support during the Cold War period). And independent Latin American and then Asian countries (decolonized in the early 1950s) were able to take advantage of this momentum, even if partially, to kick off their national development.

The situation of sub-Saharan Africa (SSA) is unequivocally different because its integration into the world economy and its independence from Europe were delayed. As a consequence, the process of structural transformation followed a slower pace and the continent remains characterized today by its "agriculture base" – with agriculture generally retaining the major role in GDP, trade and, above all, the structure of economic activity and employment.

Two of the main challenges of the present period are the acceleration of the pace of change and the growing asymmetries between the diverse but interconnected regions of the world that characterize globalization. These differentiated structural transformation processes result in a "confrontation" between different levels of productivity and competitiveness in an increasingly open economy, this confrontation effect being a blind spot in the international debate.

If we refer just to the case of agriculture, it is now commonly assumed that the world productivity gap is a minimum of 1 to 1,000, if we compare manual agriculture in many developing countries (with no Green Revolution technical package and only one agricultural cycle per year) with heavily mechanized and high-input (not to mention subsidized) farms in the developed countries (and some regions of the developing countries). Because this gap appears as a durable obstacle to competitiveness in the context of an increasingly competitive globalized open economy, there are risks of progressive marginalization for the less productive and competitive agriculture systems and places, which can increase poverty and pressure on natural resources when people cannot find alternatives to sustain their livelihoods.

THE "ICEBERG FEATURE": THE STRUCTURAL DIMENSIONS OF LIBERALIZATION

Today, trade liberalization appears like the tip of an iceberg. It is only the smaller part of a global process of change whose main characteristics are below the waterline. The consequence of an excessive focus on trade is an overestimation of the price effects (impact of tariff reductions, quota suppressions, import competition, etc.), which fits well with econometric tools but distracts attention from other drivers of change.

One of the main drivers since the early 1980s has been the progressive restructuring of the global agro-food system, which has clearly surpassed slower and difficult progress toward the liberalization of agricultural trade. The concurrence of market deregulation and privatization with the emergence of demand-driven markets boosted by a global increase in income has radically reconfigured the global pattern with new structural trends.

First, foreign direct investment (FDI) flows have rapidly increased in response to the new capital mobility fostered by deregulation, new financial instruments and communication tools, as well as companies' needs to find external sources of growth in the context of increasing competition. Privatizations were major opportunities that contributed to concentration processes related to the struggle for market share and explained by market globalization.

Second, there is an increasing demand for high-value food products, a consequence of new diets resulting from rising incomes (with a larger share of fresh fruits and vegetables, meat and dairy) that induced new quality requirements, particularly linked to sanitary issues. Simultaneously, new high-value market segments emerged that were related to the demand of customers in wealthy countries for organic, Fair Trade and other ethical products. These demand-driven trends, significantly different from the historical basic staple food supply, translated into the emergence of new norms and standards dealing with these more complex quality issues, the consequence of which is increasing transaction costs linked to compliance with these new requirements.

Third, the improvement of communications and transportation facilitated long-distance transactions and the globalization of food supply chains, both for the food processing and distribution industries. The trend toward concentration translated respectively into the vertical integration of value chains and the development of new distribution systems with the rise of the supermarket model and global procurement systems, which were a way to guarantee supply of the requested quality of products.

This deep market restructuring has radically changed the landscape of the agro-food system over the last 25 years (Reardon and Timmer, 2007). On the one hand, this evolution comes along with a growing disconnect of local farmers from their national markets, which can now be supplied from abroad. On the other hand, it allows for the integration of some local producers into global chains and provides new opportunities for growth. However, the new rules of the game resulting from this new context (and often accompanied by the development of contractualization) require significant adaptation on the producers' side. Farmers have to observe the new quality requirements that often necessitate financial capital for investments, technical skills for accurate management, and also social capital to get the right market information when information systems are deficient. Earlier chapters in this volume on shrimp aquaculture in India and Vietnam and contract farming in Madagascar illustrate these points well.

A critical issue is therefore to understand the consequences of this new pattern in terms of inclusion or exclusion of producers to/from these global value chains. This issue is critical because agriculture remains the major economic activity in the world and the primary sector of employment in the developing countries: the 1.3 billion people working in agriculture sustain the livelihoods of 2.5 billion people (40 percent of the world's population). A trend being observed in many places is a progressive differentiation or segmentation process within the agricultural sector, which allows growing insertion and inclusion for the few and progressive marginalization and sometimes exclusion for the many. The genuine question in the context of poorly diversified economies (which is the case for SSA and other least developed countries (LDCs), as well as some lower-middle income countries) is: What are the alternatives and exit options for that part of the population marginalized by these processes of global restructuring, which pertain to the hidden part of the iceberg?

DEMOGRAPHY, ENVIRONMENT AND DEVELOPMENT: THE "EMBEDDED" CHALLENGES

This progressive restructuring of the global agro-food markets and the consequences of the confrontation between different types of farming systems and productivity levels have to be put in the perspective of a rapidly evolving demographic context. According to the last United Nations projections, the world population will reach 9.1 billion people in 2050 – nearly 2.5 billion more people than today. This expected growth will put extraordinary pressure on natural resources, compounded by the effects of climate change; will accelerate global processes and their consequences; and will radically challenge the current growth model, which is based on resource consumption levels that cannot be extended to the entire world's population. Alternatives will have to be invented, and this will test the capacity of the international community to cooperate.

However, if these global challenges are well known (but barely addressed), what is less discussed is the repartition of the expected population increase between regions and its consequences on their development. Indeed, the stage in the structural transformation process strongly determines the range of alternatives and the capacity to absorb newcomers. It also defines the potential exit options for marginalized people in places negatively affected by globalization.

While Europe has the characteristics of the final stage of the demographic transition, with an aging and shrinking population, sub-Saharan Africa and South-Central Asia (the two main demographic hot spots) are still booming, even if at different rates that correspond to different sequences in their transition. The population of SSA will double by 2050, reaching 1.7 billion people; South-Central Asia will increase by 50 percent and reach 2.5 billion. This will place tremendous pressure on natural resources, both locally but also with global consequences, and present a massive challenge in terms of economic and social development.

The main concern today is the existing options and room for maneuver of the poorly diversified economies (the "agriculture-based" countries), where agriculture still involves 60 or 70 percent of the economically active population. In SSA, the yearly cohorts of additional active population are estimated at around 10 million people today, and this will reach a peak of 18 million in 2030. This is colossal pressure that offers opportunities in terms of growing domestic markets but in a context of increasing competition from the rest of the world, with a clear asymmetry in terms of competitiveness. This situation hinders the process of diversification and particularly of industrialization, which was historically the main pathway for structural change. It also implies rising pressures on natural resources as illustrated by the country case studies in this book. The chapter on Madagascar provides an illustration of how internal migration can affect traditional conservation safeguards; and the chapter on South Africa vividly illustrates the twin effects of demographic pressure and globalization on the demand for water resources. These specific circumstances where economies and societies have to deal simultaneously with their economic and demographic transitions in the context of globalization and under the constraint of increasing resource scarcity (and cost of access), are absolutely new and unique in world history. In addition, international mass migration is no longer an alternative exit option, labor markets being the major exception within the global process of liberalization.

In that context, there are risks of transition impasses where the economic marginalization of people trapped in their native places will increase poverty and pressure on natural resources, with the possible emergence (in a pessimistic scenario) of "zombie states" (Pritchett, 2006). Again, this is likely to be compounded by the effects of global climate change – which are predicted to be most negative in areas of existing poverty where the adaptive capacities of human societies are constrained, particularly sub-Saharan Africa.

THE ROAD AHEAD: REINVENTING DEVELOPMENT STRATEGIES

The best way to deal with these unique challenges and their complexity – and avoid the more pessimistic scenario – is to go back to development strategies, in order to set a framework for action and articulate the necessary public policies.

This assertion is more decisive than it might appear. Indeed, after decades of segmented policies (health, infrastructure, investment, climate, education, etc.) focused on transversal issues and largely on poverty alleviation, where market forces were theoretically taking charge of productive issues, there is an urgent need to support the global development process. This means accompanying the economic transition, supporting the structural transformation, but obviously taking into account the specific characteristics of the period (globalization), its opportunities and constraints and, particularly, the growing pressure on the environment and the shortage of natural resources. How to mitigate the risks and how to adapt to the new context?

It is easy to put forward the need for development strategies and, of course, more difficult to address their implementation because many prerequisites exist for their design. When discussing strategies, the objective is clearly not to go back to the early age of development theory when state-led policies, planning and public intervention were the rule. As Stiglitz (1998) reminds us, the objective is to focus on the processes of elaborating and preparing the strategy, which can be regarded as a public good and justify real public effort and support. It should also be an obvious area for donor support. The golden rules of a development strategy are that it must be tailor-made and owned by its stakeholders. This means a knowledge process based on a shared diagnosis of the challenges, opportunities and constraints. There is an initial need to set forth a "vision" and then to build consensus, which are prerequisites to assign objectives and discuss options to reach them. Because they must be owned to be effective, development strategies must be designed first at the local level, where the concrete vulnerabilities exist, and they must then be articulated at broader levels of concern that are important for their viability. Such processes of elaboration take time; there is a need for an updated knowledge base of what is at stake, as well as knowledge dissemination and capacity building to help stakeholders to use this information. All of this takes time and money, but it can also help to avoid costly mistakes linked to inappropriate actions.

If we now switch from methodology to substance and the primary goal of addressing the situation of vulnerable people and places, what is at stake? Without underestimating the many drivers of environmental degradation (including trade at times), it appears that one of the main concerns of the current period is the marginalization process that is a direct consequence of the confrontation of asymmetric development levels (notably capital and skills, which bear on competitiveness). In a dreadful but common sequence, marginalization increases poverty and poor people resort to the exploitation of natural resources – when they can access them – to survive. There are clear examples of this sequence in the book's case studies from India and Madagascar.

The recent World Development Report suggests three main pathways out of rural poverty: specialization in agriculture (for those who have the necessary skills and assets with respect to the period); participation in non-farm activities through rural diversification; and migration. The last two options are historical pathways out of the "agriculture world," confirmed by the statistical evidence, but they also confront the sharp reality of existing constraints at the national and global levels. Migration options rely on development and growth of other sectors within the country (only if they exist) or abroad (only if borders are open). The development of non-farm activities initially depends on agricultural growth, as shown in many countries: increasing agricultural incomes leads to greater consumption, which fosters the development of other activities in the countryside and also, through economies of scale, in the market towns or larger cities. So agricultural development is an issue that fits well with its overwhelming importance in the world's overall economic structure, and its development is decisive in those countries that have not engaged in diversification and structural change. But how to support it, and how to select the right targets?

The first option is to deal with the "big numbers." Given that the main problem faced by many developing countries is the creation of jobs and income-earning activities, the priority for policymakers is to improve the situation for the many, which initially means helping family farms (the primary farm structure all around the world) by supporting the development of food products and markets. This option doesn't mean that there are not opportunities for development of traditional, and particularly high-value, exports (which are the focus of so much government and donor attention), but food markets are clearly the most inclusive. They are open to all and are essential for income generation (the current increase in food prices is obviously a possible windfall), which directly impacts on poverty and helps to link up with other sectors thanks to increased consumption.

Strengthening the performance of local, national and sub-regional food markets can diminish the risk for farmers, improve their incomes, and directly reduce the excessive exploitation of natural resources – which is the answer to an insecure economic environment and low returns. Better revenues can thereby enable producers to invest, but also to diversify as the need for self-sufficiency declines. Finally, production growth can stimulate the development of transformation activities, create local value-adding opportunities, and facilitate so-called "cluster" development through diversification and the intensification of rural activities directly connected with the industrial urban fabric. But these developments require concrete actions related to market imperfections and particularly the excessive transaction costs that are a clear burden on farming profitability. In many cases the recent food price increases did not reach the farmgate (while input price increases did) because of middlemen and a lack of information. A better provision of public goods (especially information systems and transport infrastructure) is part of the answer.

The second option is to boost output and consequently income level through productivity increases. Best practices that target sustainability and an improvement in the economic and institutional environment of production are key themes. Public goods (research, training, rural infrastructure, natural risk mitigation, law enforcement, property rights) are again central, as is addressing some incomplete markets, typically for inputs, extension, and financial services. In the latter case, temporary public supports can help to release or jump-start private sector dynamics. It is particularly important in SSA where state withdrawal following the structural adjustment programs of the 1980s did not translate into the increased involvement of private agents.

There is of course nothing original here, because the ingredients are well known and have been noted many times before. What is essential is the way to mix them in the policy bowl to obtain a genuine strategy that addresses the priorities of each place, region or country. The increased vulnerability of people and places resulting from the marginalization within globalization, and related to the asymmetry of the historical processes of structural transformation, is a major issue. And to deal with its amplitude and its possible consequences is a major challenge that must be addressed by both local stakeholders and the international community. It clearly comes within the scope of a necessary new vision for development based on renewed values where human well-being and a sustainable environment are central. Confronting this broad range of concerns is critical. The first step is for stakeholders to take back ownership of the processes and become invested in the design of their own development strategies. And for the necessary dialogue and negotiation to happen, public support and political goodwill are badly needed.

NOTE

1. This chapter is based on arguments developed in a separate study and research program implemented by the World Bank and funded by the World Bank, the government of France, and IFAD. This three-year program (2006–09), called RuralStruc (Structural dimensions of liberalization on agriculture and rural development), was launched parallel to the WWF–World Bank trade project. It was a comparative study that focused on

the linkages between increasing integration processes in agriculture at the world level and their consequences in terms of differentiation among the productive structures in developing countries, including specialization and diversification, marginalization and migration. Madagascar and Mexico, which were part of the WWF–World Bank trade project, were also among the seven countries participating in the RuralStruc program.

REFERENCES

Lewis, W.A. (1955), *The Theory of Economic Growth*, London: George Allen & Unwin.

Mundlak, Y., D.F. Larson and A. Crego (1998), "Agricultural development: issues, evidence and consequences", in *Contemporary Economic Issues: Proceedings of the Eleventh World Congress of the International Economic Association, Tunis*, Volume 2, New York: St Martin's Press/International Economic Association.

Pritchett, L. (2006), *Let Their People Come – Breaking the Gridlock on Global Labor Mobility*, Washington, DC: Center for Global Development.

Reardon, T. and C.P. Timmer (2007), "Transformation of markets for agricultural output in developing countries since 1950: how has thinking changed?", in R.E. Evenson and P. Pingali (eds), *Handbook of Agricultural Economics (Volume 3): Agricultural Development: Farmers, Farm Production and Farm Markets*, Amsterdam, Elsevier Press, pp. 2808–55.

Rostow, W.W. (1960), *The Stages of Economic Growth*, Cambridge: Cambridge University Press.

Stern, N. (2006), *The Economics of Climate Change: The Stern Review*, Cambridge: Cambridge University Press/Cabinet Office, HM Treasury.

Stiglitz, J.E. (1998), "Towards a new paradigm for development: strategies, policies and processes", 9th Raul Prebisch Lecture, 19 October, UNCTAD, Geneva.

Timmer, C.P. and S. Akkus (2008), "The structural transformation as a pathway out of poverty: analytics, empirics and politics", Working Paper No. 150, Center for Global Development, Washington, DC.

World Bank (2007), *Agriculture for Development: World Development Report 2008*, Washington, DC: The World Bank.

Index